SLOVAK SETTLERS

THE EMOTIONAL HISTORY OF IMMIGRATION

VOLUME 1 OF 2

GLOBAL SLOVAKIA
AGÁTOVÁ 1323
905 01 SENICA
SLOVAKIA
www.globalslovakia.com

Volume I. first published in 2023
Zuzana Palovic and Gabriela Bereghazyova assert their moral right to be identified as the authors of this work.

English version © Zuzana Palovic and Gabriela Bereghazyova 2023
Front Cover Artwork © Zuzana Hudakova
Artwork © Tucker Jaroll and Sean Kovarovic
Graphic Design © Zuzana Chmelová
Editors: Margaret Bendet, Erin Lillywhite, Aaron Borrelli, Helen Fedor

ISBN 978-1-7374054-7-4

All rights reserved. No part of this book may be reproduced or transmitted in any form or by any means, electronic or mechanical, including photocopying, recording, or by any information storage and retrieval system, without permission in writing from the publisher.

44 PERSONAL STORIES OF GREAT HARDSHIP AND GREATER COURAGE

SLOVAK SETTLERS

THE EMOTIONAL HISTORY OF IMMIGRATION

VOLUME 1 OF 2

ZUZANA **PALOVIC** GABRIELA **BEREGHAZYOVA**

CONTENTS

- 7 Foreword
- 8 Prologue
- 11 Introduction

PART ONE / CHEAP LABOR AND GREAT DARING
- 14 How the Industrial Revolution Changed Everything
- 19 A Nation on the Move
- 31 The Emigration of Women

PART TWO / THE JOURNEY
- 37 Smugglers, Agents, and Fake Passports
- 45 Crossing the Ocean

PART THREE / LIFE IN THE NEW WORLD
- 52 A New Beginning
- 58 Dull, Dirty and Dangerous Jobs
- 67 Living In America
- 76 Slovak or Rusyn?
- 85 Amerikáni

PART FOUR / BUILDING A SLOVAK WORLD
- 90 The Making of Little Slovakia
- 94 Let's Get Organized!
- 101 Spiritual Oases of the Old Country
- 106 The Power of the Printed Word
- 109 Would There Have Been a Czechoslovakia without Slovak-America?
- 117 Conquering the Canadian Wilderness
- 125 Slovaks in Argentina

PART FIVE / STORIES

- 132 PERILOUS PASSAGES: LIFE AND DEATH IN A NEW LAND
  / by Ken Duda
- 152 THE SLOVAK AMERICANS
  / by Deah Partak
- 170 THE BLOOD OF VALENTÍN
  / by Paul Kostyak
- 184 AN ADVENTUROUS MATRIARCH
  / by Audrey Stucko
- 200 LEAVING HOME, FINDING HOME
  / by Jeanne M. Zulick
- 215 A SLOVAK SANCTUARY
  / by Edward Monovich
- 230 MY SLOVAK HERITAGE WAS KEPT MOSTLY HIDDEN
  / by Albert Kovanis, Jr.
- 250 FINDING MY SLOVAK ROOTS WAS A CATHARTIC EXPERIENCE
  / by Beverly Clifford
- 268 WHAT DOES IT MEAN TO BE RUSYN?
  / by Lisa A. Alzo
- 280 WHERE THE OCEAN ENDS AND A NEW LAND BEGINS
  / by María Elena Doello Jurado
  (based on the writings of Marcela Fajmonova)
- 292 IN THE CANADIAN WILDERNESS
  / by Rudy Bies
- 310 A BOY FROM FIĽAKOVO
  / by Frank Lowy
- 328 WHAT MAKES MY ROOTS SO ALIVE?
  / by John Palka

- 348 Epilogue
- 352 Afterword
- 355 Photographs & Illustrations
- 363 Bibliography
- 366 Appendix
- 370 Wall of Gratitude
- 374 Global Slovakia

FOREWORD

It is my distinct pleasure to introduce this popular history, and the life stories of 44 individuals who emigrated from Slovakia to the New World in the 20th century.

The authors did a great job in summarizing the largely Slovak immigration to the USA, Canada, Argentina, and even Japan in the last century. They included the life histories of both men and women, Slovaks, Moravians, Rusyns, and Jews.

These life histories are largely autobiographies by members of the first or second-generation immigrants and contain much useful information on the causes of immigration, the trip across the Atlantic, settlement in certain regions of the New World, the immigrants' work experiences, and their creation of institutions that would help them to survive as an ethnic group over several generations. These institutions included fraternal-benefit societies, parish churches, and a vibrant newspaper press.

It is important to remember that today approximately 2,000,000 people claim partial Slovak heritage in North America. Since today's Slovakia has a population of only 5,4000,000, one can claim that one-third of the Slovak nation lives in diaspora. This book reflects the experience of a portion of them, in their own words. It is a fitting tribute to this diaspora.

Professor M. Mark Stolarik
Chair in Slovak History and Culture
University of Ottawa, Canada

PROLOGUE

A Long Legacy to Freedom: Happy 30th birthday, Slovakia!

For centuries Slovaks have been leaving their homeland in the heart of Europe in droves. However, for much of modern history, the narrow strip of land so dear to the hearts of our people, could not be called Slovakia.

Before they could have a country of their own, Slovaks had to endure and survive unimaginable twists and turns of destiny. It is a miracle and a testimony to the hard work of our forefathers, that Slovaks were able to maintain and develop a sense of national identity against all odds.

As we matured as a nation, we faced existence in many different states—from the Kingdom of Hungary, the Empire of Austria-Hungary, Czechoslovakia, and the fascist Slovak State, to the Socialist Republic of Czechoslovakia. The collapse of the Iron Curtain and Soviet Bloc saw the re-establishment of the democratic Czech and Slovak Federative Republic, which was seen as a great victory.

But the big break came on January 1st, 1993.

That New Year's Day marked the beginning of true Slovak sovereignty. Czechoslovakia quietly split into the Czech Republic and the Slovak Republic, redrawing the map of central Europe forever. For the first time in over a thousand years of existence, Slovakia gained meaningful and genuine independence.

The opportunity came at a cost.

That great leap towards sovereignty took place within a bumpy transition from communism to democracy, from planned economy to free market, and from totalitarianism to an open and free society. As an independent country, the nation would have to take responsibility over its destiny and chart its own path into the future.

Slovaks rose to the occasion

Over the past 30 years, the country has undergone tremendous growth and change. The dark 1990s, which were marked by mafia and corruption, eventually gave way to more stability. Slovakia joined NATO in March 2004, and the European Union (EU) in May of the same year. That year the gate to the world flung fully open, as Slovaks gained the freedom to live and work in any EU country.

Since independence, our country has experienced three papal visits, Bratislava's skyline has changed beyond recognition, Slovaks became world ice hockey champions, secured 32 Olympic medals, and voted their first female president into power.

Three decades into independence, the time also came for Slovakia to restore her lost connection with millions of Slovak descendants—the progeny of Slovaks who were pushed out of their motherland by hardships, wars, and religious and political oppression. Others left in search of a better life.

In April 2022, Slovakia passed a novelization to the Citizenship Act that opened the door to citizenship for millions of Slovak descendants around the world. This novel and exciting legislation is the beginning of a new chapter in Slovakia's history.

A great deal has been accomplished in such a short span of time, yet the journey of sovereign Slovakia is only beginning. There is much to do, fight for, and improve in the years and decades to come.

But for now, let us pause and celebrate this special moment.

We are proud of you, we love you, and we know the best is yet to come.

Zuzana & Gabriela
Global Slovakia
www.globalslovakia.com

"We came here from the land of suffering and oppression. It is on this account that we hailed America like a rising sun after the dark night of humiliation. And she received us—poor, unknown, insignificant. She received us, and her sun warmed us from the first moment we set our foot on her soil—the big sun of a freer, happier life than that we had lived in our oppressed native land."

Declaration of Czech and Slovak immigrants, addressed to the American people and President Woodrow Wilson, July 4, 1918

INTRODUCTION

The history of Slovakia is a history of migration. For nearly two centuries, Slovaks have been leaving their homeland in droves.

The biggest exodus occurred at the turn of the 19th century, when an incredible one third of the Slovak population emigrated to North America. The long string of Napoleonic Wars ended on the old continent in 1815 and was followed by a wave of civil uprisings in 1848 and 1849. When these were over, a new sense of peace was reinstated in restless Europe.

On the other side of the Atlantic, the U.S. Civil War came to a close in 1865, and the rise of industrialization that immediately followed opened the American continent to newcomers. The stage was set for a migration wave of spectacular proportions. Slovaks would play an important role, becoming one of the largest emigrating European populations (per capita), second only to Ireland.

By 1920, as many as 619,866 people with Slovak roots resided in America, living in communities scattered across the Northeast and Midwest. In the 1990 census, which is the most accurate because it asked specifically about ethnicity, 1.8 million Americans reported to have Slovak ancestors according to the U.S. Census. These were the direct descendants of the pioneering Slovak settlers.

■■■

The 1990 US census produced curious result. Experts referred to it as the best American census in history in terms of identifying ethnic groups that did not have their own country. Slovakia did not claim it independence until January 1, 1993. However, having the option of 'Slovak' as a category on the census document made identifying as a Slovak possible. Some 2 million Americans self-identified as having Slovak origins. Moreover, the census validated Slovaks as a stand-alone ethnic group, distinct from the Czechs with whom they were at the time still joined in Czechoslovakia.

■ ■ ■

After the heyday of migration to America between 1870 and 1914, emigration from Central and Eastern Europe came to a halt during World War I. Many men died on battlefields, and travel became difficult and expensive. Then in the 1920s, the U.S. started to impose immigration quotas, which dramatically restricted entry for Eastern Europeans. Furthermore, the tides began to change in Europe too. The continent was reinventing itself.

When a free and independent Czechoslovakia emerged out of the rubble of the Great War, it was nothing short of a miracle.

In the difficult postwar years, the young republic quickly rose to prominence, becoming one of the most industrially and politically advanced countries in the world. This inspired many emigres to return home from overseas. At the same time, the government discouraged Czechoslovaks from emigrating to prevent further loss of skills and talent.

Czechoslovakia was the place to be, and you were lucky to be a Czechoslovak.

But peace in restless Europe was short-lived and the 'first republic' soon crumbled under the pressure of Hitler's ambitions. Czechoslovakia was dissolved, and people sensed another war was coming, more terrible and destructive than the one they had just survived. Many chose to flee the impeding danger. The most destructive war in history lasted six years.

World War II came to an end in 1945, but the relief did not last long.

In 1948, the Communist Party of Czechoslovakia took power in a bloodless coup, and hundreds of thousands fled the country as political refugees. Another wave of political escapes rocked the country in 1968, when the Soviet-led invasion of the Warsaw Pact armies stopped the budding freedom of the Prague Spring.

The end of the Cold War started a new era on the old continent. The opening of borders in 1989 offered an opportunity for people to roam beyond Czechoslovakia once again, in search of better pay and, later, in pursuit of adventure and education.

Slovaks continue to be a nation on the move. They live scattered across Europe and the world, yet some still remain connected to their homeland underneath the Tatra Mountains by an invisible but strong bond.

Part one
CHEAP LABOR AND GREAT DARING

How the Industrial Revolution Changed Everything

For the greater part of history, people lived, married, procreated, worked, and died within a very short distance of where they were born. Moving a long distance from your home was unheard of. What for and, besides, where would you go?

This was partly true because of the limited means of transport available before the era of trains, steamships, cars, and planes. But it was also a consequence of a social and political system.

Europeans, including Slovaks, lived in a feudal world. A strict caste hierarchy dominated medieval central Europe from the 9th century all the way up to 1848. In a feudal economy, most folk assumed the status of serfs, agricultural workers who were bound to the land and the will of their lord, the owner of the estate. The vast majority of serfs obtained their living by cultivating a small plot of land that did not belong to them. They paid their dues to the estate owner, the lord, usually by paying taxes, fees or agricultural produce. This payment would amount to a substantial proportion of what they produced.

It is not an exaggeration to say that the entire Middle Ages were ridden with exploitation of the common folk.

The Kingdom of Hungary, to which Slovakia had belonged since the 10th century, abolished serfdom in 1848, unshackling more than 50 million people from this bond that was not of their choosing. Though it took a while for the legal change to translate into practice in a meaningful way, people gained the freedom to roam beyond the regions and towns of their birth. They did not travel for fun, but usually for work. Truth be told, many had no choice but to move, if they wanted to survive and feed their families.

The world was changing fast in the 19th century. The second Industrial Revolution dawned, and with it came an insatiable demand for labor and many unheard-of technological innovations. Factories in Europe opened for mass production, offering thousands of new jobs to people who had worked the land since time immemorial. Slovakia, then Upper Hungary, was no different.

The steam engine gave rise to railways that allowed people to travel faster, cheaper, and easier to take up these new industrial jobs. As factories grew, more and more people left their native fields and forests behind, moving to towns and cities to find secure and stable employment. Still, in Europe there were many more people than there were jobs in factories.

Meanwhile, the stars were aligning in North America.

Slavery was abolished in Canada in 1834 and in the United States three decades later, in 1865, following the end of the Civil War. At this time, the American North was experiencing unprecedented economic growth. However, the factories, steel mills, and coal mines did not run themselves. They needed vast reserves of willing, able, and cheap workers.

The industrialists paid but a pittance to immigrant workers who labored and lived in appalling conditions. This new economic arrangement was just one step up from slavery and serfdom, and it was far from perfect.

For a good stretch of time, the Irish, escaping starvation and poverty even before the 1845 Potato Famine, took up the dirtiest and most dangerous jobs in industrializing America. They had started to arrive in the 18th century to help lay down the groundwork for the country's industrial infrastructure—from railways to streets and water canals.

By the 19th century, the Irish were America's largest immigrant group. However, as their communities matured, the Irish gained greater exposure to America's democratic ideals. They began to unionize and to claim better wages, working, and living conditions. They simply refused to work for $1.50 a day.

The owners of mines, mills, and factories were outraged. They rebuffed the demands of the trade unionists and prioritized their profit margins instead. But to meet the industrial demand, they needed to expand their pool of labor so they could replace the insubordinate Irish workers.

After the Civil War, the most immediate and accessible source of cheap labor was the newly freed black slaves in the American South. They were naturally looking to relocate to the 'free' North, but the mass migration of this population was a sticky matter.

Eventually, the industrialists of the North agreed not to employ African-Americans enmass, because the former slave owners still needed them as their source of cheap labor in the South. A 'gentlemen's agreement' was struck by which the northerners promised they would not send their labor agents to the southern states to recruit the Black workers.

The factory and mill owners would have to look elsewhere for labor supply. They set their sights on Slavic Europe, home to the hungry, desperate, and jobless masses. The fast-evolving technology worked in the favor of the Americans.

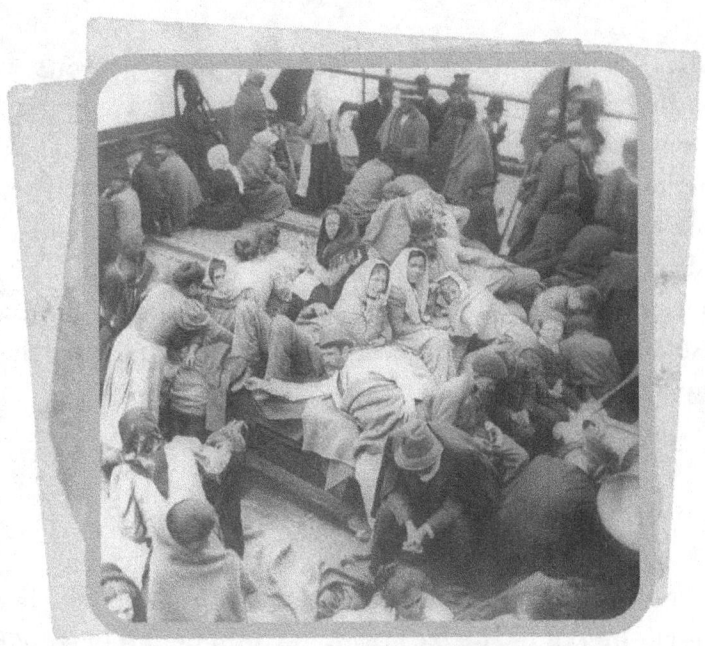

Before the first steamships set out on their maiden journeys in 1818, the transatlantic voyage from Europe to America could take anywhere from 6 to 12 weeks! Steamships shortened the crossing to under 10 days! Not only were they faster, liners propelled by steam engines also made transatlantic travel safer and more affordable for the masses. To meet the rising demand, the steamship companies kept improving their fleets to offer faster travel times. Moreover, the ships grew in size, allowing up to a thousand people to travel in steerage alone, which in turn made the tickets even cheaper.

Recruiters, the so-called 'agents' of the era, worked closely with the captains of the coal mines and steel mill industries (and later also steamship ocean liners). They crossed the Atlantic in the 19th century, tasked with finding workers willing to work for $1.50 a day. Naturally, the agents looked for people who were poor and desperate. Slovakia, then called Upper Hungary, was a good fit.

Austria-Hungary was a labor gold mine for the agents, who recruited rural and, for the most part, uneducated men and women—people who had no idea where America was—to try their luck in a faraway land. The promise of fairytale riches worked like magic and Slovaks were happy to oblige the needs of the American labor market. They would bring back American dollars that would allow them to buy land and livestock, build houses and improve their lot in life for themselves and their children.

'American fever' gripped the entire nation.

However, the outpouring of able-bodied men, especially in the east of the country, had grave consequences for the local economy and society. There were not enough people left to work the land. The lack of men could be felt beyond the domain of agriculture. The military leadership of the country grew more and more concerned as well. Conscripts were missing. The religious authorities were worried too. Their flock of followers was getting smaller and smaller, and so was the power of the church.

■ ■ ■

Flash forward a hundred years and not much has changed in Slovakia. Towns in the east of the country are still missing people. Men and women are forced to find work abroad to sustain themselves and their families, while their children are left behind to be raised by grandparents.

■ ■ ■

The Kingdom of Hungary tried to protect its interests. A law was passed in 1850 that required permits to be issued for emigration; its intention was to prevent men eligible for the draft from leaving the territory. The move failed to achieve a desired outcome, and the Hungarian government passed another law in 1881 that curbed the activities of agents who were recruiting local people for jobs abroad.

It was a strategic decision. The Kingdom needed a strong army. Even after having completed their military service, men were kept on the reserve list 'just in case'. They were not permitted to legally emigrate until they had reached an older age. Most left anyway—illegally.

A Nation on the Move

For over a hundred years, a combination of factors pushed people in Slovakia to look for work outside the country. The trend affected all of Slovakia but especially the regions of Šariš, Spiš, and Zemplín in the east.

Before Slovaks started to explore North America, they headed to Budapest, the capital of the Kingdom of Hungary, and to Vienna, the capital city of the Austrian Empire. At the turn of the 20th century, a thriving Slovak community grew in Budapest as a result of this migration. It became the largest 'Slovak city' in Europe, home to about 80,000 Slovaks.[1] For comparison, Pressburg (now Bratislava) only housed a small 15 percent Slovak minority, that did not come anywhere near in size of the Slovak community in Budapest.

With their travel options widening thanks to breakthroughs in technology, Slovaks expanded their horizons. They ventured farther than ever before in search of work, moving beyond the Kingdom, its region, and even its continent.

---

[1] Kováčová, 2014

Even before the peak of emigration, adventurous Slovaks heeded the call of faraway America.

Records indicate that Slovaks fought alongside Americans in both the War for Independence and the Civil War. The adventures of Count Móric Beňovský in the 18th century baffle even today's experts. During a time when mobility was still limited, Móric traversed the planet, making it as far as Africa, where he was proclaimed the King of Madagascar.

After years abroad, he returned to Europe and settled in Paris, where he befriended Benjamin Franklin in 1777. Their friendship grew into a strong alliance and, later, a shared mission, when Beňovský proposed to use Madagascar as a military base for the American struggle against the British Empire. In 1779, Móric relocated to Savannah, Georgia, to fight in the War for Independence.

Nearly a century later, Slovaks once again appeared on the scene when the Civil War broke out in America. In 1861, President Abraham Lincoln received a letter to approve a volunteer miliary unit from Chicago called the Lincoln Riflemen of Slavic Origin. The request stated:

"We have organized a group of soldiers of Hungarian, Czech and Slovak origin in Chicago. Since we are the first military group of these nationalities in the United States, we respectfully request that we may call ourselves the Lincoln Riflemen of Slavic origin."

The author of the letter was Gejza Mihalóci, a native of Zemplín, Slovakia. President Lincoln approved the request for the first Slavic unit, which fought on the Union forces. The unit was eventually incorporated into the Illinois state infantry that consisted mainly of European veterans forged in the fire of revolutions that swept through the old continent in 1848.

However, most of the Slovaks who emigrated left for North America between 1848 and 1918. During the time of Austria-Hungary, the largest number of Slovaks left between 1874 and 1907.[2] Most of these emigrants were from the empire's ethnic minorities; together they comprised the 52,368 Slovaks who made it to the United States in 1905 alone. This was the peak year in terms of people emigrating from Upper Hungary.[3]

■ ■ ■

Slovaks were preceded to America by other Slavs, who followed the early Irish and German immigrants. Czechs started to arrive in the U.S. as early as the 1840s, while Poles started pouring in the 1860s, laying down strong foundations for all forthcoming Slavic migrants. The first Slovak settlers stayed in Czech and Polish boarding houses and attended their churches as well.

■ ■ ■

Historians estimate that between 500,000 and 650,000 Slovaks emigrated to the New World before World War I.[4] About 30 percent were said to have returned to Slovakia.[5] Those that stayed on eventually gave rise to a sizeable descendant population. All in all, some 619,866 Slovaks were living in the United States according the 1920 US Census.

These emigrants settled in communities with an already established Eastern European presence. Pittsburgh, Pennsylvania; Cleveland, Ohio; Chicago, Illinois; New Jersey; and New York City, New York, were the most popular destinations.

---

[2] Zahra, 2016
[3] Bahna, 2011
[4] Cude, 2014
[5] Jakešová, 1997

Their coal mines, steel mills, railroads, and oil refineries were eager to receive the newly arrived workers.

Such jobs did not demand skilled labor and so they were open to anyone who wanted to do this backbreaking work. Most people arriving from Slovakia came from rural backgrounds and had never worked industrial jobs. They did not speak English, and many did not even know how to read or write in the language of their mother tongue. They were a perfect match for the dirty, dangerous jobs that were available.

The first to go were the adventurers, the pioneers and the most desperate and down on their luck people—the landless former peasants. Mostly single men emigrated, predominantly from eastern Slovakia.

At the time, Austria-Hungary lagged behind western Europe—both economically and socially. Even after serfdom was banished in 1848 and the social reforms were implemented, just 1 percent of the population continued to own more than half of everything. Theoretically, people could now buy land. In practice, few could afford it. Just like before, the ordinary people had to satisfy themselves with small 12-acre plots. Coupled with obsolete farming techniques at a time when agricultural prices were falling due to modernization, the small patches of land could simply not produce enough food to feed the large Slovak families.

■ ■ ■

By the end of the 19th century, Slovakia had become overpopulated, partly thanks to the introduction of the humble potato. Potatoes were much easier to grow than wheat or rye. One acre of land could provide more food when planted with potatoes rather than with wheat. More food and less work resulted in a population explosion. Upper Hungary went from 1.8 million inhabitants at the end of the 18th century to 2.3 million by the mid-19th

century. The potato was a mixed blessing. It warded off starvation, but more people meant that there were more inheritors to divide the land among and more competitors to vie for scant resources and jobs.

■ ■ ■

Many Slovak men and women were forced to migrate south to the fertile regions of the Kingdom and Austria, where they could find seasonal employment planting and harvesting crops. Although they made more in these jobs than they could in their native villages, they were still earning a meager sum—15 to 30 cents a day.

Beyond agriculture, there were few opportunities to earn a living. Unemployment was a huge problem in Upper Hungary, where industrialization began slowly and not until the 1870s.

Wages in American industries, as pitiful as they were by American standards, still represented astronomical sums for the former peasants and even craftsmen. More and more followed the sweet promises of the agents, who spoke of a great and abundant land on the other side of the ocean. The Slovak-American dream was born. People aspired to come to America, save a $1,000, and return home as rich men. It was said that what you earned at home in a week, you could gain in America in a single day.

Although poverty is often cited as 'the' reason why so many Slovaks left for abroad, scholars from the University of Prešov in eastern Slovakia, where mass emigration left the deepest scars, point at other factors.

For instance, alcohol.

Alcoholism disproportionately affected the local male population. The bottle provided a temporary relief from joblessness, illness, and the feelings of helplessness held by men unable to provide for their families. Or perhaps alcohol was the cause of this misery. It's hard to know which came first. Nevertheless, the reality was that the men became heavily indebted to local tavern owners, who eventually demanded that the unpaid bills be settled. The drinkers were forced to come up with a plan. With no more booze to down until debts were paid, they had no other choice but to go out and find work. America offered a way out of an impossible situation. Sadly, many continued downing glasses in the New World, where whisky was much cheaper than spirits in their homeland.

The second emigration wave depleted Upper Hungary in the 1870s. The cholera pandemic of 1872 and 1873 had catastrophic consequences in Slovakia. The disease claimed countless lives and wiped out entire villages. In the Zemplín region alone, nearly 14,000 people died in the summer of 1873.[6]

Poor weather, a bad harvest, and subsequent crop failures added to the toll, triggering a large wave of migration to the U.S. Facing a dire future at home, a great many Slovaks decided to give the coal mines and steel mills of America a chance. This second wave was greatly facilitated by the migration networks already established in America by the pioneering Slovaks.

The third emigration wave occurred at the beginning of the 20th century, when the Kingdom of Hungary found itself in a deep economic crisis. The need for cash was most acute in eastern Slovakia. The two earlier waves of migration had resulted in well-oiled migration networks by now, and the growing Slovak communities in the U.S. were ready to receive newcomers. It is hardly a surprise that this resulted in the largest emigration wave. A record number of departures was documented between 1904 and 1907.

---

[6] Derfiňák, 2016

The harsh policy of Magyrization also played a role from the 1860s onwards. Magyarization was nothing short of a forced cultural assimilation scheme, which aspired to turn Slovaks into Hungarians (Magyars). The aggressive policy did not sit well with those who did not want to part with their ethnic identity. It affected especially those who wanted to study or advance themselves professionally and socially.

Pursuing any education and especially higher education in the Kingdom of Hungary, required one to speak Hungarian. Similarly, administrative clerk positions, a dream of many, were beyond the reach of those who did not acquire education and that was not possible without speaking fluent Hungarian.

Those with aspirations beyond toiling the fields had to make a choice. If they wanted to move up the career ladder or simply improve their lot in life, they would have to adapt and accept the Hungarian language and culture as their primary identity, at least in public and at work.

It is important to note that small farmers did not feel the pressure as much as the middle classes, and so we see more and more craftsmen and professionals leaving during this period. Subsequently, during this period of homogenization, the departure of 'unwanted minorities' was welcomed by the Hungarian authorities up to a certain point.

The mass emigration of Slovaks, Croats, Ukrainians, and Rusyns was a way of reducing social and ethnic conflicts in the kingdom, exacerbated by Magyarization and the difficult economic situation.

■ ■ ■

> *Some scholars argue that most people leaving for North America from Slovakia were common folk without career aspirations. Magyarization would not have affected them as much and so it would not have been a primary*

reason for emigration. But once in America, the settlers began educating themselves. As Slovak-Americans groomed their minds and expanded their intellectual capacity, they developed an interest in politics back home.

■ ■ ■

It is possible that the theory of Magyarization pushing people out of their homeland emerged once Slovaks settled in North America, to create a greater sense of Slovak cultural sovereignty and to raise awareness about the lack of basic rights of people in Upper Hungary. Eventually, this translated into active campaigning for Slovak independence.

Up until then, the middle classes most likely spoke fluent Hungarian or German and were most hesitant to leave the safety of their homeland. Having no knowledge of English and holding education credentials that would not be recognized by foreign employers, these men and women would have to take up unsavory low-level jobs, at least in the beginning. This was an unappetizing prospect.

Whatever their reason for departure, the majority of emigrants from Slovakia did not intend to stay in North America. They went away to make money, build a nest egg, and return to their homeland able to provide a good life for their family. Uprooting and permanently settling in distant America was not their plan. After all, Slovaks were a collective, traditional, family-oriented people. Life was family. Family was life.

About one-third of Slovaks who emigrated before World War I returned. This phenomenon is known as 'birds of passage'.[7] The short-term, circular migration of Europeans was crucial to the economic boom of the United States. Many Slovaks

---

[7] Gerber, 2011

travelled back and forth multiple times, before eventually choosing to stay on in the New World. One of the reasons for this is that they had a struggle to readapt to the old conservative ways of the Slovak countryside, after they'd had a dose of freedom and capitalism in America.

■ ■ ■

> *Slovaks were said to have one of the highest return emigration rates in the Kingdom of Hungary.[8] According to U.S. Department of Labor, between the years 1909 and 1919 more Slovaks returned than actually arrived in the United States.[9] Scholars believe that around 30 percent of Slovaks returned to their homeland, and 20 percent had been to America more than once.[10]*

■ ■ ■

But this movement came to a halt when World War I broke out. In the aftermath of the war, the old empires crumbled in Europe, giving birth to new countries. The establishment of Czechoslovakia, a joint nation of Czechs and Slovaks, offered exciting opportunities. Moreover, the leadership went out of their way to attract Czechs and Slovaks to return home from North America.

On the other side of the ocean, these developments collided with the decision of the United States to cap the number of incoming persons from Central and Eastern Europe. One of the reasons behind this decision was the political desire to fully integrate the Eastern Europeans who were already in the country, in order to create a more homogenous culture and society.

---

[8] Zahra, 2016
[9] Godál, 2020
[10] Stolarik, 1988; 2012

Nevertheless, the Great Depression spurred an economic crisis that hit Czechoslovakia in the 1930s, resulting in new waves of departures once again. This time, the people were leaving for Canada and Argentina.

Migration once again came to a near halt during World War II, which claimed an unprecedented number of lives. As soon as that war ended, human mobility began again. But now it wasn't for economic reasons. Totalitarian communism took power in Czechoslovakia in 1948 and remained in place until 1989. The communist regime was responsible for more than half a million Czechoslovaks leaving the country.

When the Iron Curtain collapsed and the country's borders opened in 1989 after being sealed for four decades, people could once again travel easily. It was not just curiosity that drove them abroad to taste the forbidden West. The country's transition to a free market and democracy was bumpy and unpredictable. Many left Slovakia in 1990s to seek better pay and greater job security abroad. But this time, they settled much closer to home than their far-faring predecessors. Germany and Austria were the most popular destinations.

Another game-changer came 15 years after the collapse of communism. Slovakia joined NATO and the European Union in 2004, and for the first time in history, Slovaks could live, work and study in other countries on the continent without a visa. This spurred one of the greatest migration waves in the history of Slovakia. Young Slovaks were leaving in the hundreds of thousands. They were not being pushed out by a merciless regime or dire poverty. These people were leaving by choice, and they could leave and return, and leave again much more easily.

■ ■ ■

Though a great majority of Slovaks aspired to be birds of passage and return home with cash in hand to make their dreams happen, the departures were nevertheless emotional. The transatlantic journey was long, and family connections were maintained only through letters that took a while to arrive. One never really knew what future their destiny had in store, and there was always a chance that beloved daughters and sons, husbands and fathers, wives and mothers would not make it back.

■ ■ ■

With so many people leaving, the migration phenomenon even left an imprint on Slovak folk culture. Songs inspired by departures to America were written and sung to help the collective population digest the heavy emotions that inevitably crept in as families separated. Here is one of them.

Keď sa Slovák preč do sveta uberal,
na kopečku, na Machnáči zavolal,
zavolal on na kopečku zo dvakrát:
zbohom, otec, zbohom, mati, sestra, brat.

When a Slovak left for the big world,
He stood on a hill looking at Machnáč
(a hill in western Slovakia),
He stood on the hill and called:
Farewell father, farewell mother, sister, brother.

Povedz mi ty, môj Machnáču vysoký,
či ťa ešte uzriem o dva, tri roky,
či mi budú živí ešte otec, mať,
či ma bude moja milá spomínať.

Tell my dear Machnáč,
Will I see you again in a year or two,
Will my father and mother be still alive,
Will my beloved still remember me.

A ty naša, zem slovenská, taká si,
už na teba prichádzajú zlé časy,
tvoje deti po svete sa túlajú
a na teba, zem slovenská, nedbajú.

And you, our Slovak land,
Hard times are upon you,
Your children wander the world,
Not taking care of you.

Author: Amerikán from Zemplín, 1910

The Emigration of Women

Men, both single and married, went first to explore North America and the possibilities that it offered. They scoped out the situation, secured their footing, found jobs and places to live, and started to earn money.

■■■

Over twice as many men as women emigrated from Slovakia. In 1901 and 1902, nearly three times more men emigrated. Eventually, the number of migrating women increased and balanced out with the men, but only by the end of 1910.

■■■

The prolonged absence of so many men left a gap in the communities in the old country. With husbands, fathers, and sons away, women and children had to take up all the jobs that men traditionally had done around the home and in the fields. Everything now rested on the women's shoulders—the house, the fieldwork, the livestock, along with caring for the children and the elderly. Many women were pushed to perform tasks far beyond their knowledge or physical capacities.

Moreover, the absence of men, who were gone sometime for years at a time, led to another little-discussed phenomenon—illegitimate children. It was not uncommon for a man to return home to find a child whom he had not fathered. More often than not, this child was absorbed into the family and raised as their own son or daughter. This only fortified the desire of men to send for their wives as soon as they had saved enough to pay for the passage.

What about those who did not have wives in Slovakia? If they could, they returned home to find one, especially in the beginning of the great migration. Returning Slovaks, who were coming back to recruit more family and neighbors to come and work in America, would also use the opportunity to find a prospective bride to marry.

Once women started to immigrate, the Slovak communities in the New World could truly grow and establish themselves. After all, Slovak culture is built on and upheld by the family. First came the wives, but before long, single young women were pouring into America in large numbers. They came to earn money to support their families back home, just as their countrymen did.

■ ■ ■

> *Hungarian authorities passed increasingly restrictive laws that sought to curb emigration of men in their prime. Initially, just men eligible to be drafted into the military services were prevented from departure. But later, even men who completed their military duty were kept on the reserve list in case the army needed them.[11] In 1903, the Hungarian government banned all men over the age of 17 from emigrating without a written permission form—from both the Ministry of Defense and the Ministry of Interior.[12]*

■ ■ ■

With the movement of men restricted, women jumped on the opportunity to travel. In 1879, the first cluster of strong-willed Slovak women crossed the ocean and arrived in Passaic, New Jersey. Passaic's textile plants and garment-making factories offered plenty of jobs to women who did not shy away from hard work. The area would eventually employ many incoming Slovak women.

---

[11] De Levay, 1906
[12] Zahra, 2016

With sisters and aunts already living in the U.S., Slovak families felt safer sending their girls off. As time passed, it became more and more common for women to emigrate. Out of nearly 6,000 persons who emigrated from the Šariš region in Slovakia in the year 1905, over 2,000 were women.[13] Most found employment as servants, factory workers, and care givers.

The arrival of maidens also helped to satisfy the migrant community's need for Slovak brides. However, it was not enough for these women to marry and 'just' bear offspring. In addition to having to take care of their families, they were also expected to earn money. After all, this was America.

■ ■ ■

Although it was said that most Slovak men preferred for their wives not to work and took great pride in being the sole providers for their family, very few could afford to do it. To secure large families that commonly produced 5 to 7 children, two incomes were necessary especially in the first years and decades of immigration.

■ ■ ■

Wives and mothers would look for crafty ways to contribute to the family income.

Opening one's home to boarders became a popular approach to making ends meet for women in the U.S., and later in Canada. With so many single men working in the mills and mines, the number of men who needed a clean place to sleep and a warm meal to eat was huge.

---

[13] Megles et al, 1978

It was common to allocate company housing to migrant workers, including those coming from Slovakia. Rows of shanty housing were built to keep the men and their families close to work and to offset the low wages.

Accommodations usually comprised a four-room shack, primitive by American standards but a huge spatial upgrade for the Slovaks. In the old country, the entire family shared a one- or, at best, two-room house with a dirt floor and tiny windows.

The entrepreneurial spirit of Slovak women swiftly kicked in. They kept the kitchen and one of the bedrooms for their family, and the rest were rented out. As many bunk beds as possible were installed in each room. Sometimes, two borders would even share a single bed and a room could have as many as four beds.

Housing so many men was not easy. The housewife was expected to cook breakfast and dinner for the boarders and to prepare a packed lunch for them too. She washed their clothes by hand and sometimes even the dirty backs of the boarders who came home filthy from the mills and mines. It was hard work, and many a woman's hand would bleed under the heavy load. Some would have to take care of as many as 16 boarders at once.[14]

Boarders paid on average $1 to $2 a week for lodging and food. It was a good deal for the miners and factory workers, and a great opportunity for the housewife and her family. Thanks to the accumulated rent, they could move up the economic ladder. Still, most families relied on boarders to simply get by. A husband's salary may have been enough to pay

---

[14] Stolarik, 2012

for a wife and children back in Slovakia, but it was no longer sufficient once they joined him in America.[15]

Boarding houses became a key component in most migrant communities, housing the 'freshest' meat shipped in from across the Atlantic. Some of these women became true mavericks, building and growing their own mini-empires. The boarding house matrons as they became known, held great influence in the community. They served multiple functions—hosts to new migrants, mediators between them and their employers and even the local government, job recruiters, and personal savings banks.

The matrons were also the local matchmakers. They drew on their knowledge of the community and their networks in the old country to find wives for their boarders. One could not afford to make a bad impression on such a woman—or to not pay the rent on time. The boarder's future family happiness depended on his behaving well.

Such entrepreneurial freedoms also forever changed Slovak family gender dynamics in North America, where a woman's status was elevated to an unprecedented level. The Slovak woman, especially the boarding house matron, sometimes earned more than her husband, a stark contrast to the patriarchy in rural Slovakia, where the man was almost always the sole breadwinner and the woman was usually bound to the cradle and kitchen.

By the eruption of World War I, the migration of Slovak women caught up with the migration of Slovak men, allowing a large number of women to gain some degree of independence for the very first time. But the balancing out of

---

[15] Stolarik, 2012

men and women, also lessened the need for boarding houses for single men.

Outside of the home, employment opportunities for Slovak women in America were limited to jobs on the bottom of the career ladder. Initially, they applied their skills within the Slovak and Slavic communities, in addition to securing jobs as cleaners, servants or launderers for local Americans.

Part two
THE JOURNEY

Smugglers, Agents, and Fake Passports

Before 'American fever' gripped hundreds of thousands of people in Slovakia, ordinary folk needed to be persuaded to venture into the unknown. This was the job of the agents.

The agents were often Slavs-Czechs, Slovaks or Poles who had come to America a generation earlier, learned the ropes of capitalism, and were then sent off to seduce the European masses with the promise of the American Dream. They were the first point of contact for the people in the Old Country with the New World.

Some agents were genuine, but others were speculators. Some earnestly wanted to give people a better chance at life, an opportunity to break away from the limitations of societies still stuck in old feudal ways. But there were also agents without integrity, opportunistic predators who did indulge in lies, exploitation, and preying on the desperation of the masses.

Armed with pictures of America, dressed in fancy city clothes, and adorned with thick golden chains, the agents took the unsuspecting simple folk by storm.

■ ■ ■

The Kingdom of Hungary attempted to prevent people from leaving by passing ever stricter laws. In 1903 a new act was passed in parliament that responded to the alarming number of illegal departures taking place. Border police officers were hired to investigate the agents, and a simultaneous smear campaign was mobilized against them in the press. The government alleged that the agents took advantage of the emigrants, who were then exploited by their employers abroad.

■ ■ ■

Central and Eastern Europeans, including people in Slovakia, were susceptible to the tricks of agents especially during the first migration wave. Most of them did not know how to read or write, had no geographic knowledge of the world, and thus no ability to understand the length of the journey on which they were about to embark. It was not uncommon for locals to think that America was on the other side of the Tatra Mountains.

The agents were also creative. There are stories of agents marching into remote Slovak villages banging a large drum, vividly describing streets lined with golden coins, and an American Emperor (much like Austria-Hungary's very own Franz Joseph) who needed their help to collect them.[16]

The people were entranced. Firstly, because the American Emperor was even addressing them, and secondly because of the sheer bounty of the promised wealth. Was this God answering their prayers?

Blissfully unaware and ignorant, they sold their homes and lands to pay for the voyage. The shipping companies made fortunes on ticket sales. And not everyone who paid for a ticket,

---

[16] Pollack, 2016

actually received it. Some agents extracted people's life savings, in exchange for false travel documents.

With time, the ranks of agents expanded to include leaders of local communities. Teachers, doctors, and—most importantly—priests, were recruited to incentivize people to say 'yes' to America. Innkeepers were involved too. Men who patronized pubs to drown their troubles and numb their sorrows, accumulated drinking debts as discussed earlier. The innkeepers, looking to balance their accounts, encouraged such men to resolve their financial hardships by going to America. Each person involved in the chain received a commission on every single ticket sold.

As more people from Slovakia established themselves in North America and wrote letters back home or else returned in person to share their experiences, the need for agents subsided. Worldly returning Slovaks became the new recruiters and also the first point of contact with the new continent. They openly shared their knowledge, from practical advice about finding work in America to securing housing there. The process became more organic, and this put a stop to the dishonest practices of the agents.

Local word-of-mouth was even more effective than the silver tongue of the recruiters. Cousin to cousin, friend to friend, neighbor to neighbor and brother to brother—word of life in America travelled fast. Soon, entire villages would fall silent in eastern Slovakia. At first it was only the men who left. But later, entire families would be boarding steamships bound for North America. Experts refer to this phenomenon as chain migration.

■ ■ ■

> Daniel Šustek is known as the first Slovak travel influencer. His vivid descriptions of the New World propelled thousands of his compatriots to venture across

the ocean. Many were mesmerized by the stories of his transatlantic journey from Liverpool to New York in 1872, alongside his everyday accounts of a self-made man in America. His words single handedly inspired countless Slovaks to follow in his footsteps, dreaming of fortune and adventure in America.[17]

■ ■ ■

Returning Slovaks in fancy dress were the best walking advertisement for the coal mines, steel mills, factories, and let's not forget shipping companies. They returned home with fantastic stories of unimaginable goods, exotic foods, people of different skin colors, and buildings that touched the sky. Countless letters exchanged between Slovaks in America and their families back home only confirmed these tales.

The grass was indeed greener on the other side. Somehow, the hardships endured in the New World were glanced over. And are you surprised? With cash in hand, sometimes after years of sacrifice, the returnees chose to focus on the glory, rather than on the suffering they experienced abroad.

The visible show of financial prowess of the returning *amerikáni* (American Slovaks) was undeniable. It was hard to resist the temptation when one saw people like oneself, coming back with their pockets full of money that allowed them to turn their big dreams into a reality. Everyone and their brother wanted a piece of this fairytale wealth. Moreover, it was easier to leave home when one knew he would be received by somebody on the other side. Even the second-guessing, risk-averse Slovaks were quickly persuaded.

You might think that getting oneself from Upper Hungary to America could not have been that difficult, given how many people crossed the ocean. All you needed was a passport and

---

[17] Čupka, 2022

a ticket, right? But between making the decision to leave and boarding a steam liner lay a long and perilous process. To get that passport and ticket, you would have to jump over impossible bureaucratic and existential hurdles.

To make matters worse, you could be cheated at every step. Anyone could be a culprit. A corrupt clerk, a dishonest railway employee, or a person offering 'favorable' currency exchange rates—any of these could trick you out of our life savings.

■ ■ ■

Slovaks did their best to look out for one another. Word about fraudulent practices traveled fast in the neighborhood. Crooks could get it away with it once or twice, but then they were flagged in the eyes of the community.

■ ■ ■

To go or not to go was a life-altering decision. Once a person decided to make the big leap, they had to take a few necessary steps. First, they had to secure enough money to pay the steamship fare. Although the new ocean liners made the transatlantic travel much affordable, the $30 ticket was still a steep fee to pay for the average person in Upper Hungary.

In the beginnings of the migration wave, not everyone had to pay for their ticket upfront. The U.S. industries were so hungry for labor that sometimes the mines and mills offered to cover the cost of the ticket. The fee was then deducted from the worker's wages. But once mass migration began, the migrants had to find the money to secure their own fare.

The $30 fee was a lot of money for a people who earned next to nothing. It could take a decade to save that much. Parents, siblings, extended family, and friends all chipped in. Others resorted to selling their land and even their houses. In most cases, the purchased ticket would be valid, but there were also instances when people arrived in the German ports to be confronted with the soul-crushing news that their steamship ticket was fake.

The desperate need for fast cash created space for cheating and swindling. Opportunistic buyers offered to buy the land at a fraction of its worth, only to sell it back to migrants when they returned from America at a much higher rate.

Once you sold your land or persuaded enough family members to loan you the money, you could proceed to the next stage—facing the Austro-Hungarian bureaucracy.

At that time, people did not obtain passports in the same way we have passports issued to us today. In the latter half of the 1800s, nobody had a passport. The migrants had only recently gained the freedom to move, thanks to the abolition of serfdom. They had never needed a passport before.

As always, there was a choice—you could get a legitimate passport with all the necessary stamps, or you could go the unofficial route. Those who went by the book had to first gain a permit to leave the country. This required a letter of approval from a doctor, confirming that they were fit to travel. Of course, every single step cost money and, even worse, the complex process made room for speculators looking to enrich themselves at the cost of people who had nothing.

The Kingdom of Hungary was rocked by a scandal in 1889. It exposed the dirty practices that occurred as private companies and the public sector collided to extract money from the poorest members of the society. The Hamburg-Amerika Line, one of several transatlantic shipping companies, lined the pockets of railway employees, customs officers, notaries, policemen, doctors, and inn owners as part of an elaborate scheme. The sophisticated international network that preyed on the simplemindedness of the common folk operated as follows.

A prospective migrant would be received by a person who pretended to be employed by the local administration responsible for issuing departure permits. Upon paying a nice little fee, hand to hand, face to face, the migrant would be sent to a like-minded doctor, who would then issue the required medical permit. Here came the catch.

After a thorough medical check, the doctor would ban the migrant from leaving based on the state of his or her health. Of course, this inconvenience could be fixed with a handsome bribe. What followed was a string of other frauds, each pulling more and more money out of the would-be migrant's pocket.

When Hungary tightened its emigration law in the early 1900s, it became tricky for men of conscription age to leave the territory legally. Many wanted to emigrate not just to improve their lot in life but also to avoid military service in the Austro-Hungary army. Official records reveal that few passports were issued to men during the peak of the migration wave, suggesting that the majority of them emigrated illegally.[18]

---

[18] Javor, 2022

These men turned to the services of smugglers to get them over the border, past the patrol checks, and into Poland, on their way to the German ports. Fake passports that looked real—or real enough—were provided to the adventurers to get them aboard the ocean liners. With a little luck, these documents were not examined too closely.

Once the formal requirements were met, one way or another, and the journey to the nearest port was arranged, the migrants packed the few precious belongings they had.

Whether Catholic, Lutheran, or Greek Catholic, most could not depart from Slovakia without their rosary, Bible, or cross. A deeply religious lot, they relied on God's blessing to safely make it across the ocean. A change of clothes, food for the journey, and perhaps a family photo to remind them of home and those they were leaving behind, would also be placed into a cloth that was flung over the shoulder.

To get to the German ports, by far the most popular boarding destination, it was necessary to travel a considerable distance, leaving one empire and entering another. It was unlikely migrants would simply board a train at home and disembark in Hamburg. They first had to reach a bigger city, be it Vienna, Budapest, or Prague. People commonly covered some proportion of the journey on foot, in a horse-pulled carriage, or by some combination of the two. Making it to the bustling port was a huge relief, yet the trials and tribulations of the journey were far from over.

Crossing the Ocean

Most emigrants from Slovakia departed Europe through the ports of Hamburg or Bremen, which both had hundreds of thousands of Europeans passing through them from the mid-1800s onwards. It must have been a sight to behold. Men and women dressed in their very best traditional attire, speaking many languages, all excited, terrified, and curious as they prepared to board the ships. Hopefully, they did not succumb to the persuasive stories of swindlers who lurked around the docks offering expensive substandard accommodation in ports or unnecessary 'mandatory' kits for the journey.

When the people started to leave Slovakia in large numbers, the transatlantic voyage was much shorter and safer thanks to modern steamships. Yet, 10 days aboard a liner was not a relaxing experience for those who travelled on a budget—which

was nearly everyone. In addition, they often made stops on the way, in ports such as Liverpool, England, to pick up more passengers, which just extended the voyage.

Steerage was the least comfortable way to travel. Located at the bottom of the boat, it was the lowest category of passenger accommodation. Steerage, originally reserved for heavy machinery and livestock, was never meant to accommodate people. Steamship lines opened it to humans to respond to the massive demand of those who could not afford to travel in the regular classes.

Needless to say, most Slovaks found themselves squished in steerage together with Poles, Ukrainians and other Slavs. There were not always enough beds for the number of tickets sold, and passengers had to share bunk beds with strangers or sleep on the floor. Young women and girls travelling alone were particularly vulnerable.

Steerage passengers were separated by sex or familial status: men, women, married couples, and families. They all slept in narrow bunks, three beds across and two or three deep. The beds consisted of straw- or seaweed-filled mattresses covered with burlap.

Crossing the Atlantic in these conditions was a challenge marked by discomfort and seasickness even when the weather was good. It became a nightmare when the seas turned rough. When a storm hit, the latches to the upper deck were locked to prevent water from flooding in. This blocked access to fresh air for passengers in the steerage. What is more, they could not reach the bathrooms that were located on the upper desks. Thrashing around, the people had to rely on buckets to relieve themselves, and the buckets were then emptied into the ocean. Spilled excrement, urine and vomit would inevitably spill onto the floor. The stench was unbearable.

Regular dining rooms were difficult to come by. Sometimes, tables were replaced by shelves along the wall of sleeping compartments to save space. If there was a dining room, there were never enough tables and seats for all steerage passengers. They had to take turns eating.

At mealtimes, passengers passed in a single line before the stewards who were serving rations. Every passenger in steerage was given crude eating utensils at the beginning of the journey. They had to look after these utensils for the duration of the passage. Once they had their food, diners had to find a place to eat and to later wash their dishes. They would use a single warm-water facet or a large tub of hot water, an undertaking that required a lot of patience among hundreds of passengers doing the same thing.

The monotonous ship menu consisted of soups, stews and potatoes for dinner and cereal, bread, jam, and coffee for breakfast. Vegetables and pickles were precious, and the coffee was bad. It was said that even the few decent ingredients were spoiled by the poorly trained cooks. If you were lucky, there would also be butter and leftovers from the upper-class meals. Cheese, salami, and cakes from home were a saving grace for many.

With inadequate clean water, poor air ventilation, and dreadful access to sanitation, diseases spread easily. Steerage class was a breeding ground for influenzas and other diseases, like typhus and dysentery. Some 5,000 people died from diseases on ships bound for America in 1847 alone.[19] Legislation passed by the U.S. government in 1855 addressed the appalling conditions for the lowest class passengers. The new law stated that there had to be at least one bathroom per hundred

---

[19] Roos, 2019

passengers on all transatlantic liners. This was no sweeping victory for the people, but it was better than nothing.

In the tense atmosphere of steerage, with next to no privacy, fights broke out easily. But most passengers turned to their Bibles, rosary beads and prayers to cope.

■ ■ ■

The upper decks contrasted with the quarters below. First-class passengers paraded on the pavilion, enjoying the fresh air and sunshine. They had their own private cabins, equipped with creature comforts including their own private toilets. Three warm and tasty meals awaited them daily along with entertainment and rest. Their transatlantic crossing was a luxurious experience, earning steam liners that set sail at the beginning of the 20th century the nickname 'floating palaces'. For the rich, indeed they were.

■ ■ ■

Of course, it was not all doom and gloom in steerage. The spirit in people came alive, perhaps also because of the adversity of the conditions. There would be songs, music, dance, and storytelling to pass the long days on the open ocean. Nevertheless, by the time the ship safely pulled into the calm of New York Harbor, the migrants were overcome by relief.

Joy and excitement gripped the exhausted travelers as they sailed passed the mythical Statue of Liberty, installed in 1886, on their way to Ellis Island. Located in the mouth of the Hudson River, nested between New York City and New Jersey, this little island witnessed millions upon millions of immigrants arrive at the gates of the country where they hoped to find their sanctuary and fortune. It is estimated that around 40 percent of Americans can trace their ancestors' arrival to this gateway.

THE JOURNEY
Slovak Settlers

■ ■ ■

Before the establishment of the immigration center at Ellis Island, migrants from Slovakia disembarked in Manhattan's Castle Gardens, Kasigarda as the Slovaks pronounced it. Today, Kasigarda is a museum of migration in eastern Slovakia, scheduled to open in 2023.

■ ■ ■

Having to cope with some two thousand newcomers on an average day, the Ellis Island officials put a registration system into place. The newly arrived immigrants had to queue up, often waiting for hours, until it was their turn to meet with U.S. government officials, who conducted a medical and legal inspection.

The objective was to establish whether the immigrants were fit to enter the country. Truth be told, the job of the officers was to allow as many people in as possible, not to stop them.

Their arrival into the New World was especially tough for the pioneers, the first wave of incoming migrants from Slovakia. They had no idea what to expect on the other side of the ocean, and they were completely unprepared for the tricksters awaiting them at the ports. The most common scams revolved around money exchange rates and accommodation. For those least lucky, their money and belongings were taken from them by force.

Although Manhattan was a beacon of opportunity for many, most Slovaks journeyed further. The majority would continue by coach or train to the center of the mining and steel industry in America's Northeast. Unable to communicate in English, tags were placed on the Slovaks with names of their destinations, to enable train conductors to correctly navigate their boarding and disembarking.

Later on, more and more immigrants were greeted by families and friends once they passed the controls.

They had made it to America! What next?

Part three
LIFE IN THE NEW WORLD

A New Beginning

Many legends circulate about who the first Slovak to set foot on North America was. Rumor has it that Stephanus Parmenius came to Canada as early as 1583. Another story suggests that two Slovaks, George Mata and John Bogdan, accompanied Captain John Smith on his historic voyage to Jamestown, Virginia, in 1608. But it later turned out that these men, who are also claimed by the Poles, never existed.

The first person to reach the continent who was indisputably Slovak was Isaac Ferdinand Sarosy (also spelled Šarisský). He arrived in Pennsylvania in 1695 and lived in Germantown, where he served as a Protestant preacher. Not much is known about his destiny.

■ ■ ■

It is difficult to keep track of Slovaks arriving to the U.S. Present-day Slovakia was then a part of Austria-Hungary. Slovakia did not exist, and there was no formally recognized Slovak nation. When early immigrants arrived in America, they had no box to tick to indicate that they were Slovak. The intake forms only listed choices such as Austria or Hungary as the country of origin. Others, simply identified themselves as Slavs. Most

> *Slovaks were not even aware of being Slovak and some were not comfortable admitting to it. But with time, Slovak settlers in America began to confidently proclaim to be Slovak, and this was a game-changing moment for the old country.*

■ ■ ■

But the great migration to America kicked off only two decades after the abolition of serfdom in Austria-Hungary. As discussed earlier, the innovation of the steamship dramatically shorted the journey, and the democratization of steerage prices made the transatlantic journey that much more accessible to the masses. They went to the places where their labor was needed most, which is why the most popular destinations for Slovaks were the mines, mills, and foundries of Pennsylvania and Ohio. Others secured jobs with the railways in Chicago and many other places. But even though they had work, the first wave of settlers did not have an easy time of it.

The migration journey was unknown, difficult, stressful, and full of traps. The fact that these migrating Slovaks knew very little about where they were going made them easy prey to just about anybody. They could not speak a word of English, nor did they understand the cultural codes of the complex new world they were entering. This made them the perfect targets for an entire ecosystem of swindlers, con artists who specialized in immigrants from other countries.

Those emigrants who were not victims of crime, might lose their savings in more innocent mishaps. One story describes a man who did not know how much a dollar was worth. He handed over his US $1 bill, pointing at a ham sandwich. Much to his surprise, he received a kilo of ham rolls in turn—and, just like that, he had spent most of his precious savings upon arriving.

■ ■ ■

The trend started with a few daring or desperate individual migrants, and these were later joined by more and more Slovaks. Together, these emigrants who shared a culture started to form clusters and communities near the mines, mills, and factories. The newly established foundations made it easier for others to follow. As the unknown became known, the risk of becoming a victim of swindlers and frauds decreased and international migration became that much more common.

■ ■ ■

To add insult to injury, these Slovak peasants also looked bizarre to the Americans; the emigrants' clothes, style, and way of behaving were like something from another world. Most Slovaks showed up in the Port of New York, proudly dressed in their traditional *kroj* folk wear. Whether elaborate or simple, this attire, unique to every region of Austria-Hungary, was handmade. Every ornamental design had its own meaning and purpose, and a *kroj* was one of the most cherished possessions an individual could have. Yet to Americans, the *kroj* looked odd.

One curious story from 1879 has survived. A group of Slovaks had recently arrived in America. They had no money, and so from the Port of New York, they had to walk to their destination in Trenton, New Jersey. As was the norm, they were proudly wearing their traditional *kroj* ensembles. The locals were so confused by the colorful sight that they mistook the Slovaks for native Americans, who had returned from the prairies to claim back their lost land. The Slovaks were chased out of the town with guns and stones.

All they could do was to carry on and walk to the next town, hoping for a warmer welcome. This time the Americans ran and hid from the Slovaks. This was certainly an improvement from being shot at, but it was far from a reassuring entrance to your new country. Who knew that a *kroj* could provoke such strong reactions! Needless to say, the Slovaks shed their traditional wear as soon as they could and replaced with more appropriate cosmopolitan fashion.

Once Slovaks had found their way to their places of employment, they began working just as soon as they could. They had debts to pay and families to feed back home. America was not a holiday; it was an opportunity to make money, and they wanted to do that and return home quickly.

Many were excited about what awaited them in this strange new world, but others regretted leaving behind the idyllic, agrarian, and in many ways innocent Upper Hungary. Life in America could not be further from the alluring tales of the agents, who had promised streets covered with gold coins and nuggets. There was gold, but these men and women would have to work hard to earn it.

Although their wages were tiny, the emigrants still managed to set money aside to send home. The Slovak-American dream was to return with pockets full of dollars, but a more practical solution was to send the money home sooner and not wait to take it yourself. Considering the heavy drinking of the male immigrant population, sending money home was also a preventive measure. This way the entire week's wage did not end up in the pockets of tavern owners.

■■■

> By 1910, Slovaks in American earned around $219 million annually. Part of this was sent back to Upper Hungary in the form of remittances. It is difficult to estimate the exact sum, but experts suggest that Slovak emigrants sent back 100 million crowns ($20 million) every year. This was enough money to shift local power dynamics as Slovak farmers started purchasing plots of land from the aristocracy.[20]

■■■

Those emigrants who had wives and children in the old country were most motivated. They had to send money back to cover the daily costs of living,

[20] Čulen, 2007

and when they sent additional funds, they could be used to buy more land, more animals, and tools for the household.

In general, remittance packages were sent back to Upper Hungary twice a year—before Christmas and before Easter. However, banking was still in its nascent period, and Slovaks did not trust either banks or post offices. They were accustomed to keeping their savings hidden under a sack of hay or a mattress, and they had no experience in transferring funds across an ocean and in intangible ways. Their concerns were justified, as not all money that was sent actually arrived. Sometimes it got lost on the way; other times it did not reach the recipient simply because the address was listed incorrectly.

There were also swindlers, stealing money on the spot or applying extortionate exchange rates. When it came to sending money, the worldlier Czechs fared far better than the Slovaks, while the Rusyns faced the greatest hurdles. The poorer the migrant, the more vulnerable to exploitation. And, so, the Slovaks often opted for a more old-fashioned approach: money in an envelope. However, sending money in this way was not without problems. Although the envelopes often arrived at their destinations, the money was not always still inside.

Luckily, there was another means: the human envoy. As soon as word spread that someone in the community—a family member, a colleague, or a trusted neighbor—was about to travel to Europe, they would be asked to carry the money and deliver it in person.

■■■

> *It was a jungle out there when it came to remittances. This was an opportunity for Michal 'Mike' Bosák, who opened his first bank in Pennsylvania in 1897. He wanted to help secure the money transfers of his compatriots.*

With so many Slovaks in America, his clientele base was wide. It did not take long for Michal's banking empire to grow, and he became the president of the National Bank in Olyphant, which issued bank notes with his name on them. In 1915, he set up the Bosak State Bank in Scranton, Pennsylvania, thanks to the support and loyalty of the local Slovak community. Bosak made it possible for their hard-earned money to be delivered safely into the hands of their loved ones in Upper Hungary.

■ ■ ■

Dull, Dirty and Dangerous Jobs

Coal was the fuel behind the rise of industrial America. It was a cheap source of power for steam engines, furnaces, and forges. With coal, iron, and steel, other related industries could expand. And from the 1880s onward, they didn't just grow, they boomed—which meant that the United States needed a lot of coal to supply demand.

Advances in technology made it possible to penetrate deep under the surface of the Earth, but the search for coal also required the hands of the miners. Doing this difficult work, miners had to descend into the dark abyss of the mine shafts and to manually extract this 'black gold'. As the coalfields of Pennsylvania and Illinois began being mined, they drew countless Slovak men into their murky depths.

Most Slovaks arriving in America were low-skilled and, especially in the first few decades, also illiterate. They did not have the privilege of choosing from an array of jobs according to their liking. They often had to take the dirtiest and most dangerous jobs on the market. Being a miner required no knowledge of English; it needed 'only' the willingness to risk your life.

■ ■ ■

Slovak men were employed not only in mines. By 1909, Slovaks accounted for 10 percent of all steel and iron workers in the United States, and at their peak, 20 percent of all steel workers in America.

Homestead, Pennsylvania—site of the largest steel mill in the world—attracted countless Slovaks and Rusyns.

Carnegie Steel Mill (later, U.S. Steel) employed around seven thousand people at the beginning of the 20th century. The mill operated 24/7, and the men worked in shifts governed by strict hierarchy. The night shift was the least desirable, and so it was reserved for novices. The more seasoned workers took up the early evening shift. But the most coveted slot of all was the dayshift, exclusive to the most experienced workers.

■ ■ ■

On average, Slovak immigrants earned $1 to $1.50 a day, half of the normal wage in the U.S. The immigrants were working 10- to 12-hour shifts, 6 or 7 days a week. This was a dismal pay and long working hours for any self-respecting American, but it was a victory for the poor from Upper Hungary, who could earn 10 times more in the American mines than in the agricultural jobs available to them at home.

Miners were paid only for the weight of coal they mined until an hourly rate was introduced for those who belonged to unions. A general minimum hourly wage was introduced in the U.S. in 1938.

To earn $2 a day, which was the living wage in America at the time, this immigrant labor would have to work extremely hard. Most only managed to bring home $1.50 a day, barely enough to support a small family, let alone the large families that were a norm among Slovak immigrants.

Day in and day out, they toiled under dangerous conditions. The ceiling of the damp mines could collapse at any moment, and too often it did. Between 1900 and 1909, the deadliest decade in U.S. mining history, 3,660 coal miners perished in 133 mine accidents.[21]

Luckily for the management, dead miners were easily replaced with Eastern Europeans desperate for jobs. In the 19th century, human capital was cheap, abundant, and accessible—so why lower the profits by investing in safer work conditions?!

■ ■ ■

Coal mining was one of the most dangerous jobs on the planet. It was a fatal enterprise. Those who could, sought better employment as soon as they had sufficiently mastered the English language. Others, of course, accepted their fate. It was not easy, but their working-class jobs paved the way for their progeny, the second generation Slovak-Americans to claim the benefits of the sacrifices made by their forefathers.

■ ■ ■

A job was a job, nevertheless, and families needed the money. As soon as their sons were of age, many Slovaks would bring their children into the mines. Boys as young as 13 would work as breaker boys, separating impurities from the mined coal by hand. Sometimes, three generations of men—son, father, grandfather—all worked for the same mining company.

---

[21] Brnich and Kowalski-Trakofker, 2010

■ ■ ■

Cheap company housing made life a bit easier for miners and their families. Located right next to the mines, the rudimentary quarters were basic at best, appalling at worst. 'Company towns' also provided a company store that sold everything the migrants needed—food, clothing, diapers, work equipment. Despite their pitiful pay, the miners were expected to purchase their own tools—helmets, shovels, and pickaxes. And if that wasn't bad enough, the companies also had the local politicians in their pockets and held critical sway with the local police. Justice was hard to come by, especially in the smaller mining communities of the Northeast.

■ ■ ■

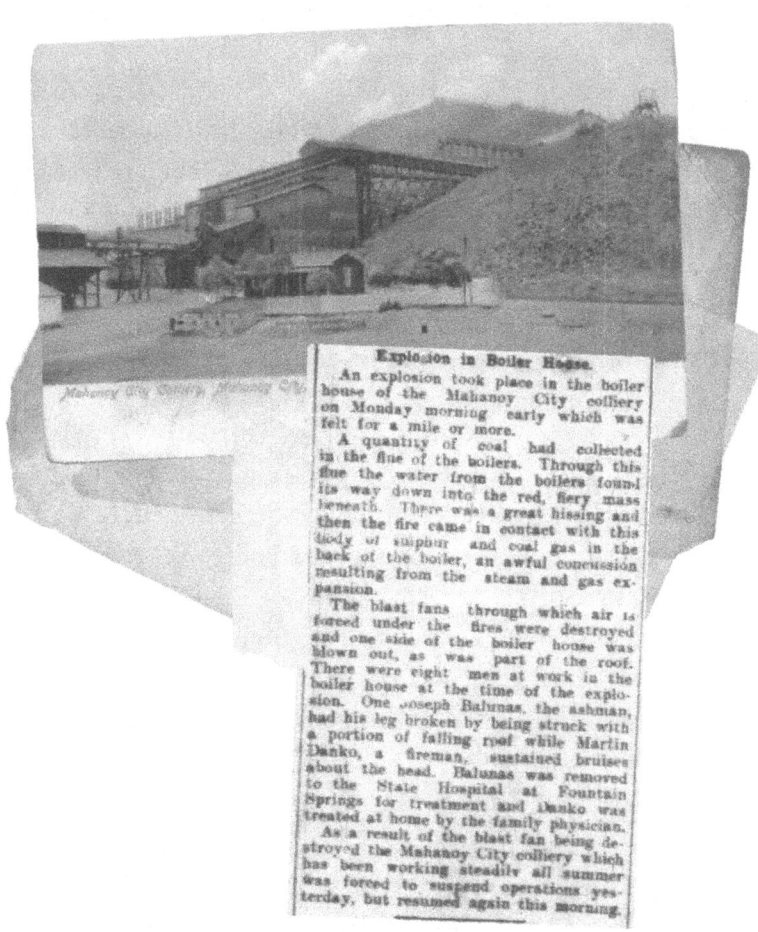

However, living and working in America empowered immigrants from Slovakia. They became aware of the injustices that they had to bear—and aware as well of their own value as workers. In time, the miners began to organize themselves into unions.

The fight for better pay preceded the arrival of Slovaks. It was the Irish who first kicked up dust, unwittingly encouraging the import of Slavic workers. The role of the Slavs was not just to replace the disorderly Irish but also to divide the English-speaking mining community from within, making it easier to control. This is partly why Slovaks and other Slavs, through no fault of their own, were so despised by other the American miners. This hostility was magnified by the unwillingness of Slovaks to join the budding unions. They were grateful to be given work, and they wanted to avoid trouble. As a result, the mines were rife with ethnic tension.

In time, the Slavs too began to organize themselves and demand better pay and safer working conditions. When the coal companies in Pennsylvania cut wages in the 1890s after a coal industry slump, this was the last straw, even for the complacent Slovaks. They knew that they, too, deserved a decent life. After all, that is why they had come to America in the first place.

As the worker strikes proliferated, mining production slowed down, compromising the profit of the mining companies even further. The stage was set for the 'labor wars'.

In 1891, around 18,000 Slovaks joined the miners who went on strike in Connellsville, Pennsylvania. Another major walkout occurred in the grimy mining town of Braddock, and 44 Slovaks were arrested. In the ensuing trial, three of them were sentenced to death by hanging: George Rusnak, Michael Sabol, and Andrew Toth. On the brink of tragedy, the Slovak community sprang into action. Slovaks across the U.S. pulled together their humble resources to appeal the court ruling. In the end, two of the men—Sabol and Rusnak—were freed. Andrew Toth served 19 years in prison.

This was just the beginning. The mining companies were not ready to part with their fat profit margins and unchecked influence. The costs of production rose with each demand for better working conditions and higher wages. The companies blacklisted defiant workers who were prone to strike, which meant they were banned from future employment in the mining industry anywhere in the region.

Consequent dismissals and further wage cuts led to ever harsher working conditions. Lower pay was combined with the rising costs of goods in company towns, and so anger and frustration rose among the workers and their families.

In 1897, the situation was about to explode in Hazleton, Pennsylvania. In August, the first 2,000 miners went on strike. Within two days, almost all the mines in the area were closed by strikes. Promises of a pay rise and fairer treatment of Slavic miners were made, but few were kept. Hence in September of that year, another 3,000 miners walked out of four mines, shutting the mines down. Within five days, 10,000 more workers joined the strike.

The mine owners were furious. They called on the county sheriff to help crush the dissent. On Friday, September 10, around 400 unarmed strikers, including Slovaks and Rusyns, marched to a coal mine that was still in operation to spread their dissent. They were met by the local sheriff and 150 armed deputies. The strikers refused to disperse, and in the ensuing fight, the police opened fire on the crowd, killing 19 miners and injuring 50 more. Many were shot in the back as they were running away from the authorities. Four Slovaks died on that fateful day, that forever changed the history of American mining. The event is remembered as the Lattimer Massacre.

Despite such challenges, the unions persisted and grew stronger. They helped to humanize the working conditions for all miners.

■ ■ ■

> Not only miners resorted to strikes to claim decent working conditions and wages. The Great Steel Strike[22] that took place across the Northeast and Midwest in 1919 was referred to as the 'Slovak strike' by some. In addition to higher wages, the men demanded that employers respect their right to gather and to hold union meetings. Company officials lined the pockets of political leaders to sabotage these rights by denying meeting permits, seizing educational literature, or harassing union leaders. The mining companies also threatened to replace the striking workers with African-Americans and Mexicans.

■ ■ ■

---

[22] Stolarik, 1997

“ *My grandmother recalled that when she was 15, the union her husband belonged to called for a strike. The mining company responded by evicting the miners' families from their homes. The miners sought refuge in the union hall, but the coal company management would keep that building, and others that sheltered the miners and their families, under surveillance to try to account for all the men. The windows of the hall were even broken by a suspected company official sent to identify them.*

Later, someone suspected to be a company official began to set off explosions near any buildings occupied by miners and their families. In a likely attempt to give the impression that the workers and their loved ones might be blown up if the striking miners did not return to work. Some of the Slovak miners retaliated by setting off explosions to scare the company representatives. A friend of my grandmother's family and an accomplice were arrested and convicted for blowing up a building. ”

Paul Dykewicz

Living In America

Besides grueling work, what did Slovak life look like in America?

New immigrants tended to form ethnic communities to soften their introduction to a foreign environment, culture, and language. These ethnic enclaves created a buffer between the strange New World and the old one. The Slovak communities were particularly strong in Pittsburgh, Pennsylvania, and Cleveland, Ohio.

The local community played an immense role in the lives of immigrants, helping them to deal with homesickness, integration, discrimination, and harassment, which came not only from Americans but also from the earlier and, thus, better established migrants—the Germans and the Irish. They made many of a joke about 'dumb Hunkies' when addressing Slavs. The most common derogatory slur was 'Hunky' for immigrants coming from Austria-Hungary.

The Slovaks, like the Irish before them, lived in poor neighborhoods where basic wooden houses were crammed together to accommodate as many people as possible. The houses

THIS YEAR LIKELY TO BREAK ALL IMMIGRATION RECORDS

LARGEST DAY, MAY 3, 1902; LARGEST MONTH, APRIL, 1902; 202,000 IN FOUR MONTHS AND NINE DAYS, AS AGAINST 402,000 IN ALL LAST YEAR.

Poles, Slavs and Italians Lead All Others Nowadays, Whereas the Germans and the Irish, Much More Desirable as American Citizens, Were Formerly in the Majority—Armenians Have Almost Ceased Coming, But Greeks and Assyrians Are Finding Their Way Here in Greater Numbers Than Ever Before.

The Influx of Slavonic Immigrants

ROPE DUMPING AGED AND UNFIT ON U. S. IN INCREASING HORDE

The "Land of the Free" Inducement Threatens to Swamp Ellis Island — 26,710 Immigrants Arrived Last Week

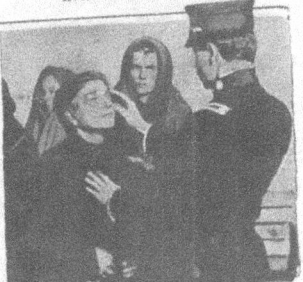

(Copyright, Underwood & Underwood.)

The type of immigrants Europe is pouring into this country in an increasing stream; aged women and children being examined at Ellis Island, New York.

BY F. M. KERBY.

Ellis Island, N. Y., March 7.—Europe is sending us her unfit—her old women and old men, her very young, and her men unfit for military duty.

Between 75 and 80 per cent of all immigrants entering the United States come through the port of New York. And the war has NOT stopped the flow of immigrants, though it has considerably reduced the stream, and has changed the character of the incoming tide.

B. H. Uhl, acting commissioner of immigration here, says:

"We are getting, now, women and children, old men, and men unfit for military duty."

"This is a natural result of the war."

"Belligerent nations have stringent restrictions upon emigration of men of military age. And we are receiving fewer young women than used to get."

During the fiscal year ended June 30, 1914, the second year of...

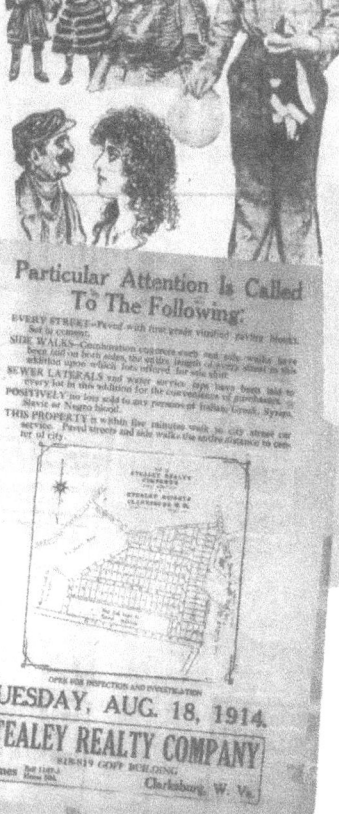

Particular Attention Is Called To The Following:

EVERY STREET—Paved with first grade vitrified paving blocks. Set in cement.

SIDE WALKS—Combination concrete curb and side walks have been laid on both sides, the width being 4 ft. every street in this addition upon which lots offered for sale abut.

SEWER LATERALS and water service taps have been laid to every lot in this addition for the convenience of purchasers.

POSITIVELY no lots sold to any persons of Italian, Greek, Syrian, Slavic or Negro blood.

THIS PROPERTY is within five minutes walk to city street car service. Paved streets and side walks the entire distance to center of city.

OPEN FOR INSPECTION AND INVESTIGATION

TUESDAY, AUG. 18, 1914.

STEALEY REALTY COMPANY

818-819 GOFF BUILDING

Phones { Bell 1140 } Clarksburg, W. Va.

had no toilets, and those who lived in them had to make do with simple latrines in what were called 'out-houses'. In cities like Pittsburgh, the streets were black from the coal dust and soot that enveloped entire neighborhoods, shielding the sun and dirtying the water. When it rained, everything turned into a muddy and slippery mess, which made the primitive conditions in Upper Hungary look idyllic in comparison.

■ ■ ■

The low quality of an immigrant's life was reflected in the child mortality rate of the Eastern European neighborhoods. Every third child died before their second birthday. Once the labor unions were able to facilitate better working and living conditions, child mortality improved.

■ ■ ■

Although living and working conditions were nothing short of appalling, there were some very pleasant surprises to life in America. Grocery store prices were much lower than in Slovakia, where having meat for dinner was reserved only for special occasions. In America, chicken and pork were affordable.

Liquor cost next to nothing. Many immigrant men found that working the grueling hours in the mills and the mines, they needed to somehow let off steam. A glass of whisky was only 5 cents at a saloon, which meant that miners and factory workers could buy quite a few on their daily pay of $1.50. To help the affordable alcohol go down and to lure in more customers, the taverns offered an all-you-can-eat buffet. The deal was impossible to resist for many a hungry and thirsty single man. As a shift would end, the dirty and depleted Slovaks poured into the streets and stumbled into their favorite taverns, no matter the time of day.

Homestead, Pennsylvania, is an example of one such town where the entire community catered to hard-working men. Taverns kept their doors open at all hours, every day. In 1902,

Homestead had 48 saloons and 22 churches competing for the limited free time of the workers. In the Slovak neighborhood of Johnstown, Pennsylvania, pubs, and saloons lined the road between the employee sleeping quarters and workplaces.

Sadly, boozing away at local saloons became a common coping mechanism for the lonely and overworked men. After the workday was over, it was common to see a row of Slovaks on the bar stools, downing one glass after another.

However, these pubs were more than just watering-holes. The taverns also created a much-needed space for the men to come together so they could relax and reminisce about their homeland. These taverns became social centers, giving their patrons vestiges of the old country in a foreign and sometimes hostile land.

But alcohol could not ease the feelings of loneliness forever. Married men wanted to bring their wives and families over to join them, and single men wanted to return to Upper Hungary to find a partner. They longed to come home to the warmth of a woman's touch, not to mention clean clothes and hot meals. Children brought responsibility, but they also brought joy into the home. They gave the hardworking men a sense of purpose. They were slaving away so that one day their children could build better lives for themselves.

Slovak immigrants preferred to marry Slovak women, and Slovak-Americans initially looked down on those who married non-Slovaks. In the beginning, returning to the old country to fetch a wife was considered by many to be a necessity. Later, there were other solutions available to those who did not have the time or money to travel back to the homeland. Women, too, began to migrate. They, too, took the big leap across the ocean to make money and support their families back home.

Slovak social dances were arranged all over America, to bring men and women together. These dances were held on weekends in local community halls, and their sole purpose was to make it possible for the young and fertile to court, commit, and become engaged quickly—if they liked one another. Men and women sometimes paired off for life after just one or two dates.

■ ■ ■

The town of Passaic, New Jersey, was known for its social gatherings and dating parties. After 1879, when single Slovak women began emigrating in large numbers, they settled in Passaic, which offered ample women-friendly employment opportunities in its textile factories. Single Slovak men started to come from far and wide, hoping to find a beautiful woman to marry. A man would usually take two days off at the end of his week to travel to

> *Passaic. He would then station himself at the factory gate and watch the girls coming to or leaving from work. If someone caught his eye, he would propose marriage to her on the spot. If she turned him down, he would try his luck with another. Once the girl agreed, the wedding would take place the following Sunday. On average, 10 to 20 weddings used to take place in Passaic every Sunday during the heyday of immigration.*[23]

■ ■ ■

Marriages arranged out of necessity were all too common as well. If a woman was widowed after her husband perished in a mining accident, she faced a bleak future. At the peak of the Industrial Revolution, the widow and her children were expected to move out of the company housing within 30 days. Most widows spoke only broken English and had little means to provide for themselves and their children. A marriage was a means for survival. To ease the blow, the single friends, cousins, or even brothers of the late husband might step in to marry the widow.

It was only when the men brought women into their lives that the Slovak communities could truly begin to establish themselves. The arrival of women dramatically altered Slovak neighborhoods, changing them by the early 20th century from places to eat, drink, and sleep to thriving communities. Slovak emigrants then developed their own boarding houses, fraternal and civic-organizations, churches, saloons, stores, schools, and Slovak language newspapers.

With their women and children beside them, the men no longer felt an urgent need to return to the old country. A year abroad slowly became five years and then a decade. Eventually,

---

[23] Čulen, 2007

the 'birds of passage' were transformed into settled American immigrants. The New World was no longer a strange and hostile place.

America became home.

■ ■ ■

In 1894, the Slovak Colonization Company in Pennsylvania purchased 3,000 acres of prairie land in Arkansas, giving rise to Slovaktown. The only settlement in the United States named after the immigrants' Slovak heritage. Following a campaign in the Slovak-American press, around 25 Slovak families plucked up the courage to take yet another leap of faith and move from industrial Pennsylvania into the grasslands of Arkansas. The inhabitants of Slovaktown originally harvested prairie hay, but by 1916 they switched to rice farming. Today, the town is officially named Slovak, Arkansas.[24]

■ ■ ■

---

[24] Čupka, 2022

Yet, for the most part Slovaks depended on the 'outside world' for their income and jobs but for little else. A person did not even have to learn to speak English to get by in America. In a Slovak community, the butcher spoke Slovak, the postman spoke Slovak, the hairdresser spoke Slovak, as did the doctor, lawyer, and banker.

Nevertheless, the birth of their progeny required that the immigrants integrate more deeply into American society. The future of their children depended on it. Then came the question of naturalization. The promise of American citizenship meant a new chapter in life, a new identity. To take this step, the migrants first had to file a petition for citizenship, and this was followed by an exam. Even though naturalization was possible, most Slovaks lived in the U.S. for decades before they even had the courage to submit their applications to become citizens.

Initially, the citizenship process was not governed by a federal law but by local regulations. Since there were no uniform standards, their was no secure process to determine who would be granted U.S. citizenship and who would be denied it. The decision was made by whichever judge presided in that area and on that day. Then in 1906, President Theodore Roosevelt signed an act to centralize the citizenship process.

Applicants would now have to provide verification of their arrival along with the names and birth information of their family members. Applicants also had to be able to speak English and be willing to pledge their allegiance to the United States by "renouncing all ties and fidelity to any foreign prince, potentate, state, or sovereignty". For Slovaks that meant Franz Joseph, the emperor of Austria-Hungary. This request wasn't hard for most Slovaks.

Once a Slovak immigrant was granted U.S. citizenship, his or her children had an easier time assimilating. Becoming an

'American' brought with it many advantages, and it opened the door to a life beyond the tightknit confines of Slovak ethnic enclaves. In order to encourage assimilation, the Slovak fraternal organizations played their part. For example, the National Slovak Society required U.S. citizenship to join the organization.

■ ■ ■

By the early 1910s, many immigrants from Slovakia or their descendants had grown tired of life in industrial America. They wanted to return to the honest life they had known back in the old country, far away from the immoral temptations and wickedness of the big cities. This sentiment was encapsulated in the popular Slovak-American slogan of the times „späť ku gazdovstvu" (back to the farm).[25]

In 1911, a small group of Slovak-Americans decided to take matters into their own hands. In the name of American spirit, they founded the Slavia Colony Company in Cleveland and used it to establish their own settlement in Central Florida. Upon purchasing 1,200 acres of farmland in Oviedo, Florida, a total of six families relocated there to begin celery farming in Slavia, Florida. The community slowly died out, also thanks to the urban sprawl. Today Slavia is seen as a ghost town. But the A. Duda and Sons family celery farm persists and, six generations later, continues to provide fresh homegrown produce to grocery stores and restaurants.

■ ■ ■

---

[25] Čupka, 2022

Slovak or Rusyn?

Slovakia is a small country, yet it is home to several thriving ethnic groups. The trials at the turn of the last century in Upper Hungary pushed not only ethnic Slovaks but also Rusyns, Hungarians, and Jews to search for a better and more abundant life—beyond the confines of their homeland. At the time, eastern Slovakia was (and still is) home to a large minority of Carpatho-Rusyns, also known as Rusyns or Ruthenians. A nation without a country, the Rusyns are an old culture whose people have survived by scattering across the borders of several countries. However, they had been living in this region long before their first appearance in recorded history, which was at the turn of the 11th century.

Today, tenacious Rusyns can be found in seven countries on the old continent. Despite a long history of being absorbed into multiple nations and various political entities, they have managed to maintain their unique identity, culture, language, customs, and spiritual beliefs.

In Slovakia, the Rusyns form the third largest ethnic minority, making up around 7 percent of the Slovak population. However, before the era of mass emigration, the Rusyns in Slovakia were a much larger population. It is difficult to gauge the exact number of Rusyns leaving Upper Hungary, but it is estimated that somewhere between 150,000 and 225,000 Rusyns left the region between the years of 1870 and 1914.[26]

Although the Austro-Hungarian Empire was generally less industrialized than other countries in western Europe, the lack of innovation was most acute in the Empire's northeast, which was home to the Rusyns. Outdated infrastructure and

---

[26] Pop, 2020

an overall lack of cashflow stymied progress in this part of the Empire. The construction of railways, a prerequisite to development in the industrial age, started only in the 1860s. The railway line was completed at the turn of the 20th century, nearly half a century after the first train arrived in Bratislava in the western part of the country.

The first few factories that opened in the Empire's east were not enough to offset the lack of land, the low crop yields, and the crippling indebtedness of the local Rusyns. They had little to lose, and so they opted to try their luck abroad. What began as a trickle, very quickly expanded to become a tsunami—hundreds of thousands of Rusyns flooding to America. Some Rusyn villages lost two-thirds of their population.

Like ethnic Slovaks, Rusyns headed to America with the intention to return. They wanted to earn enough cash—somewhere between $400 and $1,000 US dollars—that they could come back as rich peasants, with the means to secure land, build a home, and buy livestock and tools. The Rusyns, too, found employment in the mining and steel industries of America's Northeast, taking up the dirty and dangerous jobs right alongside ethnic Slovaks.

What did Rusyn life look like in America? In many ways, it continued much as it had in the old world. Similar to other Eastern Europeans, the Rusyns found themselves isolated by their economic status and inability to speak English. By 1920, nearly 80 percent of all Carpatho-Rusyns lived in Pennsylvania, New York, and New Jersey.[27] By the second generation, they had established thriving communities with Rusyn social centers and ethnic stores along with Rusyn schools, churches, and fraternal organizations.

---

[27] Magocsi, 2015

The story of Júlia Zavacká mirrors the destiny of countless Rusyn men and women. Her husband emigrated in 1913, shortly after their first baby died in infancy. Unable to follow her husband abroad until after the end of World War I, Júlia didn't reach America until 1921. Reunited, the couple settled in a Rusyn neighborhood in Pittsburgh, known as Rusyn Valley.

Like many new immigrants in the early 19th century, Júlia Zavacká lived in America without learning English. Surrounded by Rusyn shops and Rusyn neighbors, the family could get by in their native language. Devotedly religious, Julia even attended church where the Old Church Slavonic was spoken. This was the community and family to which the most famous Rusyn in the world was born.

His name was Andrew Warhola, but most people know him as Andy Warhol.

The son of a working-class immigrant family, Andy grew up in a humble two-room row house in Pittsburgh's Rusyn Valley. Few could fathom that this skinny and sickly boy would become a world-famous artist—and change pop art. Raised in a Rusyn household, Andy practiced Rusyn rituals along with attending Greek Catholic mass—celebrated in the Rusyn language—with his beloved mother.

When he became famous and the American press inquired about his origins, Andy Warhol notoriously stated, "I come from nowhere." He had never met his grandparents, who lived in Miková in present-day Slovakia. Likewise, as a second-generation American, Andy and his brothers were not necessarily interested in preserving their Rusyn connection. Instead, they assimilated into American culture, which enabled them to thrive. Yet, Andy's Rusyn roots found their expression in his art.

There is so much more to the statement "I come from nowhere" than meets the eye. It reflects a sentiment of the Rusyn experience as a whole. Although Rusyns represent a unique chapter in the history of emigration from the Austria-Hungarian Empire, they are notoriously difficult to identify and, therefore, to record. Manifest records state their country of origin as Austria-Hungary.

As a result, Rusyns were counted either as Austrians or Hungarians, and later sometimes also as Slovaks. Others put down 'Rusland' on their ship manifests and were subsequently mistaken for Russians. This identity issue was resolved for the Slovaks with the founding of Czechoslovakia, a nation of both Czechs and Slovaks in 1919.

However, it remains a sore point for the Rusyns, who live as a minority scattered across several countries in the Carpathian region.

■ ■ ■

A nation without a country

The existence on the borderland of three countries—Ukraine, Slovakia, and Poland shaped the complex history of the Rusyns. At first, they were a part of Austria-Hungary. After World War I, a great majority of them found themselves living in Czechoslovakia. Upon the eruption of World War II, the Rusyns declared independence in 1939, but that was short-lived as the Rusyn territory was later annexed by Hungary. After the end of the World War II, the bulk of the region was absorbed by the Soviet Union, and today it is a part of modern Ukraine.

■ ■ ■

The question of Rusyn identity has never been an easy one to resolve—in the old world or in the new one. But in the face of assimilation, the Rusyns would have to protect not just their language and customs but also their faith. The Rusyns founded their first parish in the United States as early as 1884. However, strengthening the spiritual backbone of the American Rusyn community was never going to be straightforward.

The Rusyns practiced Eastern Christianity, more specifically Greek Catholicism, which differs from Roman Catholicism in several crucial ways. The Roman Catholics, who comprised the vast majority of immigrants coming to America from Austria-Hungary and Europe as a whole, were hesitant to accommodate the spiritual needs of the Greek Catholics.

Why? Greek Catholic clergy did not observe celibacy, and the Roman Catholics did not approve of married priests. There was also the hope of converting the Greek Catholics to Roman Catholicism; although the Roman Catholic Church was powerful, it always sought a larger following. However, the matter of priests having sex, even within the confines of marriage, pushed the boundaries of the Roman Catholic leadership.

Attempts were made to legally prevent betrothed Rusyn priests from traveling to the U.S. Only celibates and widowed priests with children were welcome. These restrictions crossed a line, and the Rusyns of America reacted. The community consulted with their spiritual leaders in the old country, and a Rusyn priest from Austria-Hungary ended up playing a pivotal role in the history of Eastern Orthodoxy in North America.

Alexis Toth was born to a Carpatho-Rusyn family of priests in what is now eastern Slovakia. But when Father Toth arrived in America in 1889, to become the first priest of the brand new Greek Catholic church in Minneapolis, Minnesota, the local Roman Catholic Archbishop refused to recognize his credentials because he was married. Moreover, the archbishop forbade Alexis from functioning as a priest anywhere in the diocese. The main reason for this was an ongoing campaign to Americanize the Greek Catholic Church and the immigrants from Eastern Europe.

True to his resilient Rusyn spirit, Father Alexis set up his own parallel church, around which a stable community grew. And he did not stop there. He felt that something had to be done about the issue of Rusyn immigrants being told to follow Roman Catholicism. To gain allies, Father Toth converted from his native Greek Catholicism to Eastern Orthodoxy, which is followed by American Russians. There were many more Russians in the U.S. than there were Rusyns. With that, Alexis had sufficient support; ultimately, he gained a following of more than 20,000 Greek Catholics.[28]

Alexis's impact on immigrant life in America highlighted the spiritual needs and gaps of the Slavs who practiced Eastern Christianity. The Byzantium rite practiced by the Eastern Orthodox Church was unknown in the U.S., as were the onion-shaped domes of Rusyn churches from the old country. Finally, when a Ukrainian bishop was named by the Pope to care for this flock, the trouble only escalated. Ethnic tensions between Ukrainian Greek Catholics and Rusyn Greek Catholics from the Kingdom of Hungary reached a standoff. Then the Rusyns were given their own eparchy, with a Rusyn priest being ordained and appointed to serve as the first bishop of Ruthenian Catholics in the U.S.

This religious melee is just one example of the many difficulties Rusyn immigrants faced in America, over and above the usual economic struggles and assimilation pressures. The strong desire of Rusyns to preserve their cultural roots was

---

[28] Magocsi, 2015

also reflected in the rarity of intermarriage between Roman Catholics and Greek Catholics in the Slovak and Rusyn communities of Pennsylvania.

■ ■ ■

Identifying as a Rusyn is far from straightforward even today. Many Slovak descendants reading this book may struggle with the Rusyn question. Their ancestors came from the territory of present-day Slovakia, but they spoke a different language and went to different churches than other Slovaks did.

The easiest way to identify whether your ancestors were Rusyn is by the language they spoke at home. Another major indicator of Rusyn ethnicity is religion. Rusyns practice Greek Catholicism or Eastern Orthodoxy. In the past, their liturgy used Old Church Slavonic during sermons and not Slovak as the Roman Catholics did. The Rusyn faith also comes with a different annual calendar. If your ancestors were Rusyn, they may have celebrated Christmas on January 6th, rather than on December 24th like their Slovak counterparts.

■ ■ ■

Despite their differences, Slovaks and Rusyns worked together. For example, the very first Rusyn fraternal organization was a joint venture with ethnic Slovaks. The joint Slovak Roman & Greek Catholic Sick Benefit Uniformed Society of St. Stephen, King of Hungary was founded in Bridgeport, Connecticut, in 1888. It was not just cultural proximity that bound these two nations together, but also their inability to speak English. Both groups also occupied jobs at the bottom of the social and skill hierarchy. They worked side by side in the mining and steel industries of America's Northeast, which meant that they faced similar problems and challenges, working in life-threatening occupations and experiencing the same racial profiling and immigrant harassment.

The oldest and the largest fraternal society that was purely Rusyn, was the Greek Catholic Union, founded in 1892 in Wilkes-Barre, Pennsylvania. This society published its own newspaper, *Amerikansky Russky Viestnik* (American Rusyn Messenger), the longest running Rusyn newspaper in the United States. It was written in the Zemplín dialect, and for several decades it was published simultaneously in both the Cyrillic and the Latin alphabets. The fraternals, as well as the Rusyn churches and schools that offered services, classes, newspapers and publications of their own, helped to preserve Rusyn culture and language in the New World. They were also oases of respite in the alien world of America, so far removed from the fields, mountains, and mindsets of eastern Slovakia.

Beyond maintaining culture, some of the Rusyn organizations entered the political battlefield to help their compatriots back in the homeland. There as well, they joined forces with ethnic Slovaks to take a stand for their rights in the face of forced assimilation under Magyarization.

Like all immigrant communities, the Rusyns, too, would assimilate into mainstream American culture with time. Second generation Rusyns increasingly rejected the ways of their immigrant parents, including their unique language and religion. Because fewer and fewer descendants read and spoke Rusyn, Rusyn organizations would start using English and the vibrant Rusyn-language press was Anglicized to keep up with trends.

Things became even more difficult for Rusyns after Czechoslovakia fell into the Soviet sphere of influence after World War II. Because of this political alliance, Rusyns perceived American Czechs and Slovaks as their enemies, and vice versa. Not only did the Rusyn language sound closer to Russian, Rusyns also used the Cyrillic alphabet and practiced Eastern Christianity, which was all too close to what was labeled 'Russian'.

The revival of Rusyn organizations and their activities began only after the collapse of the Iron Curtain. The Slavic communities of America needed time to recover from the sting of unjust stigma. Today, more and more Rusyns are rediscovering their ethnic origins. Some estimates suggest that around 600,000 Americans have full or partial Rusyn heritage. In Pennsylvania, Rusyns remain one of the state's major ethnic groups.

There is much to be proud of if you are of Rusyn descent. The hard-work ethic, deep faith, and strong family values of Rusyn immigrants have left a profound imprint on America, just as they have shaped the eastern region of Slovakia. Although Andy Warhol is the most famous Rusyn to date, he is by no means the only Rusyn to celebrate.

Amerikáni

Journeying abroad was primarily, but not solely, about money. Experiencing a new country and a new society was both scary and thrilling!

Life in America could not be more different than existence in rural Slovakia that continued in the same rhythms and observed the same rites and rituals as it had for hundreds of years previously. In the old country, society was tightly bound to tradition and community, and one's life was inseparable from that of one's family and community. This came with certain important advantages but also with the tremendous weight of countless responsibilities. Away from home, migrants could be free from the constraints of tradition.

At first this freedom was uncomfortable, even frightening. Slovak migrants experienced a different lifestyle and witnessed different ways of dressing, behaving, and doing things. Being in America also threatened the traditional role of the family and eroded the value of community. The new bustling world tempted migrants with vices that were hard to come by at home—gambling and prostitution. Wages empowered women, who were now able to contribute to the family income. They also gained a sense of independence and a desire to self-actualize beyond the cradle and the kitchen.

When Slovaks returned to their homeland from America, they were changed. They discarded wearing their traditional folk attire with the few belongings they owned packed in a cloth slung over the shoulder. They came back confident, wearing sleek suits and carrying elegant suitcases. The surrounding society took notice, and a new term was created to label the returnees—*amerikáni*.

These young men, and later also women, had an immense impact on the local society and rural life. They had seen things that most Slovaks could not even imagine existed. Life in America shifted their worldviews and their personalities, skills, preferences, and desires.

Upon return, they helped to innovate the traditional culture of the old country. Their influence was most apparent in eastern Slovakia. Fashion, traditional housing but also intangible heritage bears the imprints of the *amerikáni*.

Before they left, most migrants lived in small sooty houses that had no ventilation or airing system to guide the smoke from cooking fires away from the living quarters. Moreover, the entire family lived with a single tiny space with a dirt floor.

When they returned, *amerikáni* no longer wanted to live in such dark, smoky, damp spaces. They had new ideas, and they had the money to turn their ideas into reality. The *amerikáni* purchased novel building materials and created larger houses with windows that could be opened, and solutions to navigate the smoke out of the house, so that it wouldn't blacken the entire dwelling. Bricks replaced wood, and shingles replaced hay. Flushing toilets appeared, and the furnishings reflected the tastes of a people who had seen more of the world.

■ ■ ■

> *Not everyone received a warm welcome in the homeland. Jealousy was at play and the Hungarian administration continued to shame those who could not speak Hungarian, making it difficult for Slovaks who returned affluent to put their ideas into action.*

■ ■ ■

Often, men sent money to their wives who then had the houses built. With the men away, it was the women who oversaw the construction, making sure the houses also looked pretty on the outside to represent the owner and his achievements. These homes still stand in Slovakia and are known to locals as the 'American houses'.

Returnees also came up with ways to make life simpler and agriculture more effective. Before, people used to plant potatoes manually, painstakingly digging holes one by one, which took a lot of time and energy. But then an *amerikáni* began planting potatoes in a furrow made by a plough.

The *amerikáni* introduced new tastes to the region, like drinking beer in northeastern Slovakia where people were traditionally used to downing shots of homemade brandies and spirits. They brought fancy city fashion to the Slovak countryside and showed an active interest in politics! The *amerikáni* bought books and newspapers to educate themselves, and to keep up to date with the world around them, an unheard-of privilege to the simple rural folk.

However, returning home was bittersweet. It created a split inside many *amerikáni*. On the one hand, they loved the money, skyscrapers, oranges and bananas, technological innovations, fashion, and thrill of individuality and freedom. On the other hand, Slovakia was their home, and it was where their family lived and owned land. Slovakia was their roots, their everything. As a result, many were leaving and returning, enjoying the best of both worlds as 'birds of passage'. But World War I halted immigration to America.

All in all, *amerikáni* had a tremendous impact in Slovakia. The era of mass migration to North America is immortalized in the many streets across the country that bear the name 'Americká' (American).

■ ■ ■

The founding of Czechoslovakia was a decisive moment in the history of emigration from the area. Tomáš Garrigue Masaryk, the first president, championed the notion of 'the patriot return home'. Married to an American woman himself, Masaryk realized that amerikáni were an asset—they had pockets full of money and heads full of ideas. Both were needed in the new country.

Masaryk called on the amerikáni to come back and invest their labor, skills, and knowledge in the building of Czechoslovakia, and creating their very own 'America' in the country. The campaign was successful. Some 200,000 Czechoslovaks returned.

But not everyone shared Masaryk's enthusiasm for the returnees. Jealousy was at play, especially in the Slovak countryside. Many received an unceremonious welcome, and some had to put up with outright disdain. The Slovak Americans were hurt. They were not 'Americans' in the United States, but they were no longer seen as 'Slovaks' in their homeland either.

■ ■ ■

Part four
BUILDING A SLOVAK WORLD

The Making of Little Slovakia

By 1920, the Slovak community in America was 620,000 persons strong.[29] The people from Upper Hungary lived especially in the industrial Northeast and Midwest. Thanks to its prospering steel mills, Cleveland, Ohio became home to the largest Slovak community in the world, prior to the establishment of Czechoslovakia and the expansion of Bratislava. At one point, more Slovaks lived in Cleveland than in any city in the old country or anywhere else on the globe.

The growth of the Slovak communities was intertwined with the arrival of Slovak women. As families established themselves, ever more men and women began to arrive in America. Moreover, families had different needs than single men, who divided their time between work and the tavern. Before long, churches, schools, fraternal organizations, and Slovak cultural centers emerged to serve the community and promote its interests.

At first the cultural centers were founded by the arriving intelligentsia and ordinary immigrants; they would request

---

[29] The 1920 U.S. Census

priests to come and serve their religiously devout community in the new Slovak parishes in the U.S. Once the priests started working in America, they realized that the migrant flock needed more than just Sunday services in the Slovak language.

These burgeoning Slovak cultural organizations offered the immigrants a sense of belonging in an alien world. But as the community matured, so did the organizations. Whether they were clubs, fraternal organizations, churches, or schools—these bodies created a space for people to discuss developments both in North America and in their homeland. They provided an important platform for Slovaks to voice their interests, concerns, and demands—domestically and internationally and come together as a culture and people.

As time went by, migrants from Slovakia were encouraged—sometimes forcefully—to advance themselves, and when they did, their communities also benefitted.

Those immigrants who had not known how to read and write acquired those skills while living and working abroad. They also learned English. They absorbed the values of democracy and became aware that, as human beings, they had personal

and collective freedoms. America was certainly not a perfect democracy, but it was much more politically advanced then the homeland. In Austria-Hungary, 'rights' had been the privilege of the affluent for most of its history. American Slovaks enjoyed much more freedom than did the Slovaks of Upper Hungary.

As a result, Slovaks in America became far more interested in the domestic affairs of Austria-Hungary than they had ever been when they lived at home. Not only were they interested; they were openly critical of the position of Slovaks in the Empire. They began to embrace migration as a means to national liberation at home.

It is said that exile is the bastion of nationalism. This may be true. It seems to be demonstrated by the political awakening of the Slovaks in America, people who left their homeland and, thereby, became more acutely aware of their own culture[30] due to the greater civil liberties they were afforded. Living side by side with many other self-actualized immigrant groups also offered a point of comparison from which to learn. By the early 20th century, Slovaks in America became a force to be reckoned with, one that went on to shape the modern history of Slovakia.

■ ■ ■

> *To this day, Slovak communities can be found in small pockets clustered throughout the United States, with the largest group living in Pennsylvania. Home to some 230,000 residents who claim to have full or partial Slovak ancestry,[31] Today, Pittsburgh is the largest Slovak city in the world outside of Slovakia. The city was once endearingly known as 'New Slovakia' in the early 20th century.*

■ ■ ■

---

[30] Poznan, 2017
[31] 2000 U.S. Census

At first, it was not necessary for Slovaks in the U.S. to speak the English language. At work, in church, and in the community, they could easily get by in Slovak. But the enlightened Slovaks realized that the long-term success of the community was contingent on its ability to integrate into the surrounding society. One of the leaders of the assimilation effort was Janko Slovenský, who published *The Practical Slovak American Interpreter* in 1887. It was the first ever Slovak-American (English) dictionary. In the foreword, Janko clearly stated his intention:

Ked človek v Amerike pokračovac chce, muši na každý pad v stave byc, še v angľickej reči vyjadric. (If a person wants to continue his life in America, they must regardless of their situation, be able to converse in the English language.)

If Slovaks wanted to stay, they would inevitably have to learn English and *The Practical Slovak American Interpreter* became the go-to tool for many.[32]

Here are some common phrases from the book in Slovak and English:

ROBOTA.

Som haviarom — **I am a miner** (aj em e majnr)
Ja som nádenník — **I am a laborer** (aj em e lejbrer)
Som robotník — **I am a workman** (aj em e vörkmen)
Dobré ráno, pane, hľadám robotu — **good morning, boss, I am looking for work** (gud mornyng, bos, aj em lukyng for vörk)
Potrebujete robotníka (pomoc)? — **do you need help?** (dú jú nýd help)
Máte neakú prácu pre mňa? — **have you any work for me?** (hev jú eny vörk for mí)
Jestli rád pracujete, vezmem vás — **if you like to work I shall employ you** (if jú lajk tu vörk aj šel emploj jú)
Potrebujem dobrého robotníka — **I need a good hand** (aj nýd e gud hend)
Akú mzdu platíte? — **what wages do you pay?** (hvat vejdžes dú jú pej)
Deväť dollárov ná týždeň — **nine dollars a week** (najn dalrs e vík)
Ako vyplácate mzdu? — **how do you pay wages?** (hau dú jú pej vejdžes)
Každú druhú sobotu — **every other Saturday** (evri adhr setrdej)

---

[32] Slovenský, 1887

Let's Get Organized!

As you have been reading, Slovaks did not have it easy in America. Without language and professional skills, they were vulnerable and they labored in dangerous jobs. With no safety net to fall back on, the Slovaks had to rely on each other to survive.

The Slovak fraternal and benevolent societies, inspired by the organizations of the Czech and Polish immigrants, were born out of need. These groups provided life insurance policies to families whose husbands and fathers risked their lives each time they went to work in the mines and the mills. Accidents and illnesses were a daily reality. They would later also provide loans for mortgages, since American banks would not lend money to Slovak immigrants.

Hardship befell the family of a man who died on the job or was unable to continue working due to an injury or illness. When a father and husband died, the family was left without their breadwinner. There was little compassion among the employers for workers who lost their lives or their health at work.

The first Slovak Beneficial Society was created in New York in 1883 to help resolve the dire predicament in which many families found themselves. As the name suggests, the purpose of the society was to help the families of the deceased or sick workers. What started with a group of Slovaks coming together in a private home, started to spread like wildfire. Similar organizations emerged in other cities and regions throughout the Northeast.

Ten years later, there were some 277 Slovak beneficial societies in the United States, out of which 148 were in Pennsylvania. By 1920, over one-third of Slovak-Americans were members of one or even several of these organizations.

■ ■ ■

Slovaks took inspiration from their Czech brethren and established the Slovak Gymnastic Union Sokol in Chicago in 1892. Sokol was an exercise movement that began in Czechia in the 19th century and helped to cultivate the human capital of the nation—physically, morally, and intellectually—through exercise, lectures, talks, and uplifting events. In America, it actively helped to build and strengthen the Slovak community.

■ ■ ■

Being a member of such an organization was not just about security. Beneficent societies provided a sense of pride and togetherness, preserving Slovak cultural and religious values and representing the rich and varied interests of Slovaks in America. They also helped the newly arrived immigrants adapt to life in the U.S. by familiarizing them with the laws, language, and ways of the New World.

Education happened formally but also informally during picnics, theater productions, dances, club meetings, and sporting events that the societies organized first in America and later in Canada. Many ran their own newspapers too, to keep their members up-to-date with current affairs both in America and the homeland.

At the beginning, fraternal organizations were male only, but later there were also those founded by women and for women. The first of its kind was established in New York in 1891 and was given the name Živena (Giver of Life). The First Catholic Slovak Ladies Association emerged one year later and is still thriving today. The purpose of these bodies was to provide life insurance for the women of the community.

It was not just the death of men that had a devasting impact on Slovak immigrant families. When a woman died during childbirth, which was common given the poor living conditions in their neighborhoods, it was a devasting blow to the family. The father had to work 10- to 12-hour shifts, 6 days a week regardless of the situation at home. If his wife died, who would look after the children?

This is when the women's benefit societies stepped in and provided the financial means to allow the widowed men to hire help, until they remarried.

Towards the end of the 19th century, the Slovak community had truly come into its own, and the small local and regional organizations started to join forces and develop into nationwide entities.

■ ■ ■

> The goals of the National Slovak Society[33]:
> - to unite persons of Slovak and Slavonic ancestry in a fraternal benefit society;
> - to cherish among its members the language and traditions of their ancestors;

---

[33] Megles et al, 1978

- to encourage respect for the land of their ancestors; and to foster pride in their ancestry;
- to preach and practice the gospel of fraternity, charity and benevolence;
- to uphold the Constitution of the United States of America and to preserve the democratic way of life;
- to assist their kinsmen across the Atlantic in their efforts to make and keep their homeland, in the heart of Europe, a land of free men with free institutions;
- to publish and circulate Slovak literature and to patronize Slovak arts and sciences;
- to protect its widowed; its orphaned; its sick, disabled, distressed, and aged.

■ ■ ■

The National Slovak Society and the First Catholic Slovak Union are two most notable examples. They went on to become fully-fledged insurance corporations with thousands of members and assets in the tens of millions of dollars. They still exist and prosper today as billion-dollar entities.

■ ■ ■

The First Slovak Catholic Union (FCSU) is still widely popular today. In addition to functioning as an insurance company and promoting Slovak heritage in the United States, the organization also promotes the Catholic faith among Slovak descendants. The slogan of its founder, the Rev. Štefan Furdek, was 'Za Boha a národ' (For God and Country). The FCSU publishes its own newspaper, Jednota, a widely circulated print during its day. In its heyday during the 1920s, Jednota counted about 100,000 members. The Great Depression hurt membership growth, as did World War II. Today membership stands a little over 40,000. A persistent problem in the recent history of fraternal societies has been garnering the active participation of third- and fourth--generation Slovak-American youth. Through time and assimilation, many intermarried with non-Slovaks and often lost the stronger sense of ethnic belonging that their predecessors shared.

■ ■ ■

Far away from the confines of Magyarization and the laws designed to nip any sign of Slovak nationhood in the bud, Slovaks could develop their own culture and politics unthreatened. A new Slovak American identity was born, which allowed Slovaks to cast themselves as culturally and ethnically Slovak but as civically American. The fight against Magyarization helped stir Slovak nationalism in the New World and helped make many Slovaks aware of who they were.

As the community became more and more established, Slovaks naturally set their sights higher.

Slovak Americans took it upon themselves to not just help, but to liberate the Slovak nation from the shackles of oppression. To do that, they would need an organization that was not just a social club or an insurance company, one that would function as a legitimate representative body for domestic and international politics.

Slovak national activism formed around the Slovak League of America (*Slovenská liga*). This was founded in 1907 in Cleveland, Ohio, where around 7,000 Slovak-Americans gathered on the occasion of the organization's National Congress. The crowd of Slovaks was so huge that they could not even fit in the assembly hall at Grey's Armory. The Slovak League quickly became an umbrella organization that helped to establish unity in the fragmented Slovak-American community. It brought together regional societies and institutions from across the United States to effectively represent the interests of Slovaks, both in America and in the old country. The League would go on to play a critical role in the founding of Czechoslovakia.

Active from its inception, the Slovak League set out to inform Slovaks about developments in the homeland.

The League also protested against Magyarization, something that Slovaks in Austria-Hungary could not do without risking their freedom or even their lives. Whenever Hungarian officials visited the United States, the Slovak League organized protests in the press and in public. Moreover, the organization maintained connections with Slovak leaders at home, and funded the political careers of those who would become leaders in modern Slovak history. Among these were Milan Hodža, the Slovak who became prime minister of Czechoslovakia, and Andrej Hlinka, one of the most important Slovak activists and a promoter of Slovak independence. It was Hlinka's imprisonment and conviction on charges of sedition that inspired the creation of the Slovak League.

■ ■ ■

Even after the liberation of the Czechs and Slovaks, the Slovak League of America continued its ambitious agenda. In 1932, the leadership decided to establish a sister organization in Canada to support, integrate, and connect Slovaks who started to migrate farther north in large numbers.

■ ■ ■

Slovak activism abroad did not end there. The politically active and self-aware settlers built cultural proxies to organizations banned at home, such as the American branch of the *Matica slovenská* (the Slovak Cultural Institute). Behind these organizations were capable, passionate, and devoted people who championed the Slovak cause. One of these leaders was Stephen Furdek, also known as the Father of Slovak-Americans. At a time when Slovaks were not sure how to call themselves in America, Father Furdek coined the identifying term "Slovak".

Furdek immigrated to Cleveland in 1883, initially, to serve the first Bohemian parish as its priest. Being the proud Slovak that he was, Furdek soon founded St. Ladislav parish to provide religious guidance to Slovak immigrants. When the Hungarian parishioners rebelled in 1891 intending to take over the church, Father Furdek persuaded the Cleveland Catholic Diocese to entrust the church to the Slovaks exclusively.

In vision, Father Furdek's faith went hand-in-hand with politics. God and nation were inseparable—for he felt that how you live is an apt expression of how you believe. In addition to tending to spiritual needs of his flock, Father Furdek also ignited the national awakening movement in the U.S.

He organized gatherings for Slovak-Americans to publicly protest against the oppression of Slovaks in Austria-Hungary and contributed greatly to the founding of Slovak schools on American soil. For this, he wrote several textbooks.

Father Furdek founded the First Slovak Catholic Union and served as the first president of the Slovak League. He devoted his life to the Slovak cause, helping Slovaks abroad maintain their identity and supporting Slovaks at home in their struggle for recognition as a nation.

It is no wonder that Father Furdek was respected, loved, and even treasured by the Slovak-American community. When he died in early 1915, the Pope himself sent sincere condolences.

Spiritual Oases of the Old Country

Slovaks were a deeply religious people and moving across the Atlantic did not change that. Religion and spiritual rituals were central to Slovak life anywhere Slovaks went.

When they first arrived in America, people from Upper Hungary attended Czech, German, or Polish parishes. But with time, they too wanted to worship and confess in their own language. As Slovak churches began to spring forth, they became the beacons of Slovak neighborhoods.

It is worth exploring the remarkable story of how these churches were founded.

As there was no Holy See to oversee the building process, the feat had to be undertaken by the immigrants themselves.

Slovakia is a majority Catholic country and 70 percent of all settlers were Roman Catholics. These were followed by Lutherans (20 percent), Calvinists (5 percent), as well as Greek Catholics and Orthodox Christians (5 percent), which were mostly ethnic Rusyns. The Lutherans and Calvinists did best when it came to establishing Slovak parishes in America. They had to face impossible obstacles and bureaucratic pitfalls beginning in the 16th century, at the dawn of Protestantism in Europe. Most of northern Hungary became Protestant in the 16th century, but the Jesuits turned the tide and reconverted most people back to Roman Catholicism. After the Thirty Years War—which was 1618 to 1648 and so hundreds of years before the first wave of emigration—the Protestants in Upper Hungary battled, with both their arms and their pens, to earn the right to build and keep their own churches. As a result, they knew exactly what they needed to know to be able to build their Slovak Lutheran churches in America. The United States being a Protestant nation softened the transition.

The Slovak Catholics had to work harder than the Protestants when it came to building their Slovak parishes and finding Slovak clergy.

But true to their Slovak nature, everyone persevered. Under the guidance of the fraternal-benefit societies, Slovak neighborhoods gathered, set up committees, and looked for suitable land to build their churches. Of course, they needed to raise funds for the buildings first, and this could take a while. The land for St. Mary's Assumption Roman Catholic Slovak Church in Passaic, New Jersey, was purchased in 1891, but construction did not begin until 1904.

■ ■ ■

The first Slovak Catholic church in America was founded and consecrated in 1885, in the anthracite mining town of Hazleton, Pennsylvania. The very first Slovak mass was celebrated there in December 1885. At the same time, Slovaks in Streator, Illinois, had also established a parish and built St. Stephen's Church, with its first Mass celebrated on December 11, 1885. In Canada, the first Slovak church opened its doors to the community in 1908, in Fort William (today Thunder Bay, Ontario).

■ ■ ■

Next came the hunt for Slovak-speaking priests. There were none in America, and so such clergy needed to be brought over from the old country. Once a church was nearing completion, advertisements were sent out to Upper Hungary, asking churches there to send over a priest. Some U.S. congregations offered money as an incentive for reluctant clergy. Priests in America could earn five times as much as the average priest in Upper Hungary.

Few immigrants realized that finding sufficient money to purchase land and to erect a church and making arrangements to bring in a Slovak-speaking priest was not going to be enough. Not versed in the rules that governed religious life in America, the founders of Slovak Catholic churches were frustrated and surprised when the local Roman Catholic dioceses asserted dominance over what they had built from the ground up.

The Slovak Catholics had wrongly assumed that if they built a church, they would also be able to choose their own priest and decide on important parish matters. In Europe, those who founded a church also held influence over this church, and the Slovak immigrants presumed that this custom extended to America. This was not the case. American bishops insisted that only they—and not the congregants themselves—had the right to create a parish and appoint its priest. The immigrants had no say in the matter.

And that was only one of a long string of problems the Slovak Catholics encountered in the U.S. and Canada.

Most Slovak parishes founded between 1885 and 1930 experienced many conflicts with the already established churches of their denomination in their neighborhoods. Whether these parishes were Irish or had been in existence from before, the established churches in America were usually unwelcoming to the new immigrants.

∎ ∎ ∎

The United States was predominantly Protestant, and Catholics faced discrimination because of that. Anti-Catholicism grew in the mid 19th century when Catholic immigrants from Ireland and Germany started moving to the U.S. in large numbers. When Slovaks and other East Europeans immigrated in the late 19th century, the older immigrant communities feared this onslaught, and viewed the new immigrants as a different race with strange cultural habits that threatened American democracy.

People gradually realized that many of their fears were unfounded, but discrimination persisted well into the 20th century. By 1906, Roman Catholics accounted for 17 percent of the U.S. population, about 14 million souls, with Catholicism becoming one of the largest denominations in the country.

∎ ∎ ∎

Politics aside, Slovak churches nevertheless became the centers of Slovak communal life abroad. They were hubs where people gathered on Sundays and on holidays to worship, but also to socialize, hold meetings, and decide on community matters in their native language. Churches acted like little oases to which weary and tired immigrants from Slovakia could retreat and forget about their worries.

Weddings, baptisms, and first communions were the highlights of Slovak communal life. Many sweet memories were made on these special occasions. At the other end of the life cycle, Slovak churches also made it possible for Slovak settlers to be buried with ceremonies in their mother tongue and in Slovak cemeteries that were often adjacent to Slovak churches. It was thanks to these familiar rites that life as they knew it from their homeland could continue in America.

Churches were not only centers of worship, they also gave their parishioners a sense of order, moral guidance, and a sense of familiarity in this foreign land. Wherever Slovak churches were built, they naturally attracted more Slovak residents into the neighborhood. For example, the city of Cleveland, Ohio, had many Slovak churches: one Calvinist, one Baptist, one Congregational, four Lutheran, four Greek Catholic, and eight Roman Catholic. All were established and paid for by the hard-working immigrants from Slovakia.

Once it became apparent that many families would remain in North America, a new need emerged—that of educating the Slovak children. Slovak schools, run by priests and staffed mostly by devoted Slovak nuns, emerged beside and often inside the churches. Founded by the Rev. Matthew Jankola, the Sisters of Saints Cyril and Methodius in Danville, Pennsylvania, became the first Slovak order of sisters. It was established for the express purpose of educating Slovak-American youths. By the mid 1920s, there were 50 Slovak Catholic parish schools in the United States, diligently instilling Slovak values and Slovak language skills into the next generation.

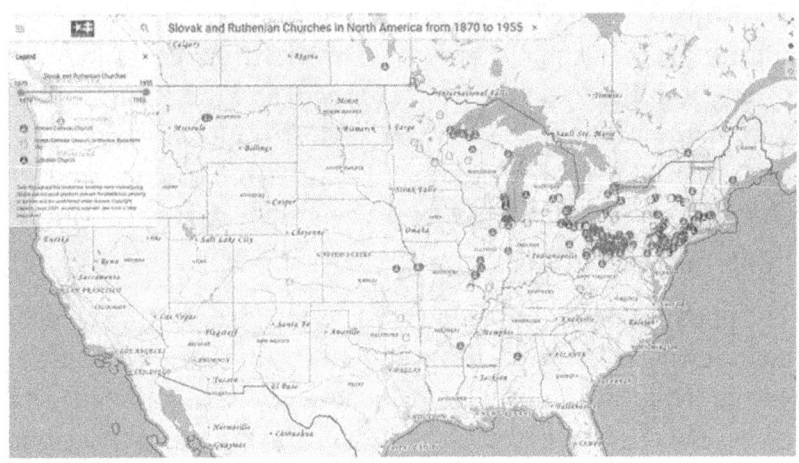

To this day the United States has the largest concentration of Slovak people outside of Slovakia. Hence, Slovak-Americans losing touch with their homeland would not affect just the Slovak communities in the United States but also the Slovak Republic.

The Power of the Printed Word

In the 19th and early 20th centuries, publishing anything in the Slovak language in Austria-Hungary was a problem. But what was not possible back home could be achieved in the New World. Books, magazines, and newspapers informed readers in Slovak about happenings at home, providing platforms for openly talking about issues that were taboo in the old country.

The pick-yourself-up-by-the-bootstraps culture of America encouraged and even prodded people to educate themselves in order to advance in their lives and careers. With more Slovak-Americans becoming literate and wanting to develop their minds, there was no shortage of readers. Unlike their counterparts in Upper Hungary, Slovaks in America had the time, the ability, and the desire to read, and they also had the money to purchase these papers. Most importantly, unlike Slovaks in Austria-Hungary, Slovak-Americans were not risking prosecution if they were caught reading pro-Slovak literature.

The phenomenon of the Slovak newspaper took off in a spectacular way in America, testament to the remarkable freedom and civil liberties enjoyed there by newcomers of all creeds and races. This freedom stood in stark contrast to the restrictions imposed on ethnic minorities back in Austria-Hungary.

Many of these Slovak-American newspapers focused almost exclusively on reporting injustices that occurred in Upper Hungary. Whether or not these accounts were accurate is a matter for debate. Some Slovak and American scholars argue that Slovak-American newspapers may have had a vendetta against Austria-Hungary and against Hungary in particular. These scholars suggest that the newspapers may have exaggerated grievances in order to fan the flames of Slovak outrage and to further the nationalist cause.

It is not surprising that all Slovak newspapers published overseas were banned in Austria-Hungary. Copies were nevertheless smuggled into the country by the returning Slovaks.

The very first Slovak-language newspaper, *Amerikánsko-slovenské noviny*, was printed in the U.S. as early as 1886. Soon, many more popped up, catering to the preferences of the eager Slovak readership. Slovak-American hero Father Stephan Furdek, joined with Ján Pankuch to establish the Slovak Press in Cleveland, while millionaire Michal Bosák published the weekly *Slovenská obrana*.

A total of 25 newspapers were available in Pennsylvania alone! Each week some 80,000 copies of Slovak newspapers were printed in the U.S. At one point there were six Slovak dailies! A total of 220 Slovaks newspapers were circulated to a combined readership of around 150,000 Slovaks in the U.S. by the early 1900s. In comparison, the Slovak press in Upper Hungary had combined readership of only 40,000.

■ ■ ■

Slovak newspapers and magazines were published by various institutions and fraternal organizations, which is why it was common to see mutual criticism of one another in their articles. After all, they were competing for the affection of the Slovak-American community.

■ ■ ■

BUILDING A SLOVAK WORLD

It is impossible to overstate the enormous significance of these newspapers, and the role that they played in cultivating the national consciousness and identity of Slovak immigrants.

Thanks to the circulation and expansion of the Slovak press in America, Slovak-Americans could strengthen their connection to Slovak ethnicity. This was critical during the 1910 U.S. Census, which allowed Slovaks to identify themselves officially as Slovaks for the very first time. This was made possible thanks to the diligent work of Slovak community leaders who successfully petitioned federal authorities to include in the census a question about language in addition to the country of origin. This pivot enabled Slovaks to identify as 'Slovak' before they had a country of their own to name.

No one realized at the time how close that dream was...

Would There Have Been a Czechoslovakia without Slovak-America?

'When the whole world slept, we were awake.'

Declaration of Czech and Slovak immigrants, addressed to the American people and President Woodrow Wilson, July 4, 1918

By the time the fatal shot was fired in Sarajevo in June 1914, assassinating the crown prince of Austria and starting World War I, Slovaks in America were already a multi-generational, well-established, superbly organized, and self-confident community.

The Slovak League of America, founded in 1907, had already brought together most of the regional societies under a single banner. This united around 100,000 diverse Slovak-Americans, whether they be Catholic or Protestant, socialist or liberal, men or women. This was a sensational accomplishment in its own right! The Slovaks were even ahead of the Czechs, who despite having arrived in America several decades earlier, had not yet formed equivalent organizations. The Bohemian National Alliance was established only in 1914.

However, from the very beginning, the Czechs and the Slovaks had gravitated towards one another. The two brethren nations had always been, and continue to be, close thanks to their cultural, linguistic, and ethnic proximity. When Slovaks first started arriving in America, they would go to Czech churches as well as Czech saloons and Czech boarding houses. Later the two ethnic groups bonded at concerts, at picnics, in bars, and at social gatherings.

When the Great War broke out, it did not take long for the Czechs and Slovaks to realize that they needed each other to make mutually beneficial things happen.

However, not everyone foresaw their future to be in a shared state. The Slovak League in America published a Memorandum in 1914 that demanded self-rule for Slovaks within the Kingdom of Hungary. Eventually, the 'Czechoslovaks' prevailed, and the Slovak League modified its mission. It was agreed that Slovaks and Czechs shared a mutual self-interest to unite in a common cause.

■■■

When WW I started, both the 'Czechoslovak' Slovaks who hoped to form a union with the Czechs, as well as those dreaming about an independent Slovakia, implored Slovak-Americans not to return home and enlist in the Austro-Hungarian army.

Although a few Slovak Americans did return to Europe in response to the war cry, they did so to join the insurgent foreign legions that formed, thanks to the efforts of General Štefánik.

■■■

The Slovaks and Czechs had a common goal—to bring down Austria-Hungary, the so-called 'prison of nations', and to create Czecho-Slovakia, a brand new country. American Slovaks were key to the liberation effort. Without their dollars and influence, Czechoslovakia may have never taken birth.

The Slovak-American community swung into full action. All available tools were mobilized to promote 'war' effort. Slovak newspapers legitimized the campaign for freedom, while the influential fraternal organizations mobilized the masses, sometimes gathering upward of 10,000 Slovaks in support of this cause.

On the diplomatic front, the Slovak League in America officially entered high politics. The raging war in Europe meant that the League now not only represented Slovak-Americans but also Slovaks on the old continent. To this end, the Slovak League and the Bohemian National Alliance gathered in Cleveland, Ohio—home to a vibrant Slovak and Czech community—to take a historic step towards nationhood.

The leadership of both organizations pledged to dismantle Austria-Hungary and to create Czecho-Slovakia on that territory, a federation where Slovaks would have autonomy. The Cleveland Agreement, a fundamental stepping stone toward the founding of a future Czechoslovakia, was signed in Cleveland on October 23, 1915.

There was, of course, a long way to go before Czecho-Slovakia could become a reality. The movement needed a strong ally. The problem was that the U.S. government was far from enthusiastic about the Czecho-Slovak cause. Washington's interests in the region were limited, and there were not enough American experts to raise awareness of the situation of ethnic minorities in Austria-Hungary.

It may have seemed dangerous to embrace the idea of Czecho-Slovakia as it could set a precedent. If the country really came into being, who was to stop other small nations from following suit in Austria-Hungary?

Practically speaking, the U.S. government preferred to deal with one large entity. Relations with one Empire was much easier than liaising with a bunch of little countries. What's more, the Kingdom of Hungary had existed for nearly a thousand years and the rulers, the Habsburgs, had been running Austria for more than six centuries. Austria-Hungary was a hallmark of stability on the old continent.

As the war unfolded, U.S. policy on Austria-Hungary eventually changed. But even after the U.S. officially declared war on the Empire in December 1917, this guaranteed nothing for the Czechs and Slovaks. The Slovak-American community needed to get involved.

When the Slovak General Milan Rastislav Štefánik arrived in New York from Austria-Hungary on June 15, 1917, he was received with enthusiasm. His job was to recruit men into the Czechoslovak Legion—men willing to risk their lives for a nonexistent country. Štefánik's appeal resulted in a mass enrollment. The local Sokol organizations were the first to send volunteers to join the Czechoslovak Legion in France and in Italy. The Legion in France, which numbered about 9,600 men, was made up of 2,309 Czech and Slovak Americans[34]. Overall, the Czechoslovak Legion—which spanned France, Italy, and Russia—numbered nearly 100,000 troops.

Štefánik also contacted the American metropolitan newspapers, working to raise awareness for the Czechoslovak cause

---

[34] Dziak, 2012

beyond the Slovak-American press. This helped to spark sympathy among the mainstream American public. Building on this effort, the Slovak League of America sent a letter addressed to President Wilson in January 1917, petitioning for an independent Czechoslovakia.

The effort escalated with the U.S. visit of Tomáš Garrigue Masaryk in the spring of 1918 when the war in Europe was turning in Czechoslovakia's favor. Thanks to the concerted work of both the Czechs and Slovaks, Masaryk was already recognized as the leader of the Czechoslovak movement. Masaryk had much to accomplish during his stay.

> *Masaryk was not unknown to the U.S. He had lectured as a professor at several prestigious academic institutions in Chicago, New York, and Cleveland. He married an American and even adopted her family name, Garrigue, into his. Moreover, Masaryk had established ties with industrialist Charles Richard Crane, the heir to the tremendous Crane family fortune, gaining his personal patronage.*

■ ■ ■

When Masaryk arrived in Chicago on May 5, 1918, he was greeted by a cheering crowd of some 200,000 Czechs and Slovaks. From there he continued to Pittsburgh, to preside over a meeting that was called on May 31, 1918. Another memorandum was produced, a watered-down version of the one originally drafted in Cleveland in 1915. Few realized that it would become the birth certificate of the Czecho-Slovak nation.

The Pittsburgh Agreement was no longer so clear on the issue of autonomy for Slovaks, but it pledged they would have their own governing body and administration, and that they would be able to use the Slovak language in all spheres of public life. The document made no mention of a federal state or a Slovak nation. Rather, it spoke of one Czecho-Slovak nation. This omission would go on to upset relations between the Czechs and Slovaks in decades to come, but at the time, the agreement legitimated the Czechoslovak movement and that was enough.

Around the same time, and perhaps due to Masaryk's personal bidding, the U.S. Department of State decided to officially change its stance towards Czechoslovakia. The American leadership had their own reasons for this shift, but still it was a major victory for the Slovaks and Czechs. They had won a battle, but the war was not over yet.

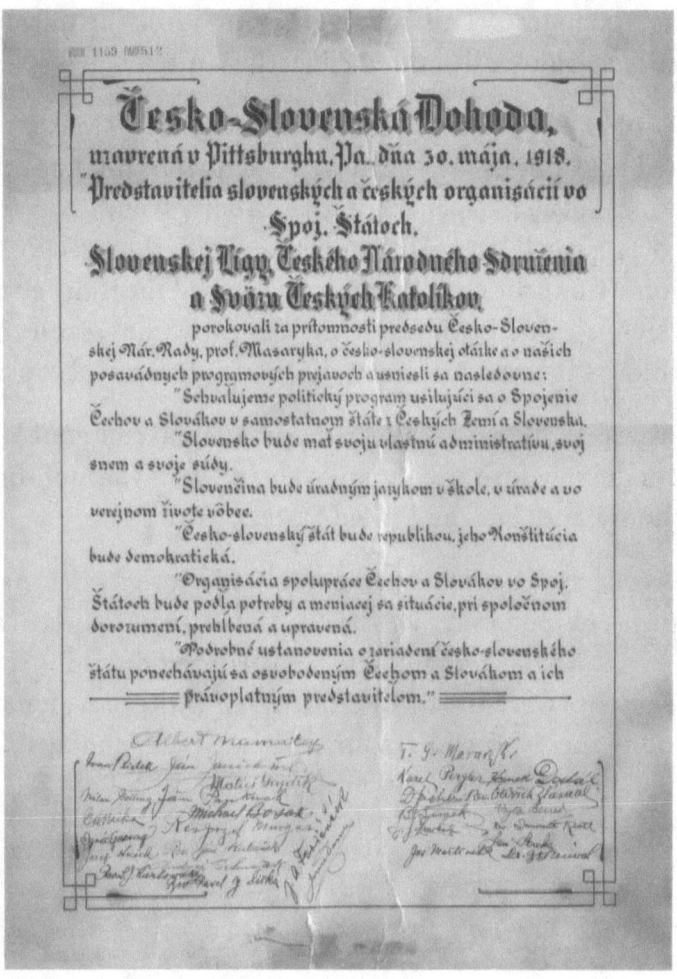

From then on, events moved forward quickly. In July 1918, American Slovaks and Czechs sent a solemn declaration to President Woodrow Wilson, appealing to the American sympathies for oppressed nations. Then the impossible happened.

On September 3, 1918, the U.S. Secretary of State announced that the United States recognized the Czechoslovak National Council. This was an unprecedented move, since there had not yet been any international recognition of Czechoslovakia as free nation. This gave a green light for the movement to proceed, now fully endorsed by the United States.

In October of the same year, Tomáš Garrigue Masaryk returned to America and personally delivered the *Declaration of Czechoslovak Independence* to President Woodrow Wilson. Just over a week later, on October 28, 1918, the Czechoslovak National Committee in Prague proclaimed the independence of Czechoslovakia. Masaryk, still in the U.S., was elected in absentia as the first president of the newly formed country.

As Professor Stolarik argues, "The principal center of Slovak nationalism before and during World War I was not the Slovak homeland, but the United States of America."[35]

The very same settlers who came to America with next to nothing, helped to make Czechoslovakia happen through their wit and hard labor. The Cleveland and the Pittsburgh Agreements were the birth certificates of the Slovak nation. Without these official statements, an independent Slovak Republic would never have been possible.

---

[35] Stolarik, 1992

Conquering the Canadian Wilderness

The first pioneers, mostly men from eastern Slovakia, started to arrive in Canada in the second half of the 19th century. The story goes that the first known Slovak to immigrate to Canada was Joseph Bellon, who came to Toronto in 1878 and established a wireworks factory. Historical evidence for this is lacking, but we do know that Bellon, whether he existed or not, was most likely not the first Slovak to arrive in the country.

Canada's western provinces received many faceless and nameless migrants during the 19th century. They travelled as far as Alberta and British Columbia to work alongside the Chinese migrants building the Canadian National Railway and later the Canadian Pacific Railway.

Carving out space in the wilderness to lay down the tracks was not just hard work; it was also dangerous. Men perished on the job, and their bodies were laid in unassuming graves next to the tracks. Work went on as normal, and only wooden crosses bearing their name and dates were left to record their presence and their sacrifice.

Despite the harsh conditions, some Slovaks chose to settle in the mining towns that the railroads connected. But a change of job did not necessarily mean greater safety or security. One of the worst tragedies to befall the Slovak-Canadian community occurred in Fernie, British Columbia on May 24, 1902, when a mining explosion claimed the lives of 50 Slovak immigrants.

Unfortunately, there are very few historical Slovak sources that document the early arrivals in Canada. One fascinating story that was preserved takes us back to the Canadian prairies in the 1880s.

The Canadian government established a land grant initiative to give away acres of free land to settlers in order to open the prairies to European settlement. The vast and sparsely populated land became the incentive offered by an eccentric aristocrat who set out to champion migrants to Canada from Austria-Hungary.

Paul Oscar Esterhazy was born in 1831 as Johannes Packh in Esztergom, Hungary. It is said that Johannesz left Hungary following the civil upheavals of 1848, served in the British army, and then went to North America. Once in the New World, Johannes adopted the surname Esterhazy in the 1860s, thereby associating himself with one of the most powerful and prestigious families from the Empire. Naturally, this came with certain benefits.

This man lived in New York City in 1868 under the name of Paul Oscar Esterhazy and offered help to would-be migrants from the old country. Count Esterhazy took a keen interest in the fate of his fellow countrymen, both ethnic Hungarians and Slovaks. He knew that they came to the United States because they struggled to make a living in their homeland. In 1885 and 1886, Esterhazy became an immigration agent.

He successfully lobbied decision-makers in Canada on behalf of the people from the Kingdom of Hungary, arguing that they had a healthy moral fabric and a good work ethic, giving them a great capacity to contribute to the young Canadian society.

In the 1880s, Esterhazy helped immigrants who had moved to the United States from Upper Hungary to relocate to Canada. He felt they would be happier there, working as farmers. Two settlements in the Canadian prairies were scouted as the perfect destinations for these Austro-Hungarian immigrants. The Hun's Valley in Manitoba and Esterhaz in Saskatchewan attracted mainly Slovak, but also Hungarian settlers, from the mining towns of Pennsylvania. Some came directly from Upper Hungary.

It was easy to persuade men and women who were tired of the industrial life in America to give rural life in Canada a try. Many migrants hoped to return to an agrarian lifestyle, which was more natural and familiar to them. Access to acres of free land was also an attractive draw for men who were being exploited by their employers in America. This was the chance they had been waiting for.

The Slovaks were welcomed to Canada, but they were given little more than the pieces of empty land. Being sent into the wilderness, they had to fend for themselves. There was no plumbing, no electricity, and no running water near the plots of land that they were given. The settlers were expected to build their own shelters from the mud and stones they could find there.

Sadly, in the long run Count Esterhazy's grand vision of building a New Hungary in the expansive Canadian landscape failed. Still, even today descendants of Slovaks and Hungarians can be found across the prairies as a result of this settlement.

This extraordinary story aside, records show that the immigration of Slovaks to Canada only became significant after World War I, when the U.S. imposed immigration quotas. According to scholars, over 20,000 Slovaks arrived in Canada between 1922 and 1927.[36] For most, Canada was not their destination of choice. Rather, they were rerouted farther north because the U.S. closed its borders to most Eastern Europeans by setting immigration quotas. These migrants found

---

[36] Mihal, 2003

employment in the docklands and factories of Ontario, or in Montreal, Quebec, where there was already a small Slovak community.

■ ■ ■

> *Without the ability to speak English or French, Slovaks had to face a great deal of discrimination. The birth of the next generation and their enrollment in the Canadian school system resulted in a greater integration into the surrounding society. Like in the U.S., Slovaks in Canada started to anglicize their names to fit in.*

■ ■ ■

The Great Depression of the 1930s had a devastating impact on the Canadian economy, and immigrants were the first to feel its blow. Slovaks, among some of the most recently arrived immigrants, lost their jobs. Like many others, the Slovak immigrants survived by joining the army of unemployed men that roamed the Canadian railways in search of work. Most would end up taking on poorly paid and intermittent farm work.

Great adversity also gives birth to miracles. During the trying years of the Depression, a unique town emerged in the Canadian wilderness. Bradlo, Ontario, became the only fully Slovak settlement in Canada.[37] It was named after the final resting place of Milan Rastislav Štefánik, a great Slovak hero.

By the 1930s, Slovaks began to trickle slowly into the settlement in northern Ontario to face the challenges thrown at them. The land was wild, the short summers hot, and the winters long and freezing cold.

---

[37] Bies, 2020

The Slovak families persevered they logged trees by hand, cleared the wilderness, built log houses, and managed, later to open a church and school to serve their community.

The possibility of earning money in logging attracted more Slovak immigrants to Bradlo during and after the Great Depression. Most were looking for a way out of the cities and factories, a way to return to nature. A neighborhood store, a post office, and a community center were added to the infrastructure of the community, and Bradlo became a little Slovak colony of 150 persons.

However, once the trees were gone, the logging ended, and life in Bradlo took turn for the worse. Settlers tried to clear the stumps to use the land for farming, but the soil and the

weather were not supportive of their endeavors. Life in the remote area offered few opportunities for the children of the original settlers, who wanted more for themselves. By the 1950s, most had moved away. According to records, the last Slovak family to live in Bradlo was in 1957.[38]

■ ■ ■

Today's Bradlo is no longer a home to Slovaks, but it is nevertheless celebrated as an iconic footprint of Slovak heritage in Canada. The descendants of the Bradlo settlers have not forgotten the great sacrifices of their predecessors. A monument in the form of an eleven-ton granite boulder was erected in their honor in 2022. Its plaque lists the name of each of the original Slovak settlers.

■ ■ ■

Interestingly, some of the Slovaks who came to Canada in the 1930s, did not immigrate from the territory of modern-day Slovakia, but rather from modern day Serbia. They were the descendants of farmers who moved to the Balkans following the Ottoman Wars that rocked Europe from 14th to the 17th century. After the Ottoman defeat, those lands were left devastated and deserted. They needed to be repopulated with people who could restore agriculture back in the region.

The opportunity was taken up by those seeking to escape the religious sanctions in Upper Hungary, where there was no peace between Protestants and Catholics. Entire families moved to the southern parts of the Hungarian Kingdom, setting up their own little Slovak colonies in Vojvodina. Flashing forward, when the Canadian Railway Agreement Act of 1925 opened Canada to farmers from Eastern Europe, Slovaks in Vojvodina saw this as an opportunity.

---

[38] Bies, 2020

Canadian agriculture was severely affected by the Great Depression. With not enough money to pay for workers, taxes, and mortgages, farms all over Canada were repossessed by the banks or the government. Instead of letting them rot, Canada introduced a plan that encouraged families from Europe to replace the original farm owners.

The on-boarding process was far from easy. It required a considerable investment, including a $1,000 cash deposit made as a down payment for the property. It required a commitment to buy the Canadian farm in full, after a period of one year. And the price of failure? Repatriation back to Vojvodina, along with loss of the original cash deposit.

Between 5,000 and 10,000 Slovaks took their chances by following this call and relocating from Vojvodina to Canada.[39]

These were not poor folk, but rather successful farmers who could afford the down payment.

Armed with faith, family togetherness, and a willingness to work hard, these Slovaks accepted the challenge. But the Canadian prairies were a devastating adversary. Despite their best effort, these Slovak immigrants often spent years of blood, sweat, and tears before life in Canada started to settle into a more balanced pace for their families. Slovak children were expected to work alongside their parents. They rarely attended school past the age of 14, giving all their energy and skills to helping the farm survive.

Today there are some 80,000 Canadians of Slovak descent.

---

[39] Mihal, 2005

Slovaks in Argentina

Not all the Slovaks who decided to cross the Atlantic to find a better existence aimed for the shores of North America. Some ventured south.

Once the U.S. started to control the number of incoming immigrants, Slovaks began to look elsewhere to start anew. The untamed vastness of South America was an interesting and seductive opportunity. For the most part, European migrants were welcomed there.

In fact, importing European settlers was a developmental strategy of several South American governments. Europeans were brought in to 'civilize' the wild and untamed landscape. This was a gargantuan task, very difficult to achieve without European agricultural know-how and perseverance. That is where Slovaks came in. They were viewed as a hard-working, agrarian people, equipped with the knowledge and resilience needed to succeed.

This was not the first time that Slovak agricultural expertise had been mobilized. When the prolonged war with the Ottomans ended in central Europe in the 17th century, parts of the Kingdom of Hungary were devastated, depopulated and in need of agricultural renewal. Slovaks from the mountainous northern regions of Upper Hungary were attracted to the fertile, but now empty lowlands by the policies of the empress Maria Theresa, and later her son Joseph. The trend was encouraged and supported even a century later.

Most Slovaks departed from the overpopulated and poor areas of Upper Hungary to present-day southern Hungary, Serbia, Romania, and Bulgaria. It is estimated that around 200,000 Slovaks emigrated in 18th and 19th centuries. It was this population that resonated most strongly with the South

American invitation to come and cultivate the wild lands. Before World War I Argentina was doing well. To be 'rich like an Argentine' was a popular expression thanks to the country's huge economic growth from the 1860 onwards. Its performance was so spectacular that Argentina was expected to become the United States of South America. Even though the first world war slowed its growth, Argentina managed to weather both the war and the Great Depression better than North America.

The interior of the country was sparsely populated, and the Argentinian government wanted Europeans to come and turn the wilderness into farmland. The Argentines also wanted to tip the ethnic scale in favor of those from European backgrounds. In the hope of civilizing the more distant provinces, the government sent out agents to Europe to persuade people to move to Argentina by promising them vast swaths of free land. Settlers could get up to 100 hectares of land.

■ ■ ■

The newly founded Czechoslovakia also felt the brunt of the global economic crisis, and many of its people concluded that their future prosperity depended on leaving their homeland. Unlike the Slovaks from the Balkans who were attracted to the countryside, Slovaks from Czechoslovakia flocked to Argentinian cities to find employment in the many industries that needed workers. Some later became entrepreneurs, opening restaurants and shops that served the needs of the Eastern European community.

■ ■ ■

The Balkan Slovaks felt as if lady luck had finally smiled on them. Gaining such large plots of land for free was a golden opportunity. This would enable them to continue their rural lifestyle, but on a larger scale and on a new continent.

Naturally, there was a catch to this deal the agents chose not to mention.

When Slovaks arrived in Argentina, they realized that the free land was not arable fields but rainforest. To till this land, they would first have to clear the jungle. The task was Herculean, and many of the migrants felt overwhelmed by it. They were not prepared for this; they had neither money nor equipment. Yet, turning around and going back home was not an option either. It took three decades for some families to turn their rainforest property into profitable fields.

What's more, Argentina had a different climate from what Slovaks were used to. The farmers would have to learn new techniques, gain knowledge of unfamiliar crops, and adopt new agricultural strategies if they were to succeed. Instead of growing an array of crops and keeping all kinds of animals, which was what they were accustomed to, they would have to change the game plan altogether and move from small family-based subsistence farming to large-scale specialized farming. Cotton and cattle led the way, and so the Slovaks worked around the clock to meet the demands of the expansive beef and textile industries.

With time, Slovaks began to feel more settled in Argentina. As their communities matured, and new children were born, new organizations also popped up. The Tatran Society established in 1923 in Buenos Aires started to open Slovak cultural centers across the country, and even beyond Argentina. More Slovak clubs, schools, and societies followed, often in collaboration with Czech immigrants.

But it was during World War II that the Slovak community in Argentina truly expanded. Slovak Jews and intelligentsia were fleeing to South America to escape the newly established Slovak State, a satellite of Nazi Germany. These immigrants were educated, self-aware, and even politically active.

As a result, the Slovak-Argentinian community received teachers, entrepreneurs, priests, scientists, politicians, and journalists who shaped the spiritual, political, and social life of the community for decades to come.

Thanks to this influx, Slovak Catholics in Argentina could attend mass celebrated in the Slovak language for the first time ever.

Among these refugees were men and women who returned to Slovakia when the war ended. Writers, artists, and poets used their experience in South America to leave a unique mark on Slovakia. These included Jozef Cíger Hronský, who became known for his imaginative and inspiring literature for children, and the Franciscan monk Rudolf Dilong, a poet who dedicated his life to campaigning for freedom through his verses and religious literature. Dilong continued his work as editor of *Listov sv. Františka* (Letters of St. Francis) when he moved in 1965 to a Franciscan monastery in Pittsburgh.

■ ■ ■

There were also those who wrote themselves into the history of Slovakia in Argentina in ways that were far from positive. Ferdinand Durčanský, the former minister of foreign affairs and the minister of interior in the wartime Slovak State, was treated as a war criminal after World War II. He was condemned for high treason in Czechoslovakia and escaped to Argentina to avoid execution, like many other high-ranking-Nazis from Europe.

■ ■ ■

Today, Slovaks in Argentina continue to cherish the culture and traditions of their ancestors. They gather frequently in Buenos Aires, but also outside of the capital, to enjoy traditional Slovak dishes, sing Slovak songs, and dance in their ancestral *kroje*. Like elsewhere in the New World, Slovaks in Argentina may no longer be able to speak the native tongue of their forefathers, but they want to know about Slovakia and are proud of their origins.

Part five
STORIES

PERILOUS PASSAGES:
LIFE AND DEATH
IN A NEW LAND

by Ken Duda

"Instantly killed while working."

Imagine abandoning a country, home, family, and lifestyle, carrying only a mother's small photograph as a last treasured keepsake, and a well-worn prayer book in your native language to offer solace and guidance in stressful solitude. Both would become tattered and faded over time, just like the connections to the homeland that gradually dissipated as each generation passed away.

My ancestors came from the scenically beautiful Spiš and Šariš regions of eastern Slovakia. The area around Slovinky was inhabited from prehistoric times, and it was a center of mining for hundreds of years. Here, only some 10 crow-fly miles southeast of the mighty Spiš Castle, heroes of my story were born.

Michal Potproč, my great-grandfather, and Anna Grabányová married in Slovakia to bear a son Mikuláš Potproč, rooted and brought up in the spirit of the Rusyn culture. Michal Potproč was the first of my lineage to arrive in the United States, leaving his wife and son behind to establish an income and life in the new country. He was not alone. His brother Ján also came to work in the coal mines—he, too, parting from his wife Anna and their children.

Men seeking employment in eastern Pennsylvania could choose from four large coal companies and 15 additional

smaller ones. The Kingston Coal Company in this Third Anthracite District employed 1,038 in mines, who were assisted by the muscles and energy of 155 horses and mules to support their mining operations. Day in and day out, Michal and Ján toiled, propelled by the dream of providing a good life for their families.

In the warm summer days of 1886, the brothers eagerly anticipated the imminent arrival of their wives and children from Slovakia.

The women travelled with their combined four children first to the port city of Stettin (now Szczecin) in present-day Poland, to board the German-flagged steamer SS *Moravia* that would take them across the Atlantic Ocean to New York. Unbeknownst to the travelers joyfully anticipating the reunion with their husbands and fathers, a catastrophe occurred in Kingston that forever changed the family.

On July 6, 1886, just 11 days before the SS *Moravia* arrived in New York, like so many of his countrymen, Michal Potproč was working as usual in the damp darkness and grime of the Kingston Coal Company No. 2 shaft. Explosives were laid to bring down a large rock, a common procedure. In that year, the Kingston Company used 19,016 kegs of powder to blast their way deep into the earth. But this time it failed to achieve the desired outcome. The laborers tried their best, but the rock refused to give way. It was Mike who was ordered to look under the rock while a second round of explosives was being prepared. But then the rocky mass suddenly came tumbling down.

The official statement in the Reports of the Inspectors of Mines describes the death of 30-year-old laborer "Michael Potprotch" in only a few terse words. "Instantly killed. While working near the left rib of breast, a projecting piece of rock fell on him. It had been sounded that morning and pronounced safe."

Still out on the open ocean, and only days away from reconnecting with her husband, Mike's wife Anna was probably tending to the children in that fateful moment when he stepped under the rock. As a newspaper article recounting the tragedy poignantly noted, "The death of her husband will indeed be sad news to her, and will cause great grief, as she expects to meet him enjoying good health, but instead she will meet him cold in death, and no loving words of welcome will greet her ears."

Sadly, Michal was certainly not the first nor the only Slovak man to meet his tragic end deep underground in the American coal mines. Such heartrending losses were all too common.

Mines were dangerous places. The official 1886 mines report[1] includes page after page of such incidents. In the process of mining nearly 35 million tons of coal in these anthracite regions during that year, there were 279 fatal and 848 non-fatal accidents among the 63,930 individuals employed inside the mines. The overall casualty rate of killed and wounded for miners was 1.8%. Almost two of every hundred! For comparison, going to war was just a little bit more hazardous than working in a coal mine!

Our first-hand family memories recall that if a miner was killed, the mining company just took the body to the house and left it there. In this time and place no compensation was given to the family for deaths or disease.

The possibility of not returning from work one day was so real that Slovaks sang songs about living with that danger and fear. There was such a consistent year-to-year loss of life that the mining authorities even kept track of the number of widows and orphans caused by mine accidents. My

---

[1] Reports of the Inspectors of Mines of the Anthracite Coal Regions of Pennsylvania, for the Year 1886

great-grandmother Anna was one of 144 new widows in the area that year, and my grandfather Nicholas became one of 452 resulting orphans.

We do not know where Michal Potproč is buried. For a long time, I wondered if perhaps his body was left in the mine under the huge rock that ended his life, but then a news article was found stating that, "A Coroner's jury also viewed the body of Michael Postbrush, a Hungarian of Kingston borough." So, the body was not just left there to rot and fade into oblivion. After all, they had to clear the rockfall to continue mining. To extract even more profit, coal companies would often "rob the pillars," cutting away at supporting columns. This caused roof collapse, deaths of miners and work animals, and loss of houses that were on the surface above.

Although the investigators seemed to suspect fatal negligence, the death of a Slovak immigrant miner became but a formality, and someone else was hired to take his place. There was no shortage of available manpower.

What happened to Anna?

It is likely that she observed the preparations for the dedication of the Statue of Liberty as her ship sailed into New York harbor in July 1886. She only learned that her husband was dead once she met his relative. Anna lost her hair in shock. It never fully regrew, but she soon found another Slovak man from Slovinky to marry.

The ethnic Slovak and religious groups were tightly cohesive and strongly supportive. Anna had much help from these groups after her arrival, in addition to that from the family of her brother-in-law John. To rapidly remarry was a matter of necessity, but it also must have been deeply satisfying and comforting for both her and her new husband Jozef Duda to meet someone from the same hometown. They remained married until parted by his death in 1929.

Jozef (Joseph or Joe) Duda was a typical miner with a lantern hat and metal lunch can. He had no shortage of mine stories to tell. One still runs on in the family about Joe carrying the lifeless body of a dead co-worker out of the mine. It was said that this fellow later came back to thank him in appreciation for the act of kindness.

Away from the mines, Joe kept church records in a book as a clerk to assist the community, and he eventually became a naturalized U.S. citizen.

He welcomed and nurtured Anna's first child Mikuláš (Nicholas), and the family gradually expanded by seven more children. When the 1900 U.S. Census was taken on June 21, Mikuláš was listed as Nicholas Potproč, but he later took the surname of his loving stepfather.

The family home had an outside water pump and no refrigerator. Meals were cooked on a coal stove, and light came from kerosene lamps. A large garden provided food and medicinal herbs. Anna also used spider webs and leeches for healing.

As if Anna had not faced enough hardships, her second husband passed away too.

The dangers in the dusty, dirty, damp, dark depths of the mines included more than rockfalls. After working there for some time, most miners likely had some degree of anthrocosis, or black lung. This leaves humans susceptible to exacerbations in chronic bronchitis, and in the pre-antibiotic era this would lead to pneumonia. Yet in these years the coal industry maintained that coal dust was harmless. The problem was so prevalent in the Wilkes-Barre area that folks referred to the persistent loud miner's cough as the "White Haven Yodel," after a sanatorium in that nearby town where pulmonary disease was treated, including tuberculosis.

Per his death certificate, Joseph died at age 64 from lobar pneumonia, thus it was a pulmonary-related death and highly likely to be a result of lung injury incurred through mining. He indicated in his will that after his wife Anna died, he desired that the family inheritance would be shared equally by the children, including his stepson, Nicholas. As a further tragedy for Anna, the house burned completely to the ground just prior to WW II. The twice-widowed matriarch lost all her money in the fire, as well as her trunk from Europe. She moved to Hazelton, Pennsylvania, and lived with one of her children until her death in 1949.

Anna rarely spoke English, and she didn't know precisely how old she was. Recalling the homeland, Anna spoke of Emperor Franz Joseph and cried when he died. Despite the trials and tribulations of life, she retained a good sense of humor throughout and was a good dancer, enjoying social gatherings enlivened by the sound of an accordion playing *csárdás*.

In addition to helping raise the children of other family members and caring for sick neighbors, Anna assisted women with childbirth and even patched up a miner after a knife fight in a local bar. One day, she stepped in to perform the religious services at the cemetery for a man when the priest refused for some reason. She simply commented that, "Nobody should be buried like a dog." Forged in the fire of tragedies, her spirit was strong and resilient.

Michael Potproč's son Nicholas, my grandfather, worked in the mines as did his stepfather, Joseph, but Nick developed a taste for adventure. He loved to roam far and wide. Perhaps travelling on a ship as a little boy created a wanderlust in him. He decided to head to Alaska and try his luck in the gold mines there.

However, along the way and in the state of Montana, he met Alžbeta Salková, an orphan born in Pavlovce, near Prešov in eastern Slovakia. He decided she was a far greater treasure. The Alaska journey was abandoned, and the couple married in Montana in 1909 where Nick began working in the local coal mines. He and Alžbeta (Elizabeth) had three children, including my father. Nick was a strong and fit miner. The family recalls that when a mine flooded, he saved a lot of the men. He got out, quickly located a cart and donkey, and used these in lantern light to maneuver and save his colleagues.

My father Clifford was born in Montana, where he began school, and made skis from barrel staves to use on the hills next to home. It was here that his father instilled his appreciation of horses, taking him when he was four years old to a rodeo in a nearby town. A photo of this is preserved on an early postcard from the time, showing the men observing a woman riding a bucking bronco. Cliff became an excellent rider himself, and he introduced me to horse riding too, as well as to shooting, baseball, football, ice skating, and other sports.

After leaving his initial mine work in Pennsylvania, for several years Nick worked in mines in Iowa and Montana. He saved his earnings as much as possible, and in time, Nick acquired his own mine in Lehigh, Montana. But when the town's economy collapsed, and the money owed to him was never paid, it was time for them to move elsewhere in search of greener pastures. Today, Lehigh is a ghost town.

The Nick Duda family adventurously drove eastward across the U.S. and was encouraged at each overnight stop to stay and become permanent residents. Nonetheless, they carried on and settled in Detroit, Michigan, buying a house one block away from the convenient Mager corner grocery store.

The stage was set for two families that hailed from towns only 50 miles apart in Slovakia to meet for the first time in faraway North America. The rest of the Potproč/Duda family had by now become well-established in and around Sheppton, Pennsylvania, while the Mager clan was thriving 500 miles away in Detroit.

My maternal grandfather Ján Mager was born and raised in Kurima, near Bardejov. When Ján and his siblings became orphaned, to avoid living with a "mean witch" relative they started to leave the heart of Europe in the hope of finding a better life in America. As the family trickled in, they settled in western Pennsylvania. Ján arrived in 1901 when he was about 17 years old and went straight to work in the mines.

Back in Slovakia, Anna Dulajčinová left the same village as Ján and eventually found work at a church rectory in Pennsylvania. But it was in the New World and at the tender age of sweet 16 that Ján, now John, Mager saw her for the first time. Soon there was a wedding, and the family grew to nine children in the years to come, including my mother, Elizabeth.

John would escape the dreary mine work when his brother Tom persuaded him to come to Detroit to try his luck in the

booming car industry. The trip from Pennsylvania with eight children in tow alongside a very pregnant wife must have been quite tense! And to add to the pressure, Anna gave birth to her last child, Irene, the day after their arrival in Detroit. The family settled among ethnic Slovaks, and my mother attended school where the Slovak language was also taught.

Like Joe Duda, John became a naturalized U.S. citizen, and he later bought a meat and vegetable grocery store from his brother. This store provided the family livelihood for his remaining years—a huge step up from the dreaded mines and factory assembly line work. Although thriving in America, Anna was homesick. My grandmother would look lovingly and longingly at the photo of her mother that she brought from home. She planned to return to Slovakia to visit her mother but died in 1937 just before this could be accomplished. Though John lived until 1969, he never remarried. My mother began taking care of the household for the very large family and assisted in running the family business. As the women of the community were the keepers of traditions, my mother also took on the responsibility of maintaining the Slovak culinary and holiday traditions.

My memories of Grandfather John are that he was a wonderful, jovial man, always with a twinkling smile for the children. He would let me go down to the store from the lodging above and select a treat of candy or ice cream. As I developed an interest in coin collecting, my grandfather allowed me to go through the cash register and sort through the coins to look for collectible old ones and make an exchange for an equivalent newer coin. When I was almost a teenager, he included me with the men of the family in raising a toast with shots of whiskey for a special occasion. It was a rite of passage of a kind, and it was also an honor to join the men who sat in the back room of the store on beer cases and exchanged news of their lives.

By then, WW II was unleashed in Europe, and as a result, only one of my immigrant ancestors ever returned to Slovakia. Under pressure from his wife, John's brother Joseph Mager went back home when it was already evident that Europe would be set ablaze. She was either drawn back by concerns for her family, or maybe she preferred the lifestyle they had left behind in the "old country." Nevertheless, both brothers strongly counseled Joseph to remain in the U.S. and told him to get another wife if she insisted on leaving.

The Mager brothers eventually signed over their rights to the family farm in Slovakia to Joseph, and he and his wife and family returned to Šariš to meet their fate amidst the turmoil of war. Details about the farm were lost in the mists of time, as direct contacts and the remaining brothers eventually faded away.

The first-generation descendants of the Slovak immigrants mentioned in this story, including my father, stood and pledged allegiance to the U.S. flag with their right hands over their hearts every day as schoolchildren in America. They did not shirk when called upon by their nation to defend liberty and release countries and peoples from the devastation of Nazi and Japanese cruelty. They joined the Allies in the push to liberate Czechoslovakia.

At 26 years of age, my father Cliff Duda was a relatively old soldier among his warrior counterparts in 1942. Nevertheless, outdoor activities in the freezing winters and hot summers of Montana prepared him well for what was to come.

In the 1st Infantry Division under command of General Patton, Cliff experienced the early U.S. onslaught in North Africa, where he engaged with fierce opposition from the Axis forces as the American army pushed toward Tunisia. His group also led the amphibious assault on Sicily to commence the penetration north through Italy. The Mager family took part

as well, in the Pacific against the Japanese, and in England against the Germans. Fortunately, no immediate family members were killed in this horrendous conflict.

Cliff's wartime experiences brought him near Slovakia, but not in pleasant circumstances. He was captured alongside other members of his platoon in Sicily, as they confronted a German tank without adequate weapons. As prisoners of war, the men were transferred to what is now northern Poland, west of Gdansk. Germany had claimed the region in 1939, and so my father spent nearly two years behind enemy lines on a farm work detail, or *Arbeitskommando*, at *Stalag II-B* — a German prison camp. He wrote to the family saying, "It sure is a tough world we are living in today, but I haven't seen a Duda that couldn't take anything yet."

Cliff survived a Nazi-forced mid-winter death march in early 1945, when the Germans tried to escape the advancing Soviets. They pushed the emaciated, poorly clothed prisoners to walk hundreds of miles westward at gunpoint in extremely frigid conditions. Others were not so lucky, succumbing to starvation, disease, cold, or a bullet from a German when they could no longer keep up. Eventually, my father was liberated by U.S. forces and returned home to recuperate in Michigan, a place he reckoned he never wanted to leave again. The 1st Division pushed on to liberate western Czechoslovakia.

It took five years before Cliff was able to move on from the trauma of war. He developed a relationship with his childhood Mager friend, Elizabeth, and they married in 1950 on the 4th of July. It was a precious moment, and it must have felt like the whole nation was celebrating with them! They had a son and a daughter Nancy. I am that son who records these recollections.

Some of my most treasured memories are of time spent with my grandparents, Nicholas and Elizabeth Duda. Being with them in their home on a large acreage that they acquired for retirement was a treat. We always arrived to a bowl full of sugar-coated donuts and left with a trunk full of all types of fresh garden produce. I could shoot arrows at targets there with my dad's hunting bow, golf with my grandfather's wooden clubs, explore the land with a toy machine gun, and quench my thirst with water from a rain barrel. The place was also a focal point for large family gatherings anticipated by all. We lost Elizabeth in 1963, Nick shortly after in 1966.

I must have inherited some of the inclination to roam. Like my migrant ancestors, I left my home country for many years to work in foreign lands and seek adventure around the world. But I always returned and am living again in the U.S. Throughout my global adventures, I have never forgotten the Slovak homeland, the birthplace of all twelve of my grandparents and great-grandparents.

The forces that prompt large-scale migration, like those that put so many Slovaks into motion in the late 19th and early

20th centuries, continue to this day. The recorded experiences of my Slovak ancestors provide prescient parallels to such present-day trials and sufferings, and to likely future travails to be endured by humanity.

War seems to be the historical norm, peace a welcome but fleeting anomaly. Borders change. Allies become enemies. Enemies become allies. At best, perhaps everything experienced in the past somehow provides sufficient preparation for the unknown future. But lives must be lived in the present. It is satisfying to observe that the descendants of my Slovak family immigrants became successful in a wide range of professional pursuits, thus honoring the sacrifices of their ancestors and contributing to the economic success of their country.

In 2007, I drove throughout Slovakia by myself. I visited the places my ancestors walked and loved, while I also restored family connections. It was an exhilarating experience! The long-anticipated "return" provided a deep sense of serene satisfaction and heartfelt accomplishment that remains to this day. I arrived back in the U.S. eager to share photos and stories with my mother about the birthplace of her parents. Perhaps I'll return to Slovakia again soon.

...

Ken Duda began his career leading geoscience exploration initiatives in numerous countries on multiple continents. He later managed science operations aspects of several major NASA Earth-orbiting satellite missions, and used acquired data to address key world concerns. Ken enjoys many sports, performing music with others using violin and guitar, long-distance motorcycling, and ongoing research in international affairs and family history.

Rich Dinner Rolls and Bread

- ½ cup warm water
- 2¼ – 4½ TSP active dry yeast (1 or 2 packages)
- ⅓ cup white granulated sugar
- 1 TSP salt
- 1 stick salted butter, softened
- 1 cup evaporated milk (canned)
- 2 large eggs, beaten
- 5¼ cups all-purpose or bread flour, sifted

1. Put the water in a pre-warmed cup and mix in the yeast. Stir and let stand.
2. In a large mixing bowl, combine the sugar, salt, and butter.
3. Scald milk and pour over sugar, salt, and butter mixture. Stir to dissolve, then let cool to lukewarm.
4. Add eggs and mix.
5. Add dissolved yeast and mix.
6. Add 2 cups of flour and beat until smooth.
7. Stir in remaining flour, to make a soft dough.

8. Mix with hands (or a stand mixer), then knead on a lightly floured surface.

9. Knead the dough until smooth and elastic (about 8-10 minutes, if by hand).

10. Place in a large, greased bowl, then turn the dough over in the bowl, to grease the top of the dough. Cover the bowl with plastic wrap.

11. Let the dough rise in a warm place, free from drafts, until it doubles in volume (60-90 minutes).

12. Punch down the dough to release the air, then let it rise again, until it doubles in volume (less time than the first rise).

13. Punch down the dough, and form it into your desired shapes: rolls or a loaf.

14. For rolls, divide the dough into 12 balls, then place them in a greased 9"x 13"x 2" pan.

15. Let the dough rise for a third time, until it doubles in volume.

16. Preheat the oven to 350 °F (180 °C).

17. Bake for 15-20 minutes.

18. Cool on a wire rack.

THE SLOVAK AMERICANS
by Deah Partak

"If it wasn't for their willingness to allow multiple cultures to co-exist, so much of who we are could have been lost."

"How do you know you are Slovak?," a friend recently asked me.

"What do you mean 'how do I know?'," was my confused response.

"I mean, how do you know your family is originally from there? Did you take a DNA test or something?"

"Because my family is Slovak," I simply retorted back.

The fact that this question seemed so odd to me made me realize it was worth contemplating. Not everyone has the privilege of knowing where their roots are. I should not take that knowledge for granted. It is a miracle for that heritage to be preserved. I have been told that our family name, originally spelled Partók, before it was Americanized to Partak, sounds Hungarian. That implies that the family certainly felt the pressure and became a victim of Magyarization. If this is true, our original Slovak name is a mystery, and yet here I am, a proud Slovak-American.

When my great-grandparents had arrived in the U.S., they settled in a community where almost everyone was doing the same thing. Being Slovak and knowing that one is Slovak was not seen as something special. It was only after I had moved away that I felt the absence of the Slovak traditions. I am now

on the path to never forget their legacy. My great-grandparents are my heroes, and here are their stories.

The first Partóks in America

My second great-grandparents raised their seven children in the tiny village of Jablonka in the Orava region which is now within the political borders of Poland. They were, like many Slovaks at the time, farmers. All I know is that they looked so very tired on the one and only photograph I have of my family in the "old country". Their sons, which included my great-grandfather Ján, came to America in the early 1900s. All but one sibling settled in Chicago.

Did they all work in the steel factory together? Most likely. But what is even more interesting is that there was also a young Slovak woman in Chicago at that time by the name of Mária. She too, was from Jablonka and was working as a cleaning woman at the Palmer House Hotel, now the Hilton. Family legend has it that she was there to earn money for her dowry and then head back home.

Did Mária and Ján meet in America by chance and fall in love? Or did the family plan the marriage? I like to think it was love at first sight from across the hotel lobby; however, I wager an arrangement is probably more accurate. At some point, Ján and Mária returned to Jablonka and were married. Later, they returned to Chicago to have their marriage legalized in the U.S. in 1904 at age 24 and 20. At some time before 1907, Ján and Mária headed back to Jablonka.

Ján came back to America in 1909, leaving Mária behind with three children. He worked at the railroad and lived on Garnsey Avenue in a Slovak neighborhood on the eastside of Joliet, Illinois. Like many Slovaks, he saved every penny to eventually bring his family over. Mária and the children arrived in 1911. That same year, they purchased a house at 701 E. Garnsey Avenue where the rest of the children were born. In 1914, the whole family became U.S. citizens.

Ján has been remembered as the 'character' in the neighborhood. He was always involved in something unexpected like buying an abandoned house, raising rabbits in the garage, inventing a motorized wheelchair when he lost his leg to diabetes, and buying a manual car, which his one leg prevented him from driving.

He did not shy away from taking risks. After all, he took a big chance when he left his parents, home country, and everything he knew behind to start out in America; might as well go all in! So, he took that abandoned house at 651 E. Garnsey Ave. and built a grocery store onto it. In 1929, he quit the railroad and opened the Partak's Grocery and Butchers. Ján remained the ideas guy, while Mária became the solid anchor for the family business.

"My grandma was the butcher!" my dad often says with pride. Mária's cleaver is still in our family along with her *droby* recipe; a potato sausage specific to northern Slovakia. I remember when my parents and I were visiting southern Slovakia, and our world shook when the family we stayed with had never heard of *droby*! Its uniqueness to the region makes me even more appreciative to my great-grandmother, my grandmother, and now my father for keeping the recipe alive. And I hold a special appreciation to my father, Andrew 'Sonny' Partak Jr., for altering the lard ratio in the recipe without losing the taste to help us all live a bit longer!

While Mária was busy behind the butcher's counter, local neighborhood lore speaks of Ján's escapades. Some have wondered if Ján was helping his fellow Slovaks raise a glass and *Na zdravie!* properly during Prohibition. Old family friends pondered where he got the money to build the grocery store

and to later buy half the houses on Garnsey Avenue during the Great Depression. I wish I knew! The mysterious finances and activities of the grocery store aside, it was also a nexus for cultural meetings and happenings of the local Slovak community.

At the end of Prohibition in 1933, The Partak's Grocer and Butchers turned into the Partak's Tavern. Perhaps accepting its rightful name? The Tavern, like the grocery store, was a great social gathering space for the local Slovaks as well as many other immigrants. My dad recalls, "The Tavern stayed open on Christmas because," as Grandma had put it, "everyone deserves to have a place to go at Christmas even if they don't have family here."

At the Tavern, sausage was eaten, drinks were drunk, fights were fought, and friendships were forged. In 1946, Ján passed away. Mária kept the Tavern going for years until her son (my grandfather Andrew) took over the operations with his wife Sophie (aka Stas) in 1955. Here, Andrew and Sophie raised

their three children, including my father. Mária remained at the house and tavern, until she passed away in 1966.

My father and aunts had the joy of spending much quality time with their Slovak grandmother. She would excite them with many legends and folktales from the "old country." There was the story of the boy with cat eyes who emerged from the forest or her fearful stories of vampires that justified a crucifix in every room. Mária and her generation also gave my father a healthy dose of Slovak words. My new favorite story is that of my father giggling at funerals hearing *Zbohom.* in Slovak ("Go with God.") and thinking they were saying, "Go home."

Father's mom Sophie, my grandma, is the only grandparent on this side of the family I had ever gotten to know in person. I have amazing memories of time spent cooking with Gramma and her asking me if I want more to eat. She and my father have been the link to my Slovak roots.

The first Sztas in America

My great-grandmother, Kristína, brings an air of mystery to our Slovak legacy. Father used to tell me that his grandmother was a healer who went blind. What does that truly mean? Perhaps her ability to heal others is connected to the pagan times that preceded the arrival of Christianity. Could it be that the old days and their ways were just as important to my family as the Catholic traditions?

Kristína, her husband Ján, and their two children left their home in Chlebnice, Slovakia, and arrived in America in 1910. Upon their arrival, Sztas was Americanized to Stas, and the first names also adjusted to the new country. No one really spoke of why they left. However, the few stories that were shared had a hint of desperation in them. It was said that Kristína's brother stowed away on a ship headed to New York. The story goes that he was discovered and jumped off the ship for fear of being forced to return to Austria-Hungary. Whether it is true or not, my family really wanted to leave Austria-Hungary behind.

They also moved to E. Garnsey Avenue, and Kristína bore four more children. While the Partaks and Stas were becoming strong Slovak Americans on Garnsey Ave., the Obšitníks were just four blocks away on the corner of Henderson and Cleveland Ave. doing the same thing in their own unique way.

The first Obšitníks in America

Juraj and Anna Obšitník are believed to have left the Košice area and arrived in America in 1892. They ended up having ten children, all born in Illinois. Juraj opened a saloon that turned into a grocery store during Prohibition and then to a tavern again at the end of it. Both Slovak and American values were strong in the Obšitník house. Their daughter, my great-grandmother Anna (Nana) was their first daughter born on American soil.

Anna Sr. never learned English well, and her father was firm in the belief that Nana must marry a local Slovak man of his choosing. Nana, on the other hand, was very much a social butterfly and fashionista. She was a modern woman who took full advantage of her American-born status. She loved everything new and was not interested in settling down, let alone to an old hunky she didn't love. Not only did Nana refuse to marry who her father had chosen, but she brought shame to the family by remaining an 'old maid' until the ripe age of 25. When she had finally found a man worthy of marriage, it was not a fellow Slovak, but an Irish Man!

Nana's desire to be happy and live as a Slovak American did not line up with her father's view of what being a Slovak in America meant. After her wedding, Juraj did not want Nana to be a part of his life. She was disowned. Nana was frequently heard saying, "I married an Irish man, so I am Irish now." Perhaps it was a phrase picked up from Juraj. However, she never disowned her Slovak identity, but instead integrated it with her American and Irish ways. Nana remained part of the overall Slovak community and part of her siblings' families. Her daughter, my grandmother, still went to mass and sang Christmas carols in the neighborhood with her cousins. But when the caroling had ended at Juraj and Anna senior's home, she and her siblings were the only grandchildren not allowed to come in and share in the traditional Slovak pastries.

Nana sent her children to St. Cyril's school, but eventually the same old-world versus new-world conflict occurred. Nana dressed her daughters in modern clothes and directed them to speak English. However, the school wanted them to speak at least some Slovak. The girls were made fun of for their non-traditional manners. Eventually, when their modern ways caught too much attention from the Slovak nuns, Nana placed her children in a public school.

Anna Sr. never gave up on Nana. They still met up throughout the years, communicating in their native tongue and keeping the cultural connection alive. If it was not for Nana, my mother would not have known it was really *Ježiško* for whom she was being good for on Christmas. We also have both Anna's to thank for the *oblátky* at the Christmas table and the egg cheese hanging from my mother's cabinets at Easter. If it wasn't for their willingness to allow multiple cultures to co-exist, so much of who we are could have been lost.

Juraj passed away in 1941. I like to think that Juraj was able to forgive Nana. I like to think that he saw his own determined spirit in her. The same strength that allowed him to embrace the journey to America was that which allowed Nana to find love and embrace America without losing her full identity.

The Slovak Americans

The three different families ended up living within walking-distance from each other in a new world after traveling thousands of miles from their homeland. This is just a small part of the migration story of my three families that gives meaning to me. Many Slovak families who left in the first migration wave and even later have shared stories we can all relate to: St Cyril, *halušky*, the mines and factory work, the port of Bremen, midnight mass, and more.

These might be small details, but it is in these details that we find the true Slovak way: support, community, meaning, and connection. It is because of these shared experiences that we are all able to have our own unique journey and to bring our Slovak heritage forward for generations to come. It is the smell of sour cabbage or potato sausage in my parent's kitchen, the pictures of my dad's mushroom haul, or the quiet comfort in seeing that the Christmas ornament from the "old country" hanging on the tree every year. There are so many of these stories, and they all bring us back to the bigger shared Slovak story. This is just mine. So, there you have it! That is how I know I am Slovak.

Ďakujem, Anna, Juraj, Ján, Kristína, Ján, and Mária for bringing your legacy to the new world.

Deah Partak *is a third-generation Slovak American originally from Illinois. She currently lives in Portland, Oregon with her wonderfully supportive husband. Aside from sharing and connecting with her Slovak culture, Deah can be found helping others at her private psychotherapy practice, relaxing with her spinning wheel and knitting needles, or caring for the many trees, plants, and vines in her yard.*

Potato Sausage

(6½ to 7 lbs. of finished product)

This is a modernized version of a traditional Slovak recipe. It's rather involved, so set aside 4-5 hours for its preparation (a double recipe takes 10 hours to complete, start to finish; a one-third recipe takes 2½ hours). Baking it in the oven avoids a kitchen full of greasy steam produced by the hour-long boiling called for in the original recipe. Using beef casing and red potatoes is essential for the success of the recipe. Also, follow the grind size given for the meats and potatoes.

- 3 lbs. thick-sliced bacon, trimmed and finely ground
- 1 lb. pork loin
- 1½ cups canola oil
- 10 lbs. red potatoes, peeled
- 2 TSP salt
- 2 TSP pepper
- 1 TSP ground marjoram
- ½-1 cup hot water
- 15-foot length beef casing (hog casing can be used, but it will change the flavor)
- 1 large onion
- 4-6 cloves garlic

1. Pre-heat a large skillet with a lid, or a cast-iron Dutch oven, over medium heat. Slowly fry the bacon with the lid on, as this prevents spattering and helps to fry the bacon.
2. Leave in all the bacon grease, to deep-fry the bacon, which should be very crisp and somewhat dry once cooled.
3. Freeze the bacon overnight. Smash it into bacon bits in a zip-lock bag.
4. Trim and finely grind the pork.
5. Heat the oil in a large skillet. Sauté chopped onion and minced garlic. Add the bacon and the pork, working the meat mixture with a spatula to break up clumps of meat. The mixture should have the texture of very-small-curd cottage cheese.
6. Coarsely grate the potatoes and thoroughly rinse them in cold water 3-5 times (until there's no more foam), to remove the surface starch. (When rinsing the ground potatoes, do not pour the rinse water down the kitchen sink drain—it will clog it up. Rinse them into a large bowl, pour the water into a bucket, and pour into the toilet, or even better, into the garden.)
7. Add the salt, pepper, ground marjoram, hot water, and the undrained meat mixture to the ground potatoes, and mix thoroughly.
8. Preheat the oven to 375 °F (190 °C).
9. Rinse and prepare the beef casing.

10. Stuff the casing loosely and tie it with string into 3-link lengths of sausage, with each link approximately 8" long. Do a double tie about an inch apart after every three links to allow cutting into 3 link sections.

11. Do not allow the uncooked sausage to come into contact with aluminum foil or an aluminum pan—it will cause the potatoes to turn black.

12. Place 1 layer of sausage in a 9" x 13" glass baking dish, adding ½" of water.

13. Use a needle to pierce the links 3 or 4 times, to prevent them from bursting.

14. Cover the dish with aluminum foil that's tented, so as not to touch the sausage.
15. Bake for 1 hour or until the casing is light brown.
16. Cool the sausage, place it in plastic bags, and refrigerate or freeze.
17. To serve, thaw the sausage and brown it in a frying pan, or heat it in the oven at 350 °F (180 °C) until browned (approximately 20-30 minutes).

THE BLOOD OF VALENTÍN

by Paul Kostyak

> "I found an abundance of historical events that clearly helped to define my family's history and the tenacious character of the Slovaks."

I was not fortunate enough to know my grandfather, John Kostyak, who died in 1944, 12 years before I was born. It took much luck, determination, and the aid of top-notch Slovak genealogists to uncover what happened to him and my family in Lendak at the base of the Tatra mountains.

When I began to explore my family history, all I knew was that my ancestors were humble farmers from Slovakia. It seemed a familiar story. On the surface, the destiny of my predecessors was similar to most other Slovak families. They suffered from hunger, disease, and death. They reacted to the difficulties of life with Slovak values—tradition, hard work, determination, perseverance, family, and faith. But as I delved deeper into my bloodline, a pattern seemed to emerge. My ancestors were not only reactive but proactive. Throughout the generations, they appeared to be imbued with just an extra touch of boldness. They didn't just adapt to the latest problem; they tried to anticipate and get ahead of life's problems. This is the bloodline we share—what I call "the blood of Valentine."

My genealogical journey began as I uncovered the story of Valentín Kostyak, my great-great-grandfather who was born in 1808. Marriage, baptism and death records from both local and national sources, including the local parish and 1869 national census carried out in the Kingdom of Hungary and other civic records, revealed a very sad tale. The whole process required proper detective work as some of the records were difficult to read; most were in Latin, and some even in Hungarian in addition to Slovak.

As I mentioned above, my family's history was typical of other Slovak families and villages. However, while many families might only rely on the stories passed onto them—their oral history—I have the luxury of knowing the details of what actually unfolded back in the old country—the written history. I found an abundance of historical events that clearly helped to define my family's history and the tenacious character of the Slovaks.

An event that captured my attention while researching my family roots speaks of a tragedy that took place in my grandmother's ancestral village. It happened after the Ottomans beat the Kingdom of Hungary in the 16th century and occupied much of its land for over a century and a half. The kingdom was in disarray, and Slovakia—a tiny sliver of unoccupied territory—functioned as a buffer zone between the two spheres of influence.

Conflicts and skirmishes unfolded especially along its southern border. Competing factions fought for power, and the little Slovak copper mining town of Štilbach paid dearly for it. It was ransacked by the Ottomans, and its inhabitants were massacred. Those who survived fled into the woods and never returned. Horrors like this were nothing unusual in the Middle Ages. Your and my Slovak ancestors are the descendants of these survivors. It is no wonder Slovaks are so resilient. They went through hell all too often.

My great-great-grandfather Valentín never fought the Ottomans, but he experienced hell nonetheless. His family nest was in the village of Lendak, in the mountainous Slovak north. Life there was far from a stroll in the park. Everybody was poor, and people often went to bed hungry, scared and numbed by the perils of life during this treacherous time in history.

A story runs in the family that the poverty was so dire that when a mother died, the family put the baby on her corpse. They hoped the baby could get some milk from the breast of the dead woman, since there was so little food to go around. Another tale says the situation was so grave, the family split a single strawberry among four members. It was all they had for dinner.

Despite these dire conditions, Valentine had foresight. According to the 1715 Lendak tax records, there were no Kostyak landowners. Somehow along the way, Valentín (or his father, Ján, or grandfather, Jakub) obtained property (prime real estate!) across from the church and built a house that would be used by five generations. Don't get me wrong, Valentín's family home was modest. It had a sleeping room, a small vestibule and a pantry. Outside was a shed, a barn and two stalls. The family owned ten sheep, a pig, a cow, and two oxen for plowing the fields nearby. These animals made them wealthier among the small farmers, but their existence was still humble and life was tough. If I may add a little family lore, it was clear that Valentine was concerned with the community—he was a respected man with vision and faith. And boldness. The "blood of Valentín."

Valentín married Anna Lizáková in 1838 and the couple had five children. In 1851 Anna died, leaving five-year-old Michal and two-year-old Gašpar motherless. Valentín muddled along as a single father for ten years before marrying his second wife, Helena Gallíková. He was 53 and she was 23. Valentín and Helena were blessed with five additional children, but only one—Vincent—made it to adulthood. (Vincent was five years old when my grandfather was born, so he certainly helped raise my grandfather early in his life at the family homestead). Nevertheless, this surviving prodigy, Vincent, was enough to plant the seed from which many hundreds of descendants would sprout in the years and decades to come. These are my half-cousins; we all share the same blood—"the blood of Valentín."

In 1869, Michal (the oldest of all of Valentine's children) married and moved two houses away to the family home of his bride; while Gašpar lived with his father, Valentín, in the old family home.

Life went on as you might expect in the rural countryside until cholera hit Lendak in 1873. Dying from cholera was horrendous. Uncontrollable diarrhea tortured people for days. Imagine facing this nightmare in the heat of summer with no running water or electricity. Helena contracted the disease in October of that fateful year. One day later, Valentín got sick, too. The next day, Helena died, and Valentín followed to his heavenly reward the following day. On that chilly Sunday, Gašpar, now 24, was left alone with four much younger half-siblings all under the age of 12.

After burying his father and stepmother in the cholera cemetery—a non-descript acre of land—Gašpar must have been beside himself trying desperately to keep his sanity and not crumble under the heavy weight of responsibility that now rested on his young shoulders. The animals still needed care. The fields still needed tending. The young children needed attention and care too. But here is where we see the boldness of Valentín shine through. It would have been acceptable for Gašpar to farm his four half-siblings out to other family or friends following the deaths of both parents. But Gašpar stayed. I believe this was not just obligation and religious values but Gašpar's vision for his family and community. It was a bold step for a very young man, reflecting the "blood of Valentín."

But the household needed a mother badly and so, not even a month after the family tragedy, Gašpar took Alžbeta Kostyaková Kostyaková (both maiden and married name) as his wife. Her family lived eight doors away. It was a joyful event when their first son was born, finally, after the merciless string of deaths. But shock would follow soon. Alžbeta, the fresh mother and young wife, died of a lung infection.

Again, the family was left without a woman and so again, Gašpar married quickly. The choice fell on Alžbeta's younger sister, Julianna (my great-grandmother). Another disaster struck when Gašpar's baby son died. But life had to go on and another baby was soon born. A year and a half later, the family was expecting the arrival of yet another baby, who would be my grandfather, John. But before he saw the light of the world, his brother died of smallpox. Such was life in the 19th century. Death was never too far way. In fact, by the time John was born, all but three of Valentine's 10 children had perished.

Because my great-grandparents, Gašpar and Juliána, now only had one mouth to feed—my grandfather, Ján—they could devote their lives, money, energy and love only to him. So Ján did not suffer the fate of so many other family members. He did not die young. He made it.

Ján learned the trade of a tailor, and perfected his craft as an apprentice to a German tailor nearby. This was yet another example of family proactivity and boldness. Gašpar helped his son obtain a lifelong art, something that would be in demand in many places and situations. Likewise, Ján, "The Tailor from Landok", abandoned his ready-made life in Lendak and, instead, made three trips to the United States in 1900,

1902, and 1908. Ján stood to inherit the family property but boldly chose to leave for the unknown—probably safe in the knowledge he had a profession to market but also a boldness, the "blood of Valentín." In 1908, I envision Gašpar and Juliána walking with Ján to the shrine at the end of the village to say their final goodbyes. I can only imagine the overwhelming sadness my great-grandparents must have felt as they saw Ján off for the last time. But the grief was accompanied with joy and hope of Ján making a new life for himself and his new bride-to-be: fellow Slovak Mária Miskovičová, in Pittsburgh, Pennsylvania.

In the old records, the Kostyak name was spelled 16 different ways, so identifying John's genealogy had to be done through the vital records. When Ján and Mária were married in 1909 in the Strip District of Pittsburgh at St. Elizabeth's—the Slovak mother church—the pastor sent a notice of the marriage to the local priest back in Lendak, who added a note in Ján's birth record (30 years after his birth!) of his spouse's name, alongside the date and place of the marriage.

Uncovering the history of my family's marriage and census records allowed me to peek into the lives of my ancestors. Back then, it was common to choose a spouse from among the neighbors who lived nearest. And these records now prove it! They really did not move far at all to marry, baptize, and bury one another.

In the past, I used to wonder whether Ján and Mária married because they knew each other from the old country. But after conducting the genealogical research, I now strongly suspect that even though their villages were only 30 miles apart, they were brought together for the first time in Pittsburgh, on the other side of the planet, by cousins in the U.S. (though there is now evidence that Mária actually had some roots in Lendak).

Ján's new bride, Mária, was less than five feet tall, beautiful and fertile. There were shadows in her past too. The records show that Mária's mother drowned in the creek in her village. The story was told that she was taking food to the workers in the fields. Maybe she slipped and hit her head or perhaps she had a stroke or a heart attack. We will never know, but I walked barefoot through that creek. It is ten feet across, with quick moving water, and a mossy, slippery bottom.

Ján and Mária, who became known as John and Mary in their new country, married in 1909, and the babies started coming along. Petite Mary bore seven children. John worked as a tailor at several places in downtown Pittsburgh, while Mary raised the children. Their last two children, born in 1923 in a difficult childbirth, were twins: my father, Frank, whose broken leg left him in a body cast for months, and Charles, who died six months later.

John and Mary lost two of their seven children—a painful reminder of the fragility of life that is not unique to Slovakia. Records state that the cause of death of one of the babies, John Jr., was malnutrition at age six months. He simply could not take nourishment. It must have been horrendous for John to watch his namesake die and not be able to change his fate.

Frugal Mary was allotted $8.00 per week for the family grocery budget. She made everything by hand. Even in later years, with children grown, she spent hours in the kitchen. I can still see the back of her standing at the kitchen sink, turning only occasionally to smile at me! My grandmother never learned to speak English—no one is sure why—but it meant that I could never have a real conversation with her. Sadly, my father couldn't either, each speaking a different language.

But Mary's hard work and John's good sense allowed John to save enough to buy a house in the Mount Washington neighborhood of Pittsburgh. He also bought the house next door to

rent to further support his family. John continued to make good business decisions. He became a member of the fraternal organization of the National Slovak Society—not just to get insured, but to nurture his Slovak essence and ease his homesickness. When the organization almost went bankrupt during the Great Depression—thanks in part to ill-advised management—many members quit. But not John.

While in the U.S., John became a part-owner of the family homestead in Lendak and soon sold it with furniture and equipment to his brother, Vincent, via a Power of Attorney for 30,000 koruna. Vincent raised his family there until the house burned down in 1946, along with 70% of the other homes in Lendak. They were wooden, and once a spark was lit, the fire spread quickly. My family agreed to give this family parcel to the church, and the church, in exchange, relocated my family to another home in Lendak.

The Great Depression, beginning in 1929, strained everyone including John and family. The pain was compounded in 1931 when he learned that his mother, Julianna, had died from

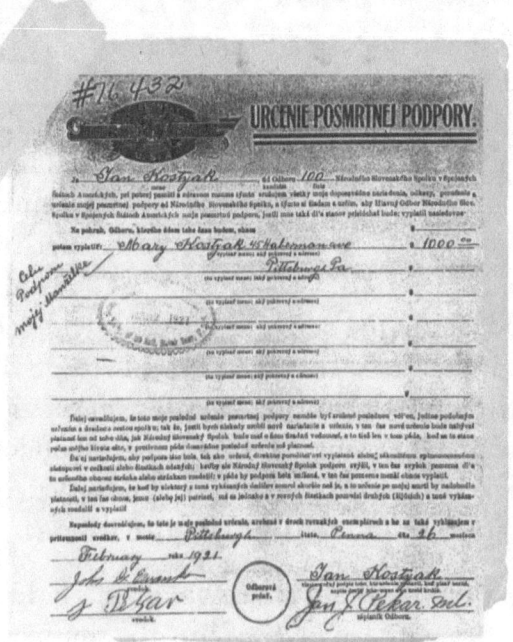

"dropsy" (excess water swelling) in Lendak. Unable to attend her funeral, John was forced to mourn her from afar. Somehow, John was able to hold the family and property together until his death from kidney failure in 1944 at the age of 66. Mary received a $1,000 death benefit from the life insurance company. He was buried at the Slovak St. Michael's cemetery. A glance at the sign-in book from the funeral shows that he was loved by his Slovak family and friends.

Despite losing her husband, my grandmother would go on to live nearly another three decades. She struggled at the end of her life with dementia. She occasionally wandered away from home and had to eventually be placed in Mayview, a mental hospital in Pittsburgh. This was apparently a very tough decision for my family, as Mary could only speak Slovak and was very frightened in the unfamiliar surroundings. My father was the only driver in the family so she had few visitors. When Mary passed away in 1971, I was honored to be a pall bearer at her funeral along with her other five grandsons.

John was a Slovak and never abandoned his roots. But he wanted his children to thrive in America, so he insisted that they learn to read and write only in English and limited the family traditions to foods and holiday celebrations. My father, Frank, followed the path of the typical American working-class kid. He attended Catholic school, played pick-up games, did odd jobs in the neighborhood, and hung out with friends. But the boldness was there. He enlisted in the Army and again in the Air Force during WW II, worked at jobs that were sometimes dangerous, and married a Londoner, my mother, Patricia. I am pretty sure the "blood of Valentín" ran through my father's veins too until he died in 2003.

I would like to believe that I share Valentín's bold spirit as well. I was working by age 10, traveling the southern U.S. in my 20s, and bypassing the usual route for a job by seeking out the CEO of the company I wanted to work for. I now have two children of my own, and I'm hopeful the "blood of Valentine" is alive in them as well.

Three of John's children raised families, and there are dozens of his descendants thriving in the world today because

our ancestors did not give up. They suffered terribly, but kept moving forward. They always chose life no matter what.

I visited Lendak for the first time in 2013. It was magical and miraculous. My family instantly grew so much as I reconnected with scores of my cousins. They were as delighted as I was to restore our family bond. I also had the incredible fortune to meet my half-cousins who lived in the old family home, making my great-great-grandparents' and great-grandparents' history a little more tangible. Thank you, Valentine, Casper, John and Frank for your Slovak perseverance. I am proud to be a descendant of such a bold bloodline.

. . .

Paul Kostyak *is a native of Pittsburgh, Pennsylvania, USA, where he resides with his wife and two children. He is a retired financial planner, avid guitarist, amateur cook, and numismatist. But his real passion is exploring his Slovak heritage, a task he has pursued over the past 30 years.*

AN ADVENTUROUS MATRIARCH

by Audrey Stucko

> Being an independent and spirited young woman, Eva preferred to choose her own husband. This could be much easier done in the New World, where women experienced a great deal more freedom.

As a young girl, I was told that my paternal side of the family was of Ukrainian heritage and that my paternal grandmother, Eva, was born in the Austria-Hungary Empire. In later years, through my own interest in genealogy, I learned that my Nana was more than just a Ukrainian, she was a Carpatho-Rusyn born in the village of Mokre in Austria-Hungary, today located in southeastern Poland. Thanks to DNA testing, I also learned that my grandmother's maternal ancestors came from eastern Slovakia. This is a story in honor of her, my Nana, based on my research, DNA tests, family annecdotes, and my very own childhood memories.

Eva Szamra grew up on a farm in Mokre where she was born in 1893. She was an adventurous and independent young girl. Moreover, living on a farm came with many responsibilities that proved useful in the development of Eva's inner strength and resilience.

At a very young age, she was tasked with tending to the family's cows. She often took them out to graze in a grassy pasture across a small nearby river. But one day, while the cows were grazing, the skies opened up and released a great deal of rain.

There was so much water that the banks of the river overflowed and made it impossible for Eva and the cows to return home that day. Eva spent the evening in the pasture all alone with the cows gazing up at the stars above.

While today's United States Bill of Rights prevents the quartering of soldiers in private homes, no such restriction existed in Austria-Hungary in the early 1900s. Occasionally, when military officers traveled through Mokre, they used Eva's home for temporary lodging, and Eva and her family had to move into the barn. On one such occasion, two soldiers arrived late in the day and requested that Eva tend to their horses. These two magnificent stallions were nothing like the family's old farm horse. Eva's adventurous spirit got the best of her and once the soldiers were out of sight, she mounted the strongest of the equines and galloped across the fields. The thrill and excitement of this experience was something she would never forget.

The village of Mokre is conveniently located along the river San. As travel along the river increased in the 1800s, so did the development of a railroad system. Mokre was fortunate as it gained its very own train station.

One of Eva's uncles was employed by the railroad company, and he often traveled to glorious places, such as Vienna, Austria. Each time one of his nieces or nephews came of age, usually around 12 or 13, he would take them on a train trip to Vienna for their birthday. Eva was enthralled with her celebratory trip to the imperial city. The grand buildings and cafés were nothing like the small farm structures back in Mokre.

On another occasion, Eva traveled with her neighbors by train, to Hungary. She was mesmerized by the vast acres of beautiful green vegetables and the rich black soil that she saw as she stared out her train window. She longed to live in a place where green vegetables were abundant, and the soil was rich—there was a lack of both in Mokre. Both train adventures opened Eva's eyes to a whole new world and perhaps inspired her to emigrate to the United States at a very early age. Most of the people she knew never travelled further than to the next village to attend church. But unlike them, Eva already had a good idea of just how big and wide the world beyond her home was.

By 1909, Eva's parents, Andre and Xenia Wadja, made the decision to pay for Eva to emigrate to the United States in the hope of finding a better life. There were probably many reasons for this decision. After all, they had only one farm and many children. That meant that only one of them could inherit the farm and that would not be Eva. There were not many opportunities for young women in Mokre, and Eva was reaching the age where the local matchmaker would soon start the process of finding her a suitable husband.

Being an independent and spirited young woman, Eva preferred to choose her own husband. This could be much easier done in the New World, where women experienced a great deal more freedom. And so, arrangements were made, and my Nana who was in her mid-teens at the time, was sent to travel by railroad to Hamburg, Germany. There she boarded a steamship and traveled alone across the Atlantic Ocean to New York. From there Eva continued to Pittsburgh, Pennsylvania, where she would live with her older sister Mary for a while; the two sister were always close, and their special bond would last a lifetime.

The Pittsburgh community where Eva lived was populated with many Ukrainians, as well as other Rusyns. There was no need for her to learn English, so she routinely spoke in her native tongue. Even the local Greek Catholic churches communed in Rusyn. By 1913, Eva married Elias Hriszko (also known as Alexander Reiscow) in a church wedding in

New Britain, Connecticut, another strong community populated with Ukrainians and Rusyns.

Why they relocated to Connecticut is unknown. Most likely it was the opportunity for employment. There were many factories hiring at the time. It was not too long before Eva and Elias would temporarily return to Pennsylvania to have their first child, a baby girl. More than likely, this was to allow family members to assist the new mother and her baby. Soon after returning to New Britain, the family bliss was interrupted by the breakout of WW I. Elias, then known as Alexander, enlisted in the United States Army as a wagoner and traveled to Germany to fight on the ground, face-to-face.

Days and months passed, but Elias was still not returning home. Eva assumed he died at war, like countless other fathers, brothers, and husbands. She was now living in a boarding house with her daughter Mary.

Eva worked several different jobs while in New Britain. At one point she was employed by a silverware manufacturing factory. When it came time to leave the company, she was presented with a full place setting of silverware that she cherished for many years. It became a family heirloom that was eventually passed onto the offspring.

Eva also worked in an ammunitions factory where she produced bullets used by the United States military during WW I. When Eva became aware that she was making less money than men who were performing the same job, she was not happy. Eva, apparently a woman ahead of her time, marched into her foreman's office and demanded equal pay. After much discussion, the foreman increased her salary to a sum equivalent to that of her colleagues, under one condition—she could not tell anyone. Eva agreed.

At the boarding house that became Eva's home for longer than she had anticipated, a fellow boarder befriended her.

His name was Dmytro Sztuka. He would eventually become my grandfather. While Dmytro, later known as Metro, was several years older than Eva, they still had much in common. Both were of Rusyn ancestry, spoke the same language, shared a common religion, and came from neighboring villages back in the old continent. By 1921, Eva and Metro were a family, welcoming their first child—a daughter named Catherine. The family relocated to the Minersville, Pennsylvania area where Metro pursued employment as a coal miner.

In the early- to mid-1920s, the Sztuka family lived in a home owned by the local mining company. The whole time, Eva was uncomfortable living in that particular house and greatly feared for the safety of her children. She could hear the miners in the tunnels below and had a premonition that the house would one day sink into the ground. It was then and there that Eva gathered up her children and marched into the office of the mine manager, demanding that he find them a safer home. He did, albeit reluctantly, relocate them to another house. Soon after, a portion of the mine collapsed, and their previous house was destroyed. A credit to Eva's intuition and no doubt the many life lessons she had endured and surpassed since she was born.

Thanks to a stable home and a secure income, the family grew and grew until there were five children, now adding Suzanne, Michael, and George to the family. While Metro worked in the mines, Eva produced moonshine which she sold to the miners on Friday evenings as a means of bringing in a little extra cash for the family. A product of her circumstances, Eva knew how to survive and double a penny.

For example, when she realized that the mining company's store was expensive, she refused to purchase anything there. Instead, she traveled the steep hills, by bus, to shops where the groceries were less costly. On one of her return trips, the bus experienced brake problems. The driver ordered everyone out of the bus fearing it might crash. While the bus was still in motion, Eva threw her groceries out the door of the bus and then she courageously followed. She miraculously survived this ordeal to return home to her family with groceries in hand. It is this kind of resilience that is bred into people from the heart of Europe.

No matter the time of day or year, Eva was always a busy bee. She dutifully cooked her family's favorite Rusyn and Ukrainian meals and shared her pysanky egg decorating skills with friends and loved ones at Eastertime. Eva was very resourceful too, as evidenced when she was unable to find a pysanky stylus—a tool used to apply the wax to the egg—she fashioned her own out of wood and some metal wire. Eva also continued to attend religious services and baptized/confirmed all her children in the local Greek Catholic Church.

A short time after my father George was born in December 1926, the family relocated to Brooklyn, New York. Their home in Pennsylvania was condemned due to more tunnel problems in the mine below, so Metro reached out to a friend in New York City who shared his love for wood working. The two of them planned on starting a handmade-furniture business. Unfortunately, the closeness in time to the Great Depression shattered this dream. By now, the family expanded by four more children, to include John, Josephine, Metro, and Irene.

Metro continued to work hard and found employment in a variety of jobs. However, he was not satisfied with his earnings and made the decision to return to the old country, to his farm in Morochow—very close to Eva's home village. Strong-spirited Eva did not want to go back to Europe and made this quite clear to Metro. She was committed to living out the rest of her life in America. Metro tried to persuade at least two of their children to accompany him on his return home, but Eva convinced them to stay.

Metro departed back home alone in 1934, with his son George's birth cowl, a piece of membrane that can cover a newborn's head and face. Back then, superstitious people believed that birth cowls brought luck to those who possessed them. At the time of his departure, Eva was pregnant with her ninth child. Sadly, she would never meet her father. Church records in the old country reveal that Metro died in 1942, but we do not know why. Perhaps he was another casualty of war—this time WW II.

Life for Eva and her nine children continued without Metro. It was not easy; the kids missed their father, and Eva no doubt missed the support of a man. The children who were old enough had to chip in and take on jobs to support the family. While Eva sewed from home to add to their limited income, her eyes began to tire. She was not yet aware of the glaucoma that would eventually claim her sight in the end.

Despite the challenges of raising nine children as a single parent, Eva never lost her sense of humor nor her adventurous spirit. She woke every morning before dawn and baked fresh bread for the children before sending them off to school. On Sundays, Eva and her offspring would dress in their finest outfits and stroll through Winthrop Park, occasionally stopping to pose for a family photo. Whenever her sister Mary visited, Eva would insist they go to the park where they could walk and reminisce about their youth. These strolls would become a family tradition throughout their lives.

When finances allowed, usually during the holiday season, Eva made her traditional family recipes. She taught her children how to prepare her family version of *pirohy*, a wonderful dumpling filled with mashed potatoes and sauerkraut. During Thanksgiving, the family enjoyed Eva's stuffing made from kaiser rolls, eggs, onions, and seasoning. These same dishes are still made by Eva's grandchildren today. Family recipes were not the only traditions that Eva continued and

shared with her children. At Easter, she decorated eggs using the pysanky process of applying wax followed by the application of color. Her children and grandchildren continued these tradition decades later.

In addition to passing on her native culture, Eva instilled in each of her children a strong work ethic, combined with honesty, bravery, and a thirst for adventure. But above all, Eva taught her children a sense of humor. Her parenting formula proved quite successful. As adults, Eva's offspring rose to successful careers, which included a pharmaceutical employee, a draftsman, a manufacturing director, a police officer, a telephone company manager, a dry cleaning business owner, a firefighter, and a teacher.

Eva's daughter Mary from her first marriage, remained curious about her father who never returned home from WW I. She hired a private investigator who, much to everyone's' surprise, found Alexander incapacitated in a United States military hospital. Unbeknownst to Eva and Mary, Alexander became a casualty of war when he was mustard-gassed by

the Germans during WW I. Military records revealed that he lived his life in various military hospitals from Philadelphia, Pennsylvania, to Perry Point, Maryland. Eva, Mary, and a few other family members took a long ride and visited Alexander in the hospital. Shortly thereafter, in 1954, Alexander passed. It appeared that he did not want to leave this world without seeing his wife and daughter again. He was buried at Long Island National Cemetery in Farmingdale, New York.

During the 1960s, most of Eva's children were married with children of their own. By this time, Eva had lost her eyesight due to glaucoma. She adjusted to the situation as best she could with the help of her family and her daughter Josie, who lived with Eva until she passed. Rather than turning bitter, Eva faced the challenge in her very own way. When her younger grandchildren visited, she asked them to be silent. She then placed her hands on their faces and guessed their identities. Intuitively, Eva never failed to correctly identify her grandchildren in this manner.

Unfortunatley over time, Eva lost contact with her sister Mary. During the 1960s, she expressed an interest in reuniting with

her sister and asked her son Metro to drive her to Pittsburgh. He agreed and the two of them set out to find Mary at her last known address. Unfortunately, Mary was no longer living there, and the internet was not yet invented to help them locate a new address. Eva never saw Mary again...

Despite the size of Eva's family (nine children and twenty grandchildren), she always insisted that the family celebrate Christmas Eve together. On this evening, her home was filled with food, drink, family traditions, laughter, and most importantly—love. There was no excuse not to partake in this annual event—no matter how far you lived or how bad the weather. I remember my family walking in our boots through deep snow one year when my father was unable to dig out our car after a huge snowstorm. While most of Eva's children lived in the neighborhood, one or two lived with their families further out on Long Island. But this never stopped anyone from attending the Christmas Eve celebration. It wasn't unusual to see some grandchildren changed into their pajamas before getting into their cars for the long ride home. Whatever the circumstance, the food was always plentiful and eaten by candlelight. Borscht, bread rubbed with garlic, pedeheh, mushrooms, sauerkraut, barley, and beets were just a few of the items on the menu.

In February 1974, Eva left behind a loving family and an amazing life story. She was truly a remarkable women who lived life on her own terms. She was a hard worker and a woman that did not hesitate to challenge anyone who did not treat her or her family in a fair manor. She followed her dreams and never failed to inspire those around her.

Eva's offspring, her many grandchildren and great-grandchildren continue to honor her by practicing and sharing her native and family traditions. In the summer of 2008, the Stucko (somewhere along the way the spelling of the family name changed) family gathered for a reunion at the Ukrainian Lower Eastside Restaurant in New York City. Photos and stories of the family matriarch were shared by all, as were bountiful servings of Eva's favorites foods. It was an event that would have made Eva proud.

...

Audrey *was born and raised in the Greenpoint neighborhood of Brooklyn New York, amongst Irish, Italian, Puerto Rican and Eastern European immigrants and their descendants. After graduating from New York University, where she studied business administration, Audrey worked as an executive in the Federal Government and later managed her own consulting business. Audrey now spends her time researching her family history and living an active life with her husband and son in coastal North Carolina. A nearby Eastern European delicatessen allows her to continue to experience the foods of her youth.*

Eva's Holiday Stuffing

- 16 kaiser rolls with poppy seeds
- Salt
- 2 onions, finely grated
- Eggs
- Chicken broth

1. Preheat the oven to 350 °F (180 °C).
2. Tear the Kaiser rolls (absolutely must have poppy seeds for flavor) into small pieces (1"x 1").
3. Add the salt, onions, and as many eggs as it takes to make it moist.
4. Add chicken broth according to personal taste—too little is better than too much.
5. Put into a baking dish and bake until a crust forms on top.
6. The stuffing is done when a knife inserted into the center comes out clean.
7. Slice, and serve with chicken gravy.

LEAVING HOME, FINDING HOME

by Jeanne M. Zulick

Previously settled residents made it clear that they did not like these "different" people with their "different" religion. Wooden crosses were set ablaze on the hill of the cemetery near Irene and Andrew's farm. Their message was clear: You 'foreigners' are not welcome."

My grandfather Andrej Zozulič was born in 1893 in Parihuzovce, Austria-Hungary. His family was religious, celebrating as Slovak Greek (Byzantium) Catholics. The ship's manifest identifies him as Ruthenian. Life in eastern Slovakia, which belonged to the Austria-Hungary Empire, was hard. People drew life from the earth. Labor was done manually. Hay was cut by hand; fields were plowed with oxen.

Healthcare was non-existent; there were no doctors or medicine. Out of the eleven children in Andrej's family, six perished from pneumonia and other illnesses.

Andrej never had an opportunity for education. Neither he nor his ten brothers and sisters had access to schools or teachers. Andrej's mother could not read or count money. Likewise, his father, Michal Zozulič, was illiterate, but he proudly served as the popular and well-liked mayor of Parihuzovce.

Even as a young child Andrej worked on the family farm—tending to sheep, oxen, and horses. His long day would be divided into working the horses and oxen during the day, and then feeding and pasturing the animals by evening. It was a lot of work for a ten-year-old child.

In the winter, the family would make shingles and sell them to earn money for fuel. One time Andrej secretly took a few of the shingles his father had made and brought them to the market where he sold them for ten cents each. He ultimately confessed that he wanted to buy a prayer book. His father scolded him, but bought him the prayer book, telling him not to do it again. He would find the money for what was needed.

Christmas was a time of celebration. The festivities and prayer continued for three days. The family would go to the brook, chop the ice, and wash their faces as was the custom in the Byzantium Catholic culture. Then they would take a lit candle and some bread to feed the cattle in the barn before eating themselves. It wasn't just a ritual or a tradition, it was a mark of respect to the animals who were a part of the family.

The community that Andrej belonged to fended off hardships and poverty with togetherness. If a building needed to be constructed, Andrej would head into the woods with the oxen, and men would help stack wood, bringing timbers to build simple homes with straw roofs. When grain was brought in, the neighbors helped each other process and divide the produce.

When Andrej turned eighteen years old, he faced conscription into the Austro-Hungarian army and, like many others, chose to flee his homeland. Although it was illegal to leave the Empire without having completed the mandatory military service, many Slovaks felt no debt to the oppressive Magyar government who aimed to erase their culture and language.

Of course, leaving was not without its dangers. If Andrej was caught by the Hungarian guards who patrolled the country border, he would be jailed.

Andrej's older brother Ján had left for America two years earlier, having used the services of a people smuggler. Likewise, Andrej paid a man who knew where the guards were located and how to avoid them. For two days, this man led Andrej and others through the woods into Russia which then stretched all the way to the borders of Austria-Hungary.

The final European destination before setting sail to the "new world" was the port city of Trieste. It was an arduous journey from Parihuzovce, Slovakia, to Trieste, Austria, via the detour of Russia, but on December 23, 1911, Andrej arrived to board the SS Argentina. But the ship did not leave as scheduled. Apparently, the captain held its passengers hostage, requiring more money before he set off across the Atlantic. Andrej reported that the steerage was so cold that he woke to find that his clothes had frozen to his bunk.

Twenty-six days later, Andrej finally disembarked in the Port of New York. During processing, his name was changed as with many other newcomers, and this is how Andrej Zozulič became Andrew Zulick in America.

From New York, Andrew travelled to Pennsylvania to join his brother, John, to work in the coal mines. For three years Andrew dug and loaded coal for thirty cents per ton. Each morning he would leave the boarding house where he stayed before the sun was up, and not return home until after dark. He went months without seeing sunlight.

After those years, he left Pennsylvania and the coal mines and moved to Weirton, West Virginia, to live with his sister Mária and her husband. There, he worked in the steel mills for fifteen cents per hour for twelve hours per day. That was a tough job. He stayed for three years before returning to the coal mines. When the miners went on strike, he switched to the West Virginia mill again. In 1914 when the war began, Andrew registered for service in the U.S. Army but was never called.

About the same time, a girl named Irén Filyová lived with her mother, father, and three siblings in Remetské Hámre, Austria-Hungary. They lived in a one-room house with a dirt floor. There was a stove in one corner and a bed in the other. The children slept on benches or on the floor in winter and in the hay field in the summer. The family had their own piece of land where they grew grains, potatoes, and cabbage, but it was a difficult existence.

Poverty pressed the father of the family to look for other ways of earning a livelihood, so he left home, travelling to Pennsylvania to work in the coal mines. He saved all his money, sending it home, so that his family could join him. When they had enough money to secure passage, 12-year-old Irén along with her mother and siblings traveled to the Port of Bremen in Germany, where they boarded the SS Kronprinzessin Cecilie.

The time aboard the ship was difficult. The family was relegated to steerage. Irén's mother became very sick, and Irén was left to care for her baby brother. To get food, she would stand in line with a bucket to receive her family's ration. According to Irén, on the day they were distributing sauerkraut, she took the food downstairs to her family and then went back in line to get more because it was her favorite.

Wealthier families stayed on the upper decks. Wealthy children would throw pennies down to the poor kids to watch them jump to gather up the money. But Irén could not get any of the coins, because she was holding her little brother, Antal. A lady on the higher deck saw her crying. She spoke to Irén in Hungarian; Irén responded, and the woman threw her a bag of fruit. "We didn't know what to make of the banana," Irén once reported. From then on, that same lady watched for Irén and threw her a bag of fruit each day for the remainder of the trip.

After seventeen days at sea, the family arrived in New York in the summer of 1913. During processing at Ellis Island, Irén Filyová became Irene Fello. The family got on a train to Pennsylvania and received a package of food—sardines, bread, and salami that was to last them for their journey. But there was a delay, and they arrived a day late. Her father, unaware of the delay, was nowhere to be found. Not knowing what to do or where to go, all the while not speaking a word of English, the family had no choice but to spend the night in the train station. A woman walked into the station the next morning and Irene's mother tried her luck speaking Hungarian.

The lady understood and directed the family to a nearby boarding house owned by her sister. At long last, they found their father. The family was finally together again. That fall, Irene and her siblings started school. They could not speak any English. The town kids would knock them around and make fun of them calling them "green horns." The next spring, a neighbor told Irene's mother that a woman in another town ran a Hungarian restaurant and needed help. Without having completed even a year of school, Irene's mother wrapped up her daughter's few belongings and sent thirteen-year-old Irene off to work for this stranger.

Irene labored at the restaurant for two years, earning $1.50 per week before moving to Weirton, West Virginia, to work in a can factory for $12 a week. That is where she met Andrew Zulick. Andrew visited Irene's aunt's house to borrow a Sears, Roebuck and Co. catalog to order clothes. He used the opportunity to ask Irene out to the movies. She said she had to ask her aunt. He asked her "how will I know you're going to go?" She replied, "If I'm on the porch dressed up, then you'll know."

The next day Irene was on the porch, but Andrew didn't stop; he continued past the house. Irene didn't know what to do, so she followed him to the theater. After a couple of months of seeing each other like that, Andrew expressed the desire to get married. Irene replied, "Well go ahead, get married." He explained that he wanted to marry her, but Irene was only seventeen. She asked her aunt what to do. She replied, "Close your eyes and marry him." Although Irene's mother disagreed, the letter she wrote telling Irene not to get married arrived too late. Andrew and Irene were already husband and wife.

After the wedding, Andrew and Irene lived with Andrew's sister and her husband. The new family saw no future in the mills or coal mines, so when they discovered a farm for sale in Connecticut, advertised in a Slovak-language newspaper,

the two families moved to Ashford, Connecticut. They began as poultry farmers, selling eggs and baby chicks until they had enough money to buy dairy cows. Then, they sold the milk for five cents per quart.

But it wasn't enough money to support the farm and two families, so Andrew had to take on another job. Each Sunday night, he would walk twelve miles to the neighboring town of Stafford and then take a trolley to Hartford to work in a rubber plant. He always brought his food for the week—bread, eggs, and butter, to save money. On Saturday morning, he would return home to the farm to work. He would start all over again the next evening.

For three years, the two families worked as partners, but the farm could not sustain everyone. Disagreements arose and the partnership broke up in 1922. Andrew and Irene took the risk, paid off the other family, and took on the mortgage. It would take them twenty years to pay it off.

At the time, more and more immigrants were coming to Ashford to buy farms which were selling at low prices.

Some of the older residents did not appreciate this influx of newcomers, but Irene and Andrew persisted. They also made it through the Great Depression that hit in 1929. The couple continued to work their farm and raise three children. The eldest daughter Margaret recalled starting school without understanding English, because only Slovak was spoken at home. This was the norm for most immigrant families.

Citizens in town also made it difficult for newly arrived Slovaks and Hungarians to gain American citizenship. Irene had become a U.S. citizen before meeting Andrew but lost her citizenship by marrying him, because he was not yet a citizen. Eventually, Andrew gained U.S. citizenship in 1929, and Irene regained hers in 1932.

Andrew and Irene were religious. As more Catholic immigrants came to town, they wrote to the local bishop asking him to send a priest to serve the growing community. It worked, and a house in the center of town was bought, walls were removed, and a partition was made to turn it into a church. Now they just needed a priest, but the parishioners were too poor to pay any wages. So Father Dunn arrived with his own farm animals. He ultimately became a pillar of the community.

Previously settled residents made it clear that they did not like these "different" people with their "different" religion and subjected the newcomers, many of whom were Catholic, to petty attacks, heckling, and harassment. These encounters intensified, turning increasingly violent. Men, dressed in sheets, began making night-time raids at local farmhouses. The intention was to terrorize their immigrant neighbors. Wooden crosses were set ablaze on the hill of the cemetery near Irene and Andrew's farm. The message was clear: You 'foreigners' are not welcome.

Despite the best efforts of these instigators, the new priest, and the Slovak and Hungarian immigrants, did not frighten easily. After all, they were descendants of a people who survived an endless procession of wars, uprisings, and famines. Instead, they fought this prejudice with renewed strength. This included economic strength. Father Dunn helped the new immigrants form a cooperative store where parishioners exchanged their produce for groceries; the produce, in turn, was sold in city markets. The store grew and prospered, and soon trucks were needed to transport all the goods.

With patience and dedication, the Slovak and Hungarian farmers put together enough money to build a proper church. The farmers gathered stones from their own fields. These stones framed St. Philip the Apostle Church.

Father Dunn continued to help the immigrants find their place in their adopted town and country. He wanted to show them that they were welcome, and that this was their home too. He formed a band, gathered donated instruments, and planned a parade for the new immigrants to march proudly down the main street on the Fourth of July. Again, local citizens tried to prevent this, so Dunn hired a police officer to escort his new band.

Life went on and the children of Andrew and Irene grew up, married, and started families of their own. All three remained in Ashford, Connecticut, to raise their families. Today, several grandchildren continue to call Ashford home.

...

Jeanne *is an attorney and the author of several books for middle grade readers including Each of Us a Universe, A Galaxy of Sea Stars, and Ruby in the Sky. In 1991, she was one of the first Americans to teach at the Gymnázium Párovská in Nitra, Slovakia, through Education for Democracy, a program that introduced conversational English to Slovak students. She lives in Connecticut with her family.*

Angel Wings
(Božie milosti)

- 5 egg yolks + 1 whole egg
- 1 shot glass of pálenka (whiskey or good brandy)
- ½ TSP baking powder
- A pinch of salt
- ¼ cup powdered sugar
- 2 cups flour
- Vegetable oil or Crisco for frying

1. In a large bowl, beat the egg yolks, whole egg, and whiskey together until blended.
2. Mix in the baking powder, salt, and powdered sugar.
3. Add the flour and beat until the ingredients come together to form a dough, about 5 minutes.
4. Working with half of the dough at a time, roll it out as thin as possible (as thick as 2 pieces of paper), on a lightly floured board.
5. Cut the dough into 2"-wide strips. Cut these strips on the diagonal, at 4" intervals, creating diamond shapes.
6. Cut a slit lengthwise in the middle of each diamond.
7. Pick up one end of the diamond, push it through the slit, and tug it back toward its original position. This forms the diamond into "angel wings."
8. In a large, deep skillet, heat 2" of oil to 350 °F (180 °C).
9. Fry the pastries for 1 minute (or less) per side, or until golden. The pastries fry quickly, so watch them closely.
10. Remove the pastries from the oil with a slotted spoon, and place them on paper towels to drain.
11. Serve the angel wings dusted with powdered sugar.

A SLOVAK SANCTUARY
by Edward Monovich

"My grandparents' kitchen was also a chapel, a direct link to their faith. Making koláče was not a secular tradition. At the heart of this whirl of walnuts and sweet dough lived prayers."

On a hillside near Pittsburgh, Pennsylvania, deep in coal-mining country, the view stuns me: my Slovak sanctuary burned to the ground. This is the former site of my paternal grandparents' home, which is now in ruins. Eduard and Elena haven't lived in this space since the 1990s, but the scene still shocks me. After a series of neglectful tenants and mysterious circumstances, only the charred foundation remains.

As I descend the hill, I instinctively count the irregular concrete steps that connect the street to the front door. They make a familiar, syncopated rhythm. When I arrive at what used to be my grandparent's kitchen, my feet stand on their surprisingly well-maintained checkerboard floor. I have a sudden flashback; the alternating cream and rose-colored squares recall the rich smells of *holúbky* and *koláče* that met me upon arrival during previous visits.

Though the floor looks the same, everything else is gone. Without the walls and accoutrements, I can absorb the actual dimensions of the kitchen. It measures only 4 by 3 meters. Somehow, meticulously polished cabinets, a crystal light fixture, religious icons and impeccably organized rolling pins, pans, and utensils, had convinced me that the space was much

bigger. From an emotional point of view, the space is enormous. It comprises the beating heart of my identity; a savory blend of religious mysticism, Slovak tradition, and familial closeness.

As a boy I was stunned to hear my father, while standing in that kitchen, spontaneously argue in an unfamiliar language. I had no idea that my dad even spoke Slovak! This was my first clue to a much bigger story lurking behind this unassuming space.

Sadly, I didn't learn to speak Slovak. During my grandparents' lives, conversing in their native tongue was severely frowned upon by most Americans. One's status was influenced by their command of the English language. In my experience, this prejudicial point of view constitutes a profound weakness in America's "melting pot" ideology. By forcibly stripping immigrants of their language, innumerable good ideas were lost. Furthermore, learning another ethnicity's language nurtures empathy. It offers an antidote to the cultural warfare that currently plagues the United States. It remains a goal of mine to learn Slovak and to gain access to the subconscious river of poetry, songs, and oral histories of my ancestors.

Nevertheless, I did manage to pick up a few useful phrases over the years spent in my grandparents' kitchen. On one occasion, I put this knowledge to good use for a secret mission. I recruited my best friends to play a joke on our least favorite elementary school teacher. Each day, we ran by her classroom during lunch and sent a special message... Slovak-style. Hustling by our nemesis's door, we yelled in unison, "Ísť do pekla!" ("Go to hell!"). After the third episode, while sitting in our homeroom, we heard an authoritative knock on the door. It was our school principal. We were busted! He escorted our group to his office and punished us with one week of after-school detention. As the ringleader, I received extra days. Thankfully, he didn't understand that we were actually cursing the teacher; otherwise, the penalty would have been stiffer. I never told my parents the real story behind the punishment.

More importantly, my grandparents' kitchen provided spiritual nourishment. Around the holidays, and especially Easter, my grandmother cooked traditional Slovak food. My favorite of these recipes is a type of nut roll called *koláč*. During the holidays, my grandmother would reserve several days to assemble a mountain of *koláče*. It was important to my family to have plenty of this dish on-hand, so that they could share it with visitors throughout the holiday season.

The nut roll was an excuse for connecting, for sitting together, and for sharing stories. With the importance of this ritual, it is not surprising that our family has guarded and carefully passed down the original recipe. Making and sharing *koláče* still centers our family today. Now, when we deliver nut rolls to our best friends, we call it sharing 'Slovak magic'. We (jokingly) characterize our relationships, as they grow closer, as becoming '*koláč*-worthy'.

We work to find the perfect ratio of nuts to dough for nutrition, flavor, and aesthetic impact. Over the years, our family has pondered the nuances of this beloved dessert. We actively seek to distill the purist form from the scribbled notes in our ancestors' cookbooks. Our recipe has more raisins than most, which I highly recommend. The perfect fresh yeast is essential. A *koláč* with too few nuts is deemed 'stingy' and will not make the cut. When we finish with rolling and rising, it is critical to apply the correct amount of egg wash to each *koláč* before baking, so they achieve an attractive, burnt-sienna shine. Like a fine baroque painting, we make sure that each nut roll attains a balanced composition.

My grandparents' kitchen was also a chapel, a direct link to their faith. Making *koláče* was not a secular tradition. At the heart of this whirl of walnuts and sweet dough lived prayers. After baking, my grandfather neatly arranged *cirak* (Slovak Easter cheese), *klobása,* and *koláče* in a basket. He invited me to sculpt the butter into Easter-themed shapes before adding it to the mix. Grandpa carried this basket directly to the local cathedral for a blessing. Eating was not allowed until after sprinkling the food with holy water. For my grandfather, this constituted a festive occasion where he remembered the sacrifices of his ancestors and his current privileges.

As much as I love nut rolls, Grandpa's gift of gratitude nourishes me even more. I still feel a tangible link between food and faith which stretches all the way from our ancestral basilica in Bardejov. In this way, our Slovak traditions connect my modern-day kitchen in Boston to my grandparents' kitchen in Pennsylvania, and all the way to my great-grandparents' kitchen in Slovakia. Making *koláč* is simultaneously time-travel and teleportation. Thanks to my grandpa, these are not abstract connections to me. He brought me along for his rituals. When we went to the cathedral, in addition to blessing the basket of food, Grandpa introduced me to his community which seemed enormous.

Grandpa was a popular guy. At the same church, he sang in the choir for 50 years and wove crosses from palm fronds that decorated the walls of his kitchen. I attribute my passion for art, to the rituals and aesthetics that were first experienced there.

These cultural seeds grew inside of me. Now, I create paintings and performance art that welcome sacred elements into everyday life. I even incorporate ashes from my grandfather's palm weavings into my paint.

Though I didn't realize it at the time, space was extremely tight in the kitchen. This forced my grandparents to be creative. Even the surface for rolling *koláče* was retractable.

When finished with the cooking, grandma would stow away her tools with the efficiency of a Murphy bed. My grandfather hand-washed, dried, and polished all the dishware, cabinets, and countertops. Each element was placed carefully on a tray and organized in the cabinets. Each utensil felt valued. Even though their efforts were disciplined, an easy-going vibe pervaded. Their process introduced me to mindfulness at an early age. Every step was equally appreciated. For Grandpa, washing dishes was part of the pleasure. After cleanup, the stainless-steel surfaces and glass cabinets shined.

The kitchen glowed, even though it was built into a hillside with little natural light. For me, the space was a magic grotto festooned with shimmering gemstones. Though meticulously organized, it never felt inaccessible. Nothing was off limits to me. This well-maintained little kitchen perfectly represented my grandparents' worldview. They were grateful for their gifts and were eager to share them. I was readily welcomed to delight in all their wares, even though they were earned at a steep price, with blood and coal. I learned later that the bright light of my Slovak sanctuary existed in stark contrast to Grandpa's dark and dangerous day job in the coal mines.

I am named after my grandfather, who was named after his father. Desperate poverty drove him to bring his young family to western Pennsylvania, in pursuit of new opportunities. They settled in Brownsville, Pennsylvania, in 1913, when my grandfather was just one year old. This decision is difficult to comprehend from my present-day vantage point of relative wealth and privilege. Soon after his emigration, my great-grandfather paid for his audacity with his life, deep in the coal mine.

With a reputation for nimbleness, he volunteered to be a brakeman, an extremely dangerous task. In the process of coupling or uncoupling, brakemen would stand between the sharp-edged, metal, coal cars while traveling at high speed.

One slip, or error in timing meant death. Though the circumstances are unclear, an error during coupling led to my great-grandfather's decapitation. In addition to their incomprehensible loss, my grandfather's family also faced the painful stigma and superstition associated with such a terrible event. Grandpa never forgot chasing gawking children away from his father's open casket, which revealed the nature of the incident.

At that time, the family lived in overpriced company housing, where the miners were essentially indentured servants. Their meager salaries were calculated to keep them slaves to their house payment and to the inflated prices of the company store. Amidst stifling poverty and fresh catastrophe, my great-grandmother, rifle in hand, defended the family from thieves who wished to profit from their misfortune.

Sadly, the coal mine stole even more from my family. While still a young man, my grandfather lost an eye during a mine collapse. This inspired him to get involved in union activism. When promoted to a leadership position, Grandpa received a commemorative clock from the president of the United Mine Workers Association. For all the years that I knew him, this clock was placed prominently on Grandpa's dresser. It currently resides in my art studio. My passion for social justice finds its roots in Grandpa's struggle to provide safe working conditions and fair compensation for his immigrant community.

Understandably, my grandpa never spoke much about the loss of his father, which was clearly a deep wound. The lasting stigma from this loss seemed to haunt and quiet my otherwise talkative grandpa. For such an open person, his silence on the matter made a salient contradiction. Though part of me wants to join in the generational silence, it is also important to share the miracle of my great-grandfather's indelible love for his family which was formidable. It transcended death and fueled my grandpa to persevere, with an overflowing heart. As a result, my dad grew up a generous and happy man. I hope to pass on this family tradition to my children, to honor my great-grandfather's sacrifice.

At a time when many struggle with generational trauma, I am blessed with an easy sense of appreciation that stems from the grounded, loving approach of my progenitors. Though blessed with my grandpa's friendship well into my adulthood, I regret not pressing him for more details about his father. I would have liked to have understood the idiosyncrasies of the man that brought our family to America.

My Slovak heritage, embodied by the family kitchen in Brownsville, compels me to this day. Even though their sacred space was destroyed, I still see life through my ancestors' lens. I share their appreciation for small moments, like the shine of a stainless-steel countertop or the spiral in a fresh walnut *koláč*. Their aesthetic commitments to culinary traditions and music inspired me to study art. My artwork draws from my family history and digs deeply into my personal psyche. It searches for ancient vestiges of wisdom that were erased by contemporary society and intercontinental migration. A current project seeks to recreate long-lost Slovak rituals with collaborators in the U.S. and Slovakia. In this way, the passions of my grandparents will manifest in new art that reunites me with my homeland.

Edward Monovich *grew up in Kalamazoo, Michigan. He received his MFA from the University of Texas at Austin and his BA in biology from Kalamazoo College. Edward is an interdisciplinary artist who lives and works in Boston. His works combine performance art, drawing, ecology and folklore. His interactive projects have exhibited in Europe, Central America and throughout the US. Ancient cultural rituals and Slovak heritage provide key inspiration. Edward currently teaches Illustration at Massachusetts College of Art and Design in Boston.*

Monovich Sacred Koláč (Nut Roll)

(Makes 3 koláče and 1 paska)

While holding hands with your fellow bakers, express your gratitude to our predecessors for passing down this recipe. Invite them to join you while you bake. Afterwards, before you eat them, take the nut rolls and the *paska* to church for blessing, or privately offer up a message of gratitude. And remember, nut rolls are better when shared—and they go quickly!

Dough:

- 2 cups milk
- 1 cup raisins
- ¾ cake (or 1½ oz.) fresh baker's yeast, preferably Red Star Fresh Yeast (thaw on counter first, if frozen)
- ¼ cup warm water, or less (to dissolve yeast)
- ½ cup unsalted butter, at room temperature
- ¾ cup sugar
- 3 eggs + 2 eggs, beaten and reserved separately
- 6 cups flour
- 1 TSP salt
- Dash white pepper

Walnut mixture:

- 1–1½ lbs. walnuts
- 1 cup sugar
- 2 TBSP unsalted butter, melted
- ½ cup unsweetened evaporated milk

• • •

1. To make the dough, scald the milk by heating it in a small sauce pan until small bubbles form around the perimeter. Do not let it boil. After scalding, place the milk into the refrigerator to cool, as hot milk will kill the yeast.

2. Put the raisins into a separate small sauce pan and add just enough water to cover them. Bring to a gentle boil, then turn off the heat and let the pot sit as is. When the time comes to add the raisins to the recipe, drain them first.

3. Dissolve the yeast in the warm water and set aside.

4. Cream the butter, then add the sugar and cream them together.

5. Put the yeast and the cooled milk in a mixing bowl, combine with an electric mixer, then add in 3 beaten eggs and mix well.

6. Next, add the flour in batches: beat in half of the flour using the mixer. Add the remaining flour gradually, along with the salt and pepper. The last of the flour should be kneaded into the mixture by hand, until the dough has a satiny (but no longer sticky) finish. When the dough is ready, it will no longer stick to your fingers, but will form a tidy ball.

7. Place the dough in a large bowl in a warm place and cover it with a towel, letting it sit until the dough doubles in size.

8. While the dough is rising, prepare the walnut mixture by grinding the walnuts fine with a food processor (pulse, to avoid overprocessing and creating a nut butter) or an old-fashioned hand grinder.

9. In a bowl, mix the sugar, melted butter, and nuts into a paste. Set aside.

10. Preheat the oven to 350 °F (180 °C).

11. After the dough has risen and doubled in size, divide it in half and set aside 1 of the halves for the paska. Divide the other half into 3 equal balls.

12. Using a heavy rolling pin, roll one of the balls into a very thin rectangle that measures approximately 18" x 12" (see illustration).

13. Spoon € of the nut mixture onto the dough and spread it evenly, using a butter knife or an offset spatula, to within ½" of all the edges.

14. Divide the drained, plumped raisins into 2 equal portions, and set aside 1 portion for the paska. After spreading the walnut mixture evenly over the dough, distribute € of the nutroll raisins evenly over each roll's nut mixture.

15. Using gentle and feathery finger motions, roll the rectangle towards yourself, along the long edge. Be sure to keep the spiral tight. Once the roll is completed, tuck both ends underneath, so that no nuts are showing.

16. Place all 3 nut rolls (seam side down) onto a greased cookie sheet, cover them with a towel, and set them in a warm place, to rise for a second time (the top of the preheating oven is a good location). When the rolls expand so that they nearly touch each other, they are ready to bake. Do not let the dough rise for too long, because nut roll is better when the pastry is thin.

17. Brush the entire surface of the risen nut rolls with a beaten egg, for a shiny crust.

18. Bake the rolls for approximately 45 minutes, until the top is golden brown. Be careful not to burn the bottoms.

* * *

1. To make the paska, divide the second half of the dough into 3 equal pieces and use your hands to roll each piece into a long strip of even thickness.

2. Divide the remaining raisins (half of the original amount) into 3 portions, and press one portion's worth into each strip.

3. Braid the three strips tightly, then coil the braid into a greased, circular bread pan that is deep enough to accommodate the rise of the dough.

4. Place the pan in a warm location, cover it with a towel, and allow it to rise to loaf size, approximately double.

5. Brush the risen loaf with a beaten egg, then bake it at 375 °F (190 °C) for approximately 25 minutes.

6. Remove from the oven and allow to cool.

MY SLOVAK HERITAGE WAS KEPT MOSTLY HIDDEN

by Albert Kovanis, Jr.

> "At our first meeting in Gbely, one of my relatives pointed to the ground and in a proud voice said to me, "This is your home!"

I am the second child in a family of twelve children born between 1947 and 1971. My early life was shaped by the faith and guidance passed on to me from my parents and grandparents. My mother's family had roots in several European countries, but my father's parents, who were more recent immigrants, were proud to state in their soft-accented voices that they were Slovak.

My school geography lessons taught that Slovaks and Czechs lived in the country of Czechoslovakia, based on the system of Soviet communism that was much different from the democracy we lived in. Czechoslovakia was an ally of the Soviet Union which made it our 'enemy' during the Cold War.

Although my Slovak grandparents were smart, hardworking, and loving, I was uncomfortable telling anyone that they came from Czechoslovakia. As a result, my Slovak heritage was kept mostly hidden. I didn't try to find out more about the origins of my family. It was enough for me to know that I was American. It wasn't until later that I discovered the rich Slovak culture and felt proud of my Slovak family legacy.

...

Felix Kovanič and Johana Kovárik left the comfort of their family to come to America at the beginning of the 20th century. With confusingly similar surnames, perhaps it was in their destiny that they would end up together. They could not have foreseen or predicted the events and great adventure that their futures would bring. This humble couple from simple peasant stock would live extraordinary lives.

Their home was the region of Záhorie in western Slovakia, between the Little Carpathian Mountains in the east and the Morava River in the west. Politically it had been part of the Kingdom of Hungary for centuries. It was also home to diverse ethnic communities that preserved their identities as Slovaks, Czechs, Germans, and others. This is not just historical trivia, but a legacy that lives on in my blood.

The family history of my grandfather Felix is no less intricate. Felix Kovanič, the seventh child of his parents, was born in 1895 in the small village of Burszentgyorgy. Today, this village is known as Borský Svätý Jur. The local records of nearby Malé Leváre reveal that the surname was present in this part of Slovakia for at least a half dozen earlier generations of serfs tied to the land. However, it is very possible that these people had been living there for much longer than that.

The area received Croatian settlers in the 16th century when the mighty Ottoman armies sprawled across the Balkans and even invaded the Kingdom of Hungary. As they advanced in the direction of Slovakia, they pushed people from the conquered lands north. Many found refuge in modern-day Slovakia, then known as Upper Hungary, which never fully fell into Ottoman hands.

Does the "ič" ending of my family name indicate that its origins are in the Balkans? Were my forefathers among those who escaped the invaders and settled in Slovakia?

Felix's father Juraj married Genovéva Horn from an ethnic German family that lived in a nearby village. The issue was that Genovéva had an illegitimate son. During a time when single mothers had to face much prejudice and judgment, perhaps it was easier for the couple to move away and start anew.

Eventually, they settled in Borský Svätý Jur where my grandfather was born. Once the family had a permanent home, Juraj travelled to America for work. When the father of the house was away, the responsibility to look after the family rested on the shoulders of Genovéva and the eldest son Mikuláš.

Sadly, in 1898, when my grandfather was only three years old, his mother died from tuberculosis. His brother Mikuláš was no longer living with them. He had married and moved to Vienna, Austria, to be close to the family of his wife. Felix's father understood he needed someone to care for his children, and so he re-married quickly. Juraj chose a widow with children of her own before he returned to America to work. Soon after, he received a letter telling him that Felix was bullied by the children of his stepmother.

Being far away in America, Juraj swiftly dispatched his son Mikukáš to check out the situation. Mikuláš told his stepmother to pack Felix's clothes and took his young brother to Vienna where he raised him as a member of his own family. Later in life, when we asked granddad about his early years, he would smile and simply say, "Aah... Vienna!"

Mikuláš who went by name Nicolas in Vienna, ran a grocery store in a prosperous neighborhood near the imperial palace Schönbrunn. Nicolas and his wife Juliana had six children, and Felix was raised by a loving family. He learned to speak and write German fluently which became a useful skill when he came to America. He also helped in the grocery store, and his big brother made sure he received a good education.

Felix was enrolled in a prestigious trade school in Vienna where he learned mechanical skills. When he graduated in the fall of 1912, he was at the age for conscription into the Austrian army, but Georg stepped in and arranged for his youngest son to join him in America. He believed America offered much better opportunities than the Austro-Hungarian army.

Unlike many others, Felix did not leave from a German port, but rather travelled via the French port Le Havre in January of 1913. He disembarked in New York City and continued to Wheeling, West Virginia to join his father.

Now let's take a pause and trace the story of my grandmother Johana Kovárik. Johana was also born in Záhorie to the family of a forest ranger. Johana was a sturdy young woman and her mother made sure she learned all the skills necessary for running a successful household. Gram would tell us that life in Gbely was not easy for the Slovaks. Her school classes were taught in the Hungarian language, and she was forbidden to speak in her native tongue. Getting caught talking Slovak in school led to a whipping; a stern warning not to do so again. So, Johana stopped going to school and stayed home with her mother instead.

At that time, many were leaving the village to seek better opportunities in the New World, including Johana's cousin. She wrote to Johana and invited her to visit. She promised there was much to see, and they would have a great adventure in America together. Resolutely, Johana's parents told her no, but she persisted in asking and finally gained their permission to go. Johana's oldest brother, Ján, agreed to loan her enough money for the journey if she promised to repay him. She took the money, and Ján was later repaid to the last cent.

As Johana was leaving for her trip, she received a valuable final piece of advice from Ján. "Don't believe all the things the boys will tell you!" And with that, the great adventure began. Johana traveled in a group with seven others from the village, chaperoned by a second cousin.

The youth made their way to Hamburg, Germany and boarded the ship appropriately named America, a good omen. The ship was filled with people from all over the place, but Johana kept to herself with the other Slovak passengers under her chaperone's watchful eye. Traveling in steerage, the part mostly below the ship's waterline, was the first test of her resolve. Light came in only through the ship's portholes. It was hot and smelly, and Johana would try to sneak out of her area to the upper decks whenever she could to find at least a temporary relief. This was against the ship rules, but occasionally the crew would take pity on the young girl. She was able stand on an open deck for a short time to get a breath of the fresh ocean air.

Food was scarce and would be shared within groups traveling together. Once, a fellow passenger came into possession of a banana. Since no one had ever seen one before, there was much curiosity about how to eat it. The lucky possessor of this mysterious delicacy simply bit in and ate the whole thing in a few bites, banana peel and all! There was no waste in steerage, and at least one growling belly was quieted for a short while.

It took two exhausting weeks to cross the ocean, and all the passengers were happy beyond words when they finally sailed into port past the Statue of Liberty. Everyone cheered and many eyes filled with tears when they saw this wonderful sight. Johana successfully passed through the immigration control at Ellis Island pretending she was 18 when in reality, she was only 15. She then found the railroad station and boarded the train to Pittsburgh, Pennsylvania. When she got off the train, Johana was greeted by her cousin's parents, and taken to the nearby town of Carnegie.

However, this was not going to be a holiday. A few days later, Johana was told that she was expected to pay for her share of the household expenses. So, she found a job as a maid to the widow of a wealthy industrialist. Before long, her short vacation to the United States turned into months and then several years.

Although she missed her family dearly, she also enjoyed the excitement of her new home. Moreover, the eruption of the First World War made returning to Slovakia impossible. The homemaking skills that Johana had learned from her mother were put to good use. She contributed some of her earnings to support her cousin's family, and the rest was saved to repay the travel expenses and, perhaps, to buy a ticket back someday.

I do not know what 17-year-old Felix Kovanič, or 15-year-old Johana Kovárik expected to find when they set out for America, but I know that the most important thing they did was find each other.

When war broke out in Europe, Felix was working with his father in the mills along the Ohio River. Juraj wanted to return to be with his family in Hungary, but it would be dangerous for Felix to go with him because he would be drafted into military service. Felix was doing well at work and had the skills to support himself in America. He wanted to marry, not die on a battlefield!

Sunday was always a day of fun and rest. On one such Sunday, Johana and her cousin went to Bellaire, Ohio for a Slovak picnic. Bellaire was on the opposite side of the Ohio River from Wheeling, where Felix lived.

There, she met a nice young man named Felix and they were immediately smitten with each other. Soon they got engaged, and in August 1915, the young couple married in a Slovak church in the same town. It was the beginning of a happy, loving marriage that would last 53 years.

The couple settled in Carnegie, a fine place to find work and raise a family. There were many opportunities for work in the steel mills, coal mines, or railroads. Pittsburgh was just a trolley-ride away and there were plenty of fellow immigrants who formed their own churches, social organizations, and just helped one another.

Felix and Johana quickly settled into their new community. They lived in an Irish neighborhood, and although some Slovaks also lived in the area, they were few and far between. There was also no Slovak church there, a pillar of Slovak communities in other parts of Pennsylvania. Hence, the couple became active members of St. Joseph's Catholic Church that was built and supported by the local German community. Felix's ability to speak German from his Vienna days really helped them to fit in.

The Concordia Club was a favorite social spot for them. That's where local Slovaks gathered to relax after work and to meet with their friends. On Saturday nights, they sang and danced to familiar songs and downed more than one warm beer! Johana also joined the Sokol organization where she practiced gymnastics. She served on many Sokol committees and even held the office of Financial Secretary Treasurer for 55 years.

Felix had well-developed mechanical skills. It was said that he could fix anything. He worked at various mills, and when he was not at work, he installed many of the first electrical line connections to houses in the area. The couple also earned money by using their home as a boarding house for Slovak mill workers. Johana cooked for them and laundered their grimy clothes.

The Kovanič couple became a Slovak-American family when Felix Jr. was born in August, 1916. He was followed by Albert, my father, in December of 1919, and their only daughter, Irene, in November 1922. The family lived a simple lifestyle rooted in a deep faith in God's goodness.

In 1917, Felix filed a U.S. Department of Labor Declaration of Intent, the first step to becoming an American citizen. The declaration stated, "It is my bona fide intention to renounce forever all allegiance and fidelity to any prince, potentate, state, or sovereignty, and particularly to Charles, Emperor of Austria, and Apostolic King of Hungary."

When the war in Europe ended in November 1918, the new nation of Czechoslovakia was born from the ashes of Austria-Hungary. Czechs and Slovaks could finally live under their own government after being ruled by others for centuries. Some Slovaks living in America chose to return to their homeland, but Felix and Johana stayed in America. On March 16th, 1922, a Certificate of Naturalization was issued for four new American citizens: Felix Kovanic, his wife 'Jennie', and their sons.

In the following years, the American family name became 'Kovanis' instead of 'Kovanič'. The reason for the change is now unknown. Perhaps it was not wise to be associated with the defeated Austro-Hungarians. These years were filled with happy times but also challenges brought about by the great economic depression that hit the US in 1929. Despite the hard times, Felix was able to always find work and provide for his family.

Over in Europe, life was far from rosy. Johana's father and one of her brothers died during the war. Her mother was not faring well, and on top of it all, Johana received a sad letter. She discovered that the financial situation was unbearable, and it was necessary to sell the family home. Would Johana agree to sell it? Her share of the inheritance would be protected. Just like that, the sale happened. The family home was gone.

Moreover, the air on the old continent was once again thick with a threat of looming war. When the Second World War broke out and the US finally entered the conflict, Albert Kovanis enlisted in the US Army in the Field Artillery Branch.

He was deployed to Hawaii where he was having a great time, sharing his stories in regular letters that he sent to his parents. But two days after his 22nd birthday party, the paradise turned into a living hell. On December 7th, 1941, Pearl Harbor was attacked. Many American lives were lost, and Johana prayed again for the safety of her son. A neighboring family in Carnegie received a government letter informing them that their son was killed on one of the attacked battleships. No letter was received from Albert after the attack, and Johana was sick with worry. I cannot imagine the relief she felt when a note from her son arrived. Maybe it was Johana's prayers that carried the family through the war.

Felix and Johana celebrated their Golden Wedding Anniversary in August, 1965. It wasn't long after that Felix suffered a stroke. He survived but was left unable to speak and lost most of his ability to move. Johana lovingly cared for him even though Felix no longer recognized who she was. My father would occasionally bring my grandparents to our house for a visit. They sat together in silence on our couch with Johana holding Felix's hand. She talked softly to him in Slovak and gently wiped his forehead with her handkerchief. Felix had a second stroke in August of 1968 that completed the journey of his life.

Felix was buried in St. Joseph's Cemetery with an adjacent plot reserved for his wife. We worried that grandmother might want to join her husband in the afterlife soon, but she stayed with us for another 26 years and graced us with much joy.

In the years after Felix's death, Johana continued to live in her own house and was always surrounded by her family. Her daughter and grandchildren lived with her and took great care of her. In return, Johana cooked, baked, and cleaned for the household. Felix Jr. lived nearby and visited often with his family. When Albert moved with nine of his children to Florida in 1971, Johana was able to escape the cold of the north's winter by going to Florida.

Although she was no longer a young woman, my grandmother's spirit for adventure was still strong. There were stories of her first solo plane journey, her first ride on a motorcycle, or the time she went into the swimming pool with the grandkids.

A special event for Johana was the ordination of my youngest brother Joel as a priest for the Diocese of St. Petersburg, Florida. As Joel was finishing his training, she proudly exclaimed, "We have a priest!" But Grandma did not live to see Joel celebrate his first mass. She passed three months before

his ordination. In March 1994, she lay down in her own bed in the house that she had shared for many years with Felix and closed her eyes forever.

After Johana died, there were many unanswered questions about the family history. I thought that we would never learn the answers. But I began to remember what Johana said after she came to America. "I never saw my mother and father again. I never saw my brothers!" I felt called to do something. There had been no contact with the family in Gbely since the late 1940s. News from Felix's family in Vienna was even scarcer. What could be done? To our great fortune, I discovered Helene Cincebeaux, whose story you can also find in this book. She and her mother led tours to Slovakia for Americans with Slovak heritage.

Helene agreed to make a side trip to Gbely during her next trip to Slovakia. She drove to this unfamiliar village with two clues. She was looking for anyone with a family name of Kovárik, and she had a photocopied sheet of some old black and white family photos. A villager directed her to a house where she was greeted by a gentleman who identified himself as Štefan Kovárik. He would turn out to be the grandson of one of Johana's brothers. When Štefan looked at the photos, he identified himself as the young boy who was posed with several adults including Johana's mother. A family reunion was in the making.

In the summer of 1997, a group of about 20 Kovanis family and friends made the trip to Gbely, Slovakia. The Kovárik family was physically reunited in that moment and emotionally reunited forever. A great celebration was held with photos, stories, and *slivovica* flowing in abundance.

We were told amazing stories about the remote family past. I was given a small replica axe and told that the great Austrian Empress, Maria Theresia, gave our Kovárik ancestor a sizeable grant of land near the village. The grant of land was reward for his skillful service as the royal executioner! Unfortunately, the land was lost when it was collectivized during communism.

Johana's brother Štefan was part of the conscripted Hungarian troops guarding Archduke Franz Ferdinand, the heir to the Austrian throne, when he was assassinated in Sarajevo in the run up to the First World War. As punishment, the troops were lined up and told to count to ten. Each 10th soldier would be shot. Štefan unluckily drew the number ten but was spared when a fellow villager and friend falsely swore under oath that Štefan was on sick call that day. In thanks, the home of the friend's family had been preserved, and was turned into a museum in the village. It was the very spot where our family meeting was taking place. We have made several trips to Slovakia since.

After hiding and knowing little of my Slovak heritage in my youth, I now embrace it. My family and I have reclaimed past connections to our ancestral roots. We feel the love that reminds us of our Slovak heritage. At our first meeting in Gbely, one of my relatives pointed to the ground and in a proud voice said to me, "This is your home!" It is my home indeed, and I can see the smiles on my grandparents' faces as I celebrate belonging there.

Originally from the Pittsburgh, Pennsylvania area, Al gained his MBA at Duquesne University in Pittsburgh and went on to have a long career as an accountant. He retired after 52 years and lives in Northern California with his wife. Al continues to cherish family traditions and stories and hopes that his three children and their children will continue to explore and preserve their shared Slovak heritage.

Apple Strudel

Dough:

- 2 eggs
- ½ cup Crisco
- ½ stick butter
- 4 cups flour
- 1 TSP sugar
- 1 TSP salt
- ½ cup warm water

Filling:

- 4 lbs apples
- 1 cup sugar
- 2 TSP cinnamon
- ½ cup golden raisins
- ½ cup chopped walnuts
- Flour
- ½ cup melted butter
- ½ cup plain breadcrumbs

1. Combine all the dough ingredients in a large bowl. Knead the dough until it is soft, but not sticky. Cover it and let it stand 1 hour, in a warm place.
2. Peel, core, and cut the apples into thin slices. In a large bowl, mix the slices with the sugar and cinnamon. Add the raisins and walnuts, then set the bowl aside.

3. Preheat the oven to 375 °F (190 °C) and line a baking sheet with parchment paper.

4. On the counter, spread out a thin kitchen towel, preferably with a pattern (to help you see the shape of the dough). Sprinkle it with flour.

5. Cut the dough into 4 pieces. On top of the towel, roll out one piece as thin as possible, into a rectangular shape, with a long side closest to you. Stretch the dough without tearing it.

6. Brush the dough with the melted butter.

7. Spread the breadcrumbs over the dough (to absorb some of the butter), leaving a 2" margin along the top and bottom (long edges) of the dough.

8. Use a slotted spoon to scoop ¼ of the apple filling out of its accumulated liquid, and spread the filling on top of the breadcrumbs, maintaining the 2" margins.

9. Fold the 2" margins onto the filling, then roll up the strudel from the short side, using the towel to help you roll. Tuck the ends underneath.

10. Carefully transfer the strudel to the prepared baking sheet, seam side down. Brush with a small amount of melted butter.

11. Repeat steps 5-10 for the remaining 3 pieces of dough.

12. Bake about 45 minutes, until the strudel is lightly golden on top.

13. Remove from the oven and allow to cool.

14. Cut into 1" slices and serve.

FINDING MY SLOVAK ROOTS WAS A CATHARTIC EXPERIENCE

by Beverly Clifford

"I'm here, Granny. I came to see and understand the life you led here; the sacrifices you made to leave this very place and make a new life for you and your own children, your children's children, and your great-great grandchildren."

The journey of my grandmother Mária Anna Martinková from her homeland in Visolaje, Czechoslovakia (now Slovakia) to America in 1919 at the age of 22 was the turning point for her future and the future of our family. As the oldest child of a family of 12 living in the country prior to electricity, piped water and plumbing, her family's existence depended on what they could source from the land and from within their community.

In the age of electronics, automobiles, and technology, it is difficult to imagine a world without access and the comforts of modern living. Yet, it was in that world that our ancestors undertook the great journey and dared to make a fresh start in a new and foreign land.

Mária Anna's education opportunities were limited, and so she worked as a horseback mail carrier. She was summoned by her uncle John (her sponsor) to travel to America to work with his wife in their household in Philadelphia, Pennsylvania. To this day, it still baffles my mind how one would agree to leave their homeland and their family with the knowledge that they would have a high probability of not ever seeing them again. How could you say goodbye to your mother, your father, your siblings and know that they would soon be a fading memory? I think of that decision of hers and am in awe of her bravery and enterprise.

My granny, as she was affectionately known, left her home and traveled by train to Hamburg, Germany, where she boarded a ship with $5 in her pocket. The journey to New York was thought to be about 10 days. Reaching Ellis Island, she was processed, deemed healthy, and was sent on her way to the train station to travel south to Philadelphia. Unbeknownst to her, while she was traveling from Slovakia, her uncle John died. She waited for 2 days in the train station by herself with no English skills waiting for her aunt to pick her up. She must have been terrified and questioning her decision to come to this foreign land. Unfathomable! Eventually, her uncle's widow came to collect her, only to treat her poorly as a servant in the home.

During the great migration from eastern Europe, it seems like the communities that formed in America were highly segregated by ethnicity. There was a Slovak enclave in Philadelphia, but my granny would have to wait to be introduced to it. For a time, my grandmother worked at the Campbell Soup factory and also at a cigar factory. This is where she met a man, Mr. Sokula, who introduced my grandmother to a section of the city that harbored people of Slovak descent. She then became aware of the network of communication between other communities in Pennsylvania which were primarily settled by Slovak immigrants.

Meanwhile in Schuylkill County, Pennsylvania, my grandfather John Lazovi, a miner who arrived in 1909 from the same vicinity as my grandmother, noticed her name and village on a ship's manifest list which was prominently displayed

at the neighborhood market. Through the lines of communication, he made a stab in the dark to contact someone in Philadelphia to meet my grandmother. He arrived by train to claim his bride and take her back to rural Pennsylvania. They were married in 1920 and settled in a company house owned by the mining business. After two miscarriages, my grandparents went on to raise seven children.

Taking care of a large family took some skill. The house had one faucet in the kitchen from a well. No hot water. No toilet. There was a coal stove which provided heat and hot water for cooking and bathing.

On their property, my grandparents raised chickens, pigs, ducks, and once a cow. They applied their survival skill set from the "old country" to use their property to farm their own vegetables, berries, and fruit. The land provided for all their needs. Before the first refrigerators appeared on the market, granny preserved vegetables and fruit for the winter months, and grandfather had a smoke house to cure the meat. Their sons were hunters who provided deer and pheasant meat for the household.

My mother, the second oldest, Ann Louise Lazovi, married my father Joseph Skrincosky (Polish/Ukrainian) in 1951. They bought a home across the street from my grandparents. Next door lived my uncle and on the lot next their home lived my eldest aunt. In a way, we lived as one large, extended family.

My mother was a working mom, and I was raised by my granny along with many of the other grandchildren. It was in her home that we learned of her homeland. She described the landscape of rolling hills, the stream running through the property, and the house with a central hearth. She described the *orech* (walnut) tree that graced the property. She told of how the girls slept in the rafters in the attic. She spoke of the feather quilts that kept her and her sisters warm. We were informed about the harvesting and fermenting of plums for the prized *slivovica*. All of this oral history was kept close in our hearts.

When granny departed from our midst, we always yearned to learn about her past and her rich Slovak culture and heritage. When the first relatives took it upon themselves to venture to the ancestral land first, we were all anxious to hear of the adventure. Their stories whetted my cousin George's appetite to seek more about where our grandparent's family originated. George's mother Mary was the oldest of my grandmother's children and fluent in the Slovak language. So, in 1994, George, his mother Mary, along with others made the trip back to Bratislava.

Staying in the capital city overnight before their adventure north to Trenčín, my aunt found it difficult to communicate, because the dialect seemed foreign to her. They almost aborted the trip because of the confusion. But then, just like her mother before her, she forged forward.

The only address they had to connect them with my grandmother's family was an old, tattered envelope that was found in the family Bible. As their train made its way north, the language of the passengers on the train became more and more familiar. My aunt beamed from ear-to-ear knowing she could communicate.

At the train station, they found the only taxi for the community. With envelope in hand, they were delivered directly to my grandmother's family in Visolaje. At the time she still had two living sisters: Anna and Gizela; both in their 90s. Several family pilgrimages to the area by my relatives followed, but I was a young working mother who could not take the time out. I lived vicariously through the eyes of my cousin George who now was the ambassador for the family.

Then in 2006, my cousin afforded me the opportunity to travel with him to Slovakia. He insisted that we leave Bratislava on the train, just as my grandmother would have done. As we made our way through the countryside and changed trains, I could see just from the population on the train how the economic conditions were changing. City people dressed in business attire gave way to the country women boarding the rickety older trains wearing scarves and carrying live chickens!

We checked into the Tatra Hotel in Trenčín, right underneath the castle! Carved into the cliff rocks behind the hotel is the oldest inscription in the territory by Roman soldiers in their crusade against Germanic tribes dating back to the 2nd century AD. Charming old world.

My cousin whisked me away to have my first introduction. My grandmother's nephew Jozef was the first to greet me. Even though he spoke no English, his eyes sparkled, and he heartily hugged this American relative. Then came the celebratory shots of *slivovica*. I was knocked on the floor by the high proof! But the shots kept coming and I struggled to keep up! In Slovak, he announced to his family: Bev—not good Slovak! Thank God that his wife presented us with an incredible meal of homemade soup, fresh baked bread, a roast, dumplings, salad, potato pancakes, blood sausage, pickles, sauerkraut, and the courses kept coming! Then the gorgeous desserts—all from scratch in an incredibly small kitchen hardly bigger than a closet—a testament to Slovak hospitality and resourcefulness.

There was a sad moment too. My grandmother's sister Anna, Jozef's mother, was in the hospital and not expected to live. Gizela had passed away already. So Anna was the last remaining relative who knew my granny from Slovakia. I had to see her.

Entering the geriatric ward of the hospital, I was taken back by the 1950s-type equipment—metal syringes, medicines in brown glass bottles, wooden potty seats next to the beds. As we entered the room, I could see a familiar face in that bed. Smaller framed, but the same features as my grandmother. When she spoke, tears ran down my face. The same voice, tone, as my beloved grandmother. I embraced her and she smiled.

Anna was a young girl when my granny left Slovakia. To think that I was close to not having met my grandmother's last living sibling. My own mother is her namesake. No words can describe the emotion of connecting with her. It was overwhelming in the most beautiful way. Anna passed away shortly after my visit.

The next day came amid a whirlwind of activity. Apparently, from far and wide, the extended family was notified that the Americans were in town. As we went from town to town, we were greeted with *slivovica*, open-faced sandwiches and sweets. They were all so proud to host us, giving us the very finest food that they could afford.

The last home in Visolaje included a trip to the church where my grandmother worshiped as a child and a visitation to her parents' graves. The honor and reverence that Slovaks afford their deceased relatives is evident in the beautiful graves—covered with slabs of granite, graced with flowers and candles, and tended with love. We attended mass at the ancient church, and I was in wonder of its simplicity, and the awe-inspiring spirit that rose from there. The tradition of the men in the upstairs choir balcony and the women downstairs gave me a sense of their rituals.

The highlight of the stay was visiting grandmother's home which was still standing. In my head that night I recalled all the conversations with my granny and her recollection of her family home. There were so many emotions coursing through me in anticipation of finally seeing the actual place where this long journey began.

After my granny passed away, I put my pen to paper and wrote a poem to try to embrace the feelings that would have been in my grandmother's heart as she made her goodbyes and began her trek across Europe. Then boarding a ship across the vast Atlantic full of people speaking many languages. "Babylon relived." The thought of her arriving in Ellis Island and being herded through the customs and immigration, I tried to put myself in her shoes. I tried to imagine how a 22-year-old woman could brave this adventure by herself and not having the comfort that money afforded. It was unfathomable the terror and fear that she must have had.

When morning came, we set off to Visolaje. In my hand, I clutched a copy of my poem. I was finally going to see with my own eyes and walk the same path on the land of my ancestors.

Off the paved road we turned onto a long, winding dirt road, past bushes and trees that encroached the road. As we continued, I was able to feel the remoteness; I could smell the earth under our vehicle; my mind was alive with vicarious thoughts of living this primitive life.

With every bump of the road, I prayed to my grandmother— "Granny, I made it! I'm here. I feel you with me. I know you are watching and shining down on me."

At last, in the horizon, I could see the barn-like building come into sight. I saw the beautiful walnut tree that granny told me about all those years ago. The sun was shining down through the trees like a lattice on the ground. It was so bucolic; so surreal. I was really here.

As I stepped out of the car, I could feel the soft breeze, the fresh country air. And there it was at last. The rough-hewn, simple cottage. I scanned the property. There were the grassy, rolling hills, the trickle of the stream. It was all there just as it had been painted in my mind.

As my cousin George escorted me over the threshold, my feet touched the dirt floor. This I hadn't anticipated. Where was the tile, the carpet? No, my grandmother and her family of 12 lived on a bare earthen floor!

The inside square footage was incredibly small for a family of 12. The centerpiece of the home was a large white plastered hearth for cooking and heating. I glanced to the left and saw a crumbling door with a primitive lock. Through the door was an animal pen. I was told that the animals were kept in the same building for warmth!

While exploring the property, I saw a ladder on the outside of the house that led to an opening in the eave. Then it hit me, THIS IS WHERE THE GIRLS SLEPT! In the attic! After much admonition and objections from my cousins, I ascended the rickety ladder. When I peered into the cavernous darkness of the garret, I was hit with a damp, musty smell. On a whim, I aimed my camera into the blackness and used the flash on my camera to take several random pictures.

As I reentered the house one last time, I could see objects protruding from the earthen floor. With my hands, I began to do some excavation. After some tedious digging, I unearthed a glass pentagon-shaped pitcher, a porcelain bowl, a wooden board used to make *halušky*, a piece of a still, a rusty funnel, a teacup, and six shot glasses! All the while I was doing my archeological dig, the cousins were asking me to stop plowing up this junk! Well, I had intentions for this 'junk'!

As I surveyed the house for the last time, I allowed myself a moment to feel my grandmother in my bones and her life here. I approached the wall adjacent to the hearth. With

tears in my eyes, I unrolled my poem and pinned it to the wall. I said to myself: "I'm here, granny. I came to see and understand the life you led here; the sacrifices you made to leave this very place and make a new life for you and your own children, your children's children, and your great-great grandchildren."

The winter after my visit, the roof was blown off the house, and my grandmother's abode had to be razed. I had made it just in time.

Finding my roots was a cathartic experience. Knowing exactly what life must have been like at the end of 19th century Slovakia gives me such a feeling of appreciation for all my grandmother's sacrifices, her courage, her resilience, and her stamina. When there are days in my life that are filled with tragedy, hopelessness, or struggle, I look to my granny for her strength to push me through. She will always be my inspiration, and she will forever be knitted in my soul.

My four voyages to Slovakia over the years have given me a strong sense of my Slovak identity and a territorial belonging. I have come full circle with my grandmother and feel a sense of completeness.

...

Beverly Clifford *is a second-generation Slovak American, born and raised in the coal mining community of Pottsville, Pennsylvania. She was educated at Pennsylvania State University and San Diego State University. For 35 years she was an educator near the Mexican border. Beverly has three children, six grandchildren and is the widow of Jack Clifford, Founder of the Food Network. She loves cooking, and growing her own fruits and vegetables in the tradition of her Slovak grandmother.*

. . .

I would like to give special thanks to my cousin George Harris for escorting me to Slovakia four times.

All of the artifacts that I pulled from the earthen floor of the Martinka home are proudly displayed in my home in southern California as a gentle daily reminder of my ancestral beginnings.

The film that was developed from the pictures taken in the rafters depicts women's shoes and boots all lined up! A wink from my granny.

A GRANDDAUGHTER'S TRIBUTE

In loving memory of:
Granny & Grandpop Lazovi (Slovakia)
Baba & Gigi Skrincosky (Ukraine & Poland)

"Return not," the ocean cries.
The horizon beckons.
Tears trickle down your troubled face.
Torn between two loves.
Poverty reflects in your mother's face
Troubled by this adventure.
New-found friends push forward.
The sun winks in support.
At last, the boat weds the sea.
Toil and labor melt into the sunset.
Voices chime with struggle.
Babylon relived.
Time rehearscs a pirouette.
The mind unfolds yet is confused.
To the sea bows the earth.
Minarets dance to the pyre.
Never to return.
A gale licks the sore.
Beckoning, the child reaches out.
A new world awaits.

Chicken Paprika

(6–8 servings)

- 4 TBSP sweet paprika
- 2 TSP salt
- ¼ TSP ground black pepper
- 1 roasted chicken, cut up
- 2 TBSP vegetable oil
- 1–1½ cups water
- 2 medium carrots, sliced
- 1 onion, chopped
- 1/3 cup diced celery
- 8 oz. elbow macaroni, cooked
- 2–3 TBSP unsalted butter
- 1 cup sour cream

1. Mix paprika, salt, and pepper in a small bowl. Coat the chicken with the spice mixture.
2. Heat the oil in a large skillet and brown the chicken on all sides.
3. Add the water, carrots, onion, and celery. Cover and simmer for 45 minutes, or until the chicken is fork-tender.
4. Meanwhile, cook the macaroni according to the instructions on the package.
5. Remove the chicken from the skillet and keep it warm. Skim the fat from the pan juices.
6. In a large bowl, toss the hot macaroni with the butter until the butter melts.
7. Add the sour cream and ½ cup of the pan juices. Toss gently, to coat.
8. Serve the chicken with the macaroni. Pour the remaining pan juices into a gravy boat and serve on the side.

WHAT DOES IT MEAN TO BE RUSYN?

by Lisa A. Alzo

> "Despite the extensive research I had performed over the years, I never felt like a real genealogist until I took the trip of a lifetime in 2010 to visit Slovakia, the homeland of my ancestors."

I grew up in Western Pennsylvania, an area well-known for its large population of Slovak and Rusyn immigrants. From a very young age, I was aware of my Slovak heritage, yet it was not until 1991 that I started to explore this legacy for myself.

I was in my second year of the Master of Fine Arts Degree program in Nonfiction Writing at the University of Pittsburgh and was required to choose a topic for my thesis. A required reading for one of my literature courses was *Out of This Furnace*, the classic 1947 novel written by Thomas Bell that was well-known to Slovaks and Rusyns. Inspired by the story of Bell's immigrant ancestors, I asked my mother about our family history to learn about the life of my maternal grandmother, Verona Straka Figlar, who immigrated to the United States from the tiny village of Milpoš in 1922.

I wrote my thesis to tell my grandmother's story, and in 2001, I adapted the manuscript into a nonfiction book *Three Slovak Women*.

...

My maternal grandfather (I called him "Pap-Pap") died when I was nine. I remember him only as a short, stocky old man who was bald except for the thinning gray hair at the sides. He used to sit at the kitchen table and roll his own cigarettes, carefully filling each paper with tobacco from the turquoise Bugler can. There was always a deck of cards on the table because Pap-Pap played Solitaire (a.k.a. "Beat the Devil," as he liked to call it), for hours at a time.

Meanwhile, my grandmother was cooking what seemed like bottomless pots of chicken and vegetable soup, baking homemade golden-brown buns dusted with flour, making *bobálky* and *pirohy* at Christmas, and *paska* and *hrudka* at Easter. In all the years I knew my grandmother, I regret never asking her questions about her life in Slovakia or her immigration. She died in 1984.

Fortunately, my mother saved my grandparents' baptismal extracts, passports, photographs, and other documents. My foray into genealogical research began before there were genealogy databases on the Internet. Using the details from the family documents, I obtained key information about my grandparents from vital records, printed copies of ship manifests, naturalization papers, and other records from courthouses and libraries. I interviewed my mother, aunts, uncles, and neighbors to learn more about my grandparents' lives. Following the clues, I was able to piece together an understanding of my family history—or so I thought...

Surprise! You are Rusyn

All four of my immigrant grandparents were born in Slovakia and both sides of my family identified as Slovak. I had never heard anyone in my family use the term Rusyn. In 1994, I attended a meeting of the Carpatho-Rusyn Society in Pittsburgh, Pennsylvania, where I met others who were of Rusyn descent, among them the esteemed scholar Paul Magosci. I learned that the Rusyns are said to have settled in the Carpathian Mountain region of the former Austro-Hungarian Empire during the sixth and seventh centuries A.D. Due to the lack of any firm geographic identity, Rusyns have often been referred to as the people from "No Man's Land". Rusyn pop artist, Andy Warhol, famously described himself as coming from "Nowhere". I was fascinated and started to dig a bit deeper into my grandfather's family tree.

In 1896, my grandfather, Janoš Figlar (originally Figlyar), was in Osturňa, a village located in northeastern Slovakia not far from the Polish border. The area is known for its mountains. Osturňa is nestled in the Pieniny Mountains, and the High Tatras are just a stone's throw away. Originally settled by Ruthenians who came from the Lemko region of southern Poland, Osturňa was first mentioned in historical records in 1593.

The Carpatho-Rusyns came from small villages and were, in general, a poor people. The mountainous terrain that surrounded their villages prevented large-scale agricultural production, forcing most Carpatho-Rusyns to make a living through farming, forestry, and shepherding livestock.

A photo of Janoš (the youngest of 11 children) as a young boy sitting with his parents, siblings, and extended family provides a brief glimpse into their peasant existence consistent with that description. But his father died unexpectedly when Janoš was just a young boy. Several of his siblings died in infancy. That alone speaks of a tough mountain life.

Janoš's three older brothers immigrated to America before WW I while he earned apprenticeship and worked as a cartwright/assistant helper in the nearby town of Kežmarok. When he reached adulthood, Janoš had to enlist in the Austro-Hungarian Royal Army where he served in the infantry regiment as WW I was coming to an end.

On September 8th 1921, with forty-five dollars in his pocket, Janoš boarded the *S.S. Lapland* at Antwerp, Belgium, to sail to America. He arrived in New York on September 16th 1921, and from then on altered his name to Jan. He was going to join his brother Jacob, in Fairpoint, Ohio, a chief mining area for bituminous or soft coal. There he found work as a miner.

In fact, all three of his older brothers had settled in the vicinity. The town drew a large population of Rusyn immigrants, many of whom came from Osturňa. His brother Joseph was a charter member of St. Nicholas Greek Catholic Autonomic Church #362 (today St. Nicholas Orthodox Church), built as a carbon copy of St. Michael's Church in Osturňa. St. Nicholas Church was where my grandparents got married and my mother was baptized.

The young family moved around at the beginning, living with various family members before my grandfather obtained a job with the US Steel Duquesne Works. There, he worked eight hours a day in the ore yard, whether in 90-degree heat and his clothes stuck like glue against his sweat-covered body or in the biting cold of winter when he wore extra thick long underwear beneath his work pants and shirt. He prided himself in being a good worker. My grandfather took his oath to become an American citizen in 1939. He was now going by the name of "John Figlar." In 1944, my grandparents purchased their very own home.

By all accounts, my grandfather was a complex man. My mother referred to him as a "Dr. Jekyll-Mr. Hyde" personality. Like so many of his fellow steelworkers, my grandfather often stopped at the local bar after work. Alcohol offered him a reprieve from the drudgery of his job. While sober, he was a man who never missed a day on the job and worked hard to provide food, clothing, and eventually purchase a home for his family. He would stay up late to help his daughter (my mother) with a difficult math assignment; he played card games, built puzzles with her and her siblings, loved to dance, and enjoyed telling a good joke. But when he was drunk, he was full of rage. My mother recalled that liquor transformed his naturally fickle temper into a violent rage that was difficult to control which greatly impacted the family dynamics. My grandfather died in 1974 from a blood clot to his heart. As

a child, I was unaware of the impact my grandfather's drinking had on his wife and children. I wonder how much of an influence his own upbringing had on his behavior.

Despite the extensive research I had performed over the years, I never felt like a real genealogist until I took the trip of a lifetime in 2010 to visit Slovakia, the homeland of my ancestors. Unfortunately, I was unable to make it to Osturňa due to flooding. It was not meant to be. I returned in 2012 and I finally got the chance to walk in my grandfather's footsteps.

During the drive to Osturňa, I saw some spectacular views of Slovakia's countryside, especially the magnificent Tatra mountains. Together with my Slovak guide, we passed through Levoča, a former royal town that sits in the center of the Spiš region. The roads began to narrow the closer we got to Osturňa. We wound our way through hills and valleys, passing many villages along the way. I was so excited to see the sign welcoming me to the place where my grandfather was born. I had arrived!

Osturňa is one of the few places in Slovakia that has preserved the historic wooden architecture. It was like stepping back in time. The village is a monumental reserve of folk architecture. Unfortunately, there was no way of knowing which houses my ancestors lived in since I learned that the houses there had gone through a renumbering every 50 years. As we drove along, I could not help thinking of my grandfather and wondering how he managed to get from this place all the way to Duquesne, Pennsylvania!

During the night I listened to the rain hitting the windows. In the morning, I could hear bells dinging outside my window as the sheep moved about along the hillside as well as an occasional "Baaa!" The crowing of a fine rooster served as my alarm clock. I breathed in the crisp morning air. Ah… Osturňa! I imagined my grandfather waking up to those same sounds and smells.

But my genealogical search that day was not so successful. I found no graves, just a few brief mentions of the family name in historical documents. I tried another local archive in a different village, hoping to find at least the register of my grandfather's birth and a death record for my great-grandfather's brother. I had hoped to discover more, and part of me was disappointed that I could not make any family connections or get all the information. But I was also grateful and satisfied. I had done it! I was here at long last!

Later that day, I visited St. Michael's Church. I knew about the building's restoration and renovations because I had participated in a fundraiser in America to help raise money for the cause. I was overcome with emotion to stand in the church where my grandfather had been baptized. The village priest allowed me to look through the church books. While I already had information about births, marriages, and deaths for many of my relatives, I found some additional records. But there were other ancestors whose names were not in the books. I know the Figlar family moved to Podolínec at some point, so my search would have to continue there.

Would the records office in Podolínec reveal anything about my great-grandparents or my grandfather's sister, Katerina Hotáry? I knew her married name from a receipt for a money order my grandfather had sent her in 1927 after the death of their mother. The clerk found the registration of Katerina's marriage, the birth registrations of their sons, as well as my great-grandmother's death certificate.

The other office clerk who happened to be working that day told us she knew the Hotáry family and happily offered to introduce me. We walked down the road to a row of houses and knocked on the door. A woman answered. It turned out that she had a handwritten family tree with all of the descendants of Michal and Katerina Hotáry. The serendipitous meeting of cousins, an avalanche of photographs, a cemetery and house visit (where Michal and Katerina lived) followed suit. I felt like I had won the family history lottery!

Osturňa prides itself for its ability to stand on its feet, to not give up and fight for its rights. Harsh natural conditions, hard and honest work, a strong family bond, and deep faith in God were able to awaken in its people strength, steadfastness, and the will to go further. After my own journey to Osturňa, I now deeply appreciate what those words mean.

My understanding of what it means to be Rusyn continues to grow with an even deeper appreciation of the culture. But it is more than just language, religion, food, and traditions. Genealogy research and DNA testing validated my tangible connections to the people of the area known as the Carpathian Rus', but the sense of identity comes from within.

My grandfather may have identified himself as Slovak, but if I could talk with my grandfather today, I would share with him the details I had uncovered about our heritage. I imagine he would proudly quote the lines written by 19th-century Carpatho-Rusyn national awakener Aleksander Duchnovyc, "I was, am, and will remain a Rusyn."

...

Lisa A. Alzo *is a freelance writer, instructor, and internationally recognized lecturer, specializing in Eastern European research and writing your family history. Lisa is the author of eleven books, including The Family Tree Polish, Czech and Slovak Genealogy Guide, and the award-winning Three Slovak Women. Lisa has been researching her Slovak and Rusyn heritage for more than 30 years and has published hundreds of magazine articles on genealogy and family history.*

Hrudka (Easter Cheese)

The traditional Easter "cheese," with its bland but sweet taste, symbolizes the moderation Christians should have in all things.

- 4 cups whole milk
- 13 extra large eggs
- 1 cup sugar (start with ½ cup and add more, to taste)
- Dash of salt
- ¼ TSP vanilla extract

1. Place all the ingredients in a pan and combine thoroughly with a whisk or a mixer.
2. Place the pan in another pan of water (similar to a double boiler) and cook.
3. Using a wooden spoon, stir often and only in one direction, always bringing the mixture towards you.
4. When the mixture starts to firm up and looks like scrambled eggs, add approximately 1 cup of cold water and continue cooking, until it firms up.
5. Remove the pot from the heat and pour the mixture into a colander set in a bowl, with a suitably-sized piece of cheesecloth lining the colander and hanging over the rim.
6. Gather up the edges of the cheesecloth and squeeze the contents until all the "juice" is removed. Tie the cheesecloth in a knot and let it hang until firm (approximately 3-4 hours). Use a container to catch the drips.
7. Remove the cheesecloth and refrigerate.
8. Slice and serve.

WHERE THE OCEAN ENDS AND A NEW LAND BEGINS

by María Elena
Doello Jurado
(based on the writings of Marcela Fajmonova)

"There we were in Buenos Aires, Argentina. Everybody was staring at us, but I felt they were watching with admiration and curiosity. No wonder. We were dressed in our finest kroje, handmade by our grandmother."

My family hails from Veľká Maňa in southern Slovakia, a town so beautiful in my memories that I struggle to describe its charms. It had only one street, a church flanked by chestnut trees, and an antique fairytale castle surrounded by a grove. Crystal water lakes and gentle hills wrapped around the town like a handkerchief. In the surrounding forests, deer, wild boars and also bears roamed free. During the hunting season, pheasants used to fall from the sky like hail.

In the 1920s, there was only one store in the town and it sold everything, including ice during the summer months. There was a town hall with a big ballroom, which had a speaker and a gramophone, where parties and celebrations were held. It would play music so loud it could be heard across town, especially in the summer.

I have many sweet memories of the town and its people. I remember how on Christmas Eve, the town's boys and girls would sing carols door to door. The carolers would then be invited to come and share in the Christmas joy and food as guests of honor. Weddings would last an entire week, and

locals would hire gypsy musicians to play Strauss's waltzes, Hungarian czardas, or Smetana's and Listz's music that we all loved so much. None of the food was bought and all the wine came from our own vineyards. But one memory stands out.

One day, all of us school children got dressed in our Sunday best and were carrying flowers. We marched all the way to the local train station. There, a decorated train was wrapped in the flag of the newly erected Czechoslovak Republic. Our beloved president Tomas Garrigue Masaryk was leaning out of the train window, waving at us and thanking us for our love and support. In return, we showered him and the train with flowers.

That was my hometown and that was the place my grandma Maria called home.

In 1891, Maria married my grandfather, a fine and educated man who would become the local mayor. She was only 15 years old. Grandfather was fond of horses. One day, he bought a bad-tempered steed, and when he went to give it a bath in the river, the horse threw him off, killing him and making my grandma a very young widow. She was now all by herself, responsible for four children, including my mother Malonia who was her only daughter.

Perhaps it would have been a fairytale tranquil life if the WW I did not hit the family so hard. All of my mother's children had died of cholera before I was born and there was no news of my father who had gone to fight in the war. With the men gone, the women of the family (both by blood and by law) had to stick together to get by.

We lived with grandma. I still remember her house. It was big and glorious. There was a spacious yard, a dovecote, heaps of hay at the back, a barn, and beyond it were plum trees we used to climb to reach the cherry tree on the other side of the fence on the land of an aristocrat. But as the war unraveled, all the local horses disappeared. They were handed over to the Austro-Hungarian army. We were left with two cows and two foals that the army did not bother to take because they were too skinny and small to be of use to them. Everything else was swept away, and we even had to share our home with them. I remember that the officers stayed in the house while the soldiers were relegated to the stables.

Then one day my mother received my father's documents and prayer book. The army considered him dead. All she had left of him was a backpack with his belongings. I cannot imagine how traumatic it must have been for her. Not only had she lost all of her children, but now her man was gone too. It would take a while for these wounds to heal. Eventually, after years of loneliness, mother was about to re-marry but then something remarkable happened.

One of her brothers was chopping firewood in the yard when he saw the figure of a man approaching the house. When the man got closer, he recognized him. It was my father!

My uncle dropped the ax and ran towards the house shouting, "Sandor is back from the dead!" My mother was fetching water from the well when she heard the commotion. She dropped the bucket and fainted right then and there.

As you can imagine, my father had an unbelievable story to tell. He and other Austro-Hungarian soldiers were surrounded by Russian troops and taken as prisoners. He spent years as a prisoner of war in Russia. When the war ended, my father together with others in the same predicament, managed to escape by taking the colonel's wagon and horses which he had tended. He had no documents to prove his identity, so the odyssey back home was rife with obstacles and challenges, but he made it!

Miraculously, life returned to normal.

My sister was born, then me, and finally, my brother. But the war had changed my father. It awakened his adventurous spirit. Home life in Slovakia no longer satisfied him, and so he came up with the idea of going to America to try his luck there. Mother was far from thrilled. She would be left alone again with three children, but father was determined, and nothing could change his mind, not even his wife and family.

He left for South America in 1923 with the promise of returning the next year, but that did not happen. The situation was all too familiar for my mom who eventually grew tired of doing everything by herself and decided to go and search for her husband. She thought it would not take more than a few months. Grandma protested. How could she leave her young children behind? But no pleading or reasoning worked, and mother left for the Americas, too in 1926.

With mom and dad gone, we were looked after by our grandmother and stayed in her marvelous home as a result. I cherish those years and moments. They were filled with heartfelt memories but also some troubling ones.

One day in the yard, I was cracking nuts that were still green, and I ended up with stains all over my hands. Grandma was about to tell me off for getting so dirty when we heard screaming coming from the thresher. There had been an accident. My grandma covered my face with her apron so I could not see a legless woman being taken away. She ran inside with me and told me that if I behaved, she was going to buy me an orange. An orange! It was the most delicious thing anyone could give me. We used to have cherries, and all kinds of berries at home, but never oranges. Those cost one crown! Her distraction had worked, and my attention remained focused on the fruit.

Several years went by, and the only thing that came from America once in a while was a parcel or a little bit of money

and a couple of photographs of my parents who were reunited in Argentina. Once, we received new shoes. On Sunday, we put them on instead of the leather boots that grandma used to keep spotless and strode off proudly to church. We arrived a little late but went in anyway. The priest looked at us and said, "You are not only late, but also barefoot!" We had to get out of our row for the priest to take a closer look at us. He proclaimed, "How lucky these orphans are. Their parents sent them white sneakers from America."

We were the center of everyone's attention. No one had sneakers but us! However, when grandma found out that the priest had called us orphans, she got really angry and condemned his actions by not inviting him for supper at the house for a long time.

Grandma never let us feel like we were a burden. She was sweet and tender to us always.

I will never forget the day I was bathing with the other kids in the creek when I saw a rider in the distance fast approaching. It was my uncle bearing sad news. "Come home. Your grandma is dead." He said flatly. My whole world collapsed with those words.

I grabbed my clothes and ran home without getting dressed. I kept falling over and over. I fell, got back up again, and kept running. I thought that if I ran fast enough, I would be able to keep her by my side. My feet were all cut, but I did not feel any pain. I wanted to reach her and tell her to not go away, to stay with me. When I got home,

I sat in the corner of her room, looking at her lifeless body for hours.

Just like that, everything changed. Nobody wanted to take in the 'orphans', and so one of my uncles sent a telegram to my parents in Argentina asking them to come back for us. Instead, tickets were sent for us to undertake the journey across the Atlantic by ourselves. I was eight, my sister was fourteen, and my brother only seven.

Before we left, everybody in town showered us with goodbye presents. Even the priest invited us to his house and gave us a Bible. The final goodbye was for my grandma. We went to the cemetery, and as we stood by her grave, I felt her fragile silhouette beside me saying, "Be good and I will buy you an orange." Right then and there, I felt protected.

An uncle took us to Hamburg by train. We traveled for several days, landscape after landscape. Everything was different. Finally, we arrived at the docklands and were checked by a doctor. To everyone's surprise, we were declared unfit to travel as my brother had contracted measles during the trip to Germany. What should we do? Stay in Hamburg until the illness was over?

Instead, we returned to Slovakia. How wonderful it was to be back; the familiar houses, the people we knew.

I went up and down grandmother's stairs, touching all the furniture in the house, sitting again in the kitchen and the dining room which were gigantic in my view! I also visited the stables. After that, I went to my mom's house which was exactly as it had been left. I looked at my father's portrait from when he was a young man. It was the only memory I had of him. I didn't know him. I couldn't even remember his voice.

I was happy to be home, but we would not stay there long.

As soon as my brother recovered from his illness, we traveled again to Hamburg where we were met by a Hungarian couple that my uncle knew, also headed to Argentina. He hired them to take care of us.

We said goodbye to our uncle who was crying as if he was never going to see us again. He hugged us so tight and wouldn't let us go. Between laughter and tears, we first boarded a small boat that took us to the ship that was about to set sail to Argentina.

The liner was huge. It had two chimneys. I was amazed at how this enormous thing could even float. We climbed on the ship accompanied by our guardians who were thankfully loving and gentle people.

Life on board was exciting at first. We met sailors who spoke our language and made friends. We could wander into the kitchen and explore the ship.

In the morning, we got up early and went to the dining room to have breakfast. The tables, covered with white tablecloths, offered delicious toast, sweets, butter, and even croissants on some days. The tasty smell of coffee wafted all around. The ship resembled a paradise!

But as days passed by, the liner no longer seemed as huge as before. Rather, it started to resemble a walnut shell surrounded by water. Then a storm came and, the sailors knocked on the door asking us to close the portholes. Outside our cabin, passengers were throwing up, but no one was allowed to go on the decks to get fresh air. I had never been so scared in my life. The sailors pushed me back inside my cabin and forbade me from leaving the room. The ship was rolling from side to side. Things were falling off the shelves.

We spent two days rocking like that in the open ocean. When the storm had passed, everything went back to normal. There was bacon and eggs for breakfast again!

The ship eventually anchored in a port a few days later. A small boat came by, and to my amazement, it was filled with oranges. Someone threw a rope from our ship, and tied a basket to it, filled with the delicious fruit. I ran towards my sailor friends, and they gave me a few. I had never smelled anything so wonderful. I felt grandma smiling down on me. Then we were off again, sailing toward the endless horizon.

I was fascinated by the colors of the ocean that were sometimes blue and sometimes green. I loved sitting near the lifeboats, watching the watery expanse and forgetting about time. I wondered what awaited my siblings and I on the other side; where the ocean ends, and a new land begins.

Twenty-one days had gone by when our journey finally came to an end. We reached Buenos Aires, Argentina in December 1929. We hadn't seen our parents for three years. As we stood bewildered on the main deck, we heard someone calling us by our names. My sister, who was already 14, was the only one who remembered how our mother looked. She pointed to a couple in the distance and said, "That woman and that man standing over there are our parents." Mother was crying. I said to my siblings, "I am sure she is crying of happiness, but let's wait until she meets us".

There we were in Buenos Aires, Argentina. But we still had to go through the customs and immigration procedures before we were handed off to our parents. Everybody was staring at us, but I felt they were watching with admiration and curiosity. No wonder, we were dressed in our finest *kroje*, handmade made by our grandmother.

But our parents took us to a shop in the city, bought new clothes for us, and made us change right then and there. I felt different, and something close to disappointment pulled on my heartstrings. Next, we boarded a train that would take us to our new home. I was finally with my parents again. So why was I unhappy? Was it because I didn't know them or because I didn't love them?

I missed my little town in Slovakia; the hills, the creeks, the cherry trees. I missed grandmother.

When we arrived at my parents' apartment, it was so tiny I could never imagine living there. Gone was the large house of my grandma. I was forced to adapt to a new routine. Days would go on, with father leaving for work at the factory at six in the morning, then coming back for lunch at noon and returning home once again late in the evening. He would lay for a while, and then drink something through a straw. Later I learned the drink was called *mate*, a typical herbal infusion in Argentina.

Mother stayed home with us. It all seemed so strange, as if I had lost my freedom. I constantly felt like I was drowning. There was no more running in the snow on the way to school. No friends to play or bathe in the creeks with. Every day felt the same, and we did not understand the new language around us.

Months went by, each heavier than the previous one. I thought even my smile had left me. I felt like I was dying, like my wings were clipped. I could no longer run, sing, or fly like I used to. I struggled to adjust to a new life in a new culture.

Several months later, I started attending a Czechoslovak school in the morning and a Spanish one in the afternoon. I started to learn the new language, and I was relieved to be able to go out of the tiny flat. Nevertheless, it took me years to get used to this new country.

With time, I learned to love Argentina but the reminiscences of my childhood in my beloved little town in Slovakia were never erased from my memory.

...

María Elena Doello Jurado was born in 1953 in La Plata, Argentina, where she grew up and graduated as a teacher for children with special needs. She then worked at the National Institute of Statistics before retiring. It has been María's' dream to publish the writings of her Slovak mother ever since she passed away in 1994. María is happily married and has three children.

IN THE
CANADIAN WILDERNESS

by Rudy Bies

> "The Slovak Bradlo community existed from 1930 to approximately 1960. Most of its inhabitants were immigrants from Slovakia."

My parents Jan and Anna Bies rest in Canadian soil. The front of their tombstone is inscribed in Slovak and the back in English, a symbol of their eternal connection to the homeland.

...

Ján and Anna were born in the hilly region near Myjava in western Slovakia at the turn of the 20th century in the twilight years of the Austro-Hungarian Empire. The highlanders were known in Slovakia for their no-nonsense approach to life, iconic blue and white *kroj*, and high-quality plum brandy.

My father was but a boy when the WW I was proclaimed. He almost never talked about this experience, except mentioning that his older brother sustained a serious leg injury on the battlefield. It was mother who would recall every year, on Remembrance Day, that dreadful afternoon in 1914 when a crier arrived in her village.

She was only eight years old and the people around her started to weep as the crier instructed every eligible man to make his way to the train station and leave for the front. That day, pacts were made. Brothers promised brothers that should one of them die in battle, the other would look after the family.

Anna's own family would feel the pain of loss as the war ravaged Europe. Her father returned an invalid, but her uncle would not be so lucky as to see his family again.

When the Great War ended and Austria-Hungary crumbled, life started looking up again. Czechoslovakia was founded, and it seemed that peace was restored in Europe. My father told countless stories of his adventures as a boy, a teenager, and finally as a soldier in that young republic. However, the good times would not last forever. When his dad passed away at the young age of 47, the family was plunged into hardship. Could the faraway North America be a solution?

For decades, able-bodied men from all over Slovakia were leaving to work in the mines, forests, and factories of the New World. Women were going to find jobs too, they worked as nannies and care-givers in wealthy households.

As my father considered his options, he did not have to look far for guidance. In fact, he would not be the first member of the family to cross the ocean. At the turn of the century, his own mother had journeyed to the US to work as a nanny. She only returned to Slovakia when her husband could not pass the medical exam that would have allowed him to join her.

Thanks to her adventurous spirit, the journey across the Atlantic was no untrodden path for father, who was recruited by an agent in Europe in 1927 to come and work in Western Canada as an agricultural worker. He left in the second wave of Slovak immigration to Canada and was followed by his brothers Pavel and Michal as soon as he managed to put aside enough money for their passage.

Canada became a popular destination when the United States introduced an immigration quota system in the aftermath of the war. The restrictions drastically curbed the number of incoming Eastern Europeans. Meanwhile, the so-called Railways Agreement of 1925 opened Canada up to immigration. The country began recruiting agricultural and industrial laborers from 'non-preferred' European countries, including Czechoslovakia. It was an opportunity my father did not hesitate to seize.

Many times over his life, father recounted the minute details of his first journey to Canada. It was an exciting experience for a young and adventurous twenty-three-year-old man: the sea sickness, the icebergs, and the apprehension everyone faced in passing the physical examination in Antwerp, Holland when nothing was yet certain. Without the green pass from the authorities, a person would not be allowed to board the vessel for Canada. Not everyone was as fortunate as dad. Families had to be broken up when a member, sometimes a child, was turned back to their country of origin because they failed to pass the medical exam.

Father travelled on the C. P. R. Steamer *Montnairn* arriving in Quebec City, Canada in May 1927. But the journey was not over. My father's destination was on the other end of another long journey, this time by train to Luseland, Saskatchewan.

To his horror, the employer who should have greeted him at the train station was nowhere in sight when father arrived. In fact, the man never showed up. Alone in a foreign country and worn out by the travel, dad became quite distressed. His agitated behavior drew the attention of a police officer, but dad spoke no English and so he could not explain what had happened to him. The policeman took him to a restaurant where there was someone who could understand dad's language. When his predicament was understood, the officer telephoned local farmers until he found one that could give my father work. I can hardly imagine how relieved he must have been.

During his first years, Ján worked on farms in Saskatchewan and in Northern Alberta. Although it was familiar work that he had known from home, eventually he decided to move on with life and headed to Montreal in 1929 where a large Slovak community of newly landed immigrants resided. However, work did not materialize for him there, so in the spring of 1930 he departed for the great Canadian prairies of Western Canada once again, and returned in the fall.

At the time, an army of unemployed men was riding the railroads of Canada in search of work. It was at the onset of the Great Depression, and the employment conditions in the 1930s were the worst yet. My father was one of many who struggled to make ends meet.

To add insult to injury, it was November and the weather had turned bitterly cold. At Sioux Lookout in Ontario, a sympathetic train man allowed several of the men traversing the country in search of work to sleep in a box car loaded with coal. At least they could stay warm. While they were asleep, the box car that those men were in was shunted by the train crew to Hearst and left behind much to the surprise of its temporary inhabitants. They were not allowed back on the train.

Father spent a few days wandering around the town before continuing his journey. At a local store, he met several Slovaks from a nearby Slovak settlement. That was how he became aware of the Slovak colony just 11 kilometers away, which was later named Bradlo in honor of Bradlo, Slovakia which was the monumental resting place of the great Slovak hero, General Milan Rastislav Štefánik. Finally, a promising work opportunity showed up at a hydro electric project near Fraserdale, Ontario.

In order to get it, father camped on the outskirts along with hundreds of other unemployed men, hoping for Lady Luck to smile upon them. He was not alone and the gloomy days would be soothed by his brother Michal who joined him in the quest. When dad managed to get a job on the project at last, he sneaked his brother under his bed and smuggled him food from the kitchen dining room every night. Coffee, he joked, was not possible to bring.

The loneliness of single life in Canada started to wear on the brothers, and after 18 months at this lucrative job, father returned to Hrašné in Slovakia in the fall of 1931 with both his brothers. It was time to get married. A beautiful young lady had caught dad's eye before he left for Canada in 1927. He made sure to check back with her aunt to find out if the lady was still unmarried. She was, and so he started corresponding with her from Canada. It was a success and my father married Anna Hučková in a local Lutheran church in 1932, a few months after his return. For a people who had experienced the horrors and hardships of war, they did not waste time in moving forward. Soon after, their first baby, daughter Olga, was born.

Father returned in 1932, leaving his wife and daughter in Slovakia. However, it was only after his arrival back in Canada that he found out his job at Fraserdale was no longer available. After all, he had left over a year ago and jobs were still more precious than gold. So, he purchased two homesteads in the Slovak settlement of Bradlo, one for himself and one for his brother Michal. His other brother Pavel had already married and started a family in Slovakia and did not aspire to return to Canada. It must have been difficult for dad who, at the time, did not make enough money to bring his wife and baby daughter over. But pride kept him from writing to Slovakia to say how bad things truly were.

Meanwhile on the other side of the ocean, mother took the initiative to join her husband in Canada and persuaded her father to fund her passage. She arrived in Canada in the summer of 1933 and was shocked at the wilderness that surrounded her. Even so, she put her fate in God's hands and God did not abandon her. The young family set up a homestead in Bradlo, and with the $70 that was left over from mother's journey to Canada, father bought a horse for the farm.

Mom used to say that it took two to succeed. It was certainly true in Bradlo, where those who brought their wives did better than those who did not. That was true for my family, too. They were stronger together.

My parents would end up living in Bradlo for most of their lives, but they made two attempts to start anew elsewhere in Canada. The first to Dobie, Ontario in 1939 came when Slovakia became a German satellite following the 1938 Munich Agreement, a foreplay to WW II. This development would affect not just people in Slovakia, but also Slovaks who lived far away.

Slovak residents in Canada not yet naturalized were obliged to register with the Royal Canadian Mounted Police as aliens. My father was naturalized but my mother and daughter Olga were not. Olga, who was seven at the time, recalled returning home after school to find visitors there. The women were crying as was our mom. The war had started, and the family would not receive letters from relatives in Slovakia until 1941.

My father faced outright discrimination caused by the war (because Slovakia was a satellite state of the Nazis) and was forced to return to Bradlo in 1941 where he purchased a truck and worked on highway construction until 1944. In 1944, he managed to get a job working in a gold mine in Geraldton. Following an accident in the mine, in which dad was seriously injured and his partner killed, the family that was now comprised of seven children moved back to Bradlo in 1946 for good.

Bradlo proved to be a true refuge, which is how the community started in 1930, thanks to the involvement of Slovak Catholic priests in Montreal. Unemployed Slovak men were its first inhabitants, and the community grew after that. Most residents came from different parts of Slovakia. The school became the magnet where community events took place including concerts, dances, meetings, English lessons for new immigrants, and of course, a school for the children. At its peak in the late 1930s, the community had a post office, a church, a general store, a meeting hall, a school and close to 150 inhabitants. The homesteaders helped each other to build homes and to create a community. Neighbors worked together, helped one another, and celebrated together; weddings, births of children, and funerals were all a part of the daily cycle of life in Bradlo.

Life there was also marked by the seasons. Farm chores such as the seeding of crops, haying, harvesting, zabíjačky (pig slaughter), and preparing firewood for winter formed the daily rhythm. To earn money, the men would leave home to work in the surrounding lumber camps. For long periods during the summers and winters, the women would be left alone to look after the homestead. When the homestead became snowbound, there was a constant threat of chimney fires and serious winter ailments with the children. The nearest town was 11 kilometers away, and could only be accessed by snow plane or by walking.

Growing up in Bradlo was an adventure, that's for sure. Life did not feel like a hardship to me. I enjoyed the get togethers that my parents had with their Slovak neighbors. They were a generation that liked to sing. The earlier residents made their own music playing the accordion and the fiddle. Togetherness, dancing, singing, and laughing eased the pain of separation from homeland. Their folk songs spoke to my heart.

At school, I was taught little about Czechoslovakia and even less about Slovakia. I had no Czechoslovak nor Slovak heroes. It was from my parents and their friends that I learned about the homeland, the language, and the culture of the Slovaks. In the winter of 1949, our teacher announced that Czechoslovakia had just won the World Hockey Championship. She told me that I should be proud because my parents are Czechoslovaks. My parents certainly were beaming.

By far the major event of the year was the Christmas Concert. The excitement started with the building of the stage. Each year, father volunteered to construct it. The sound of the sawing, hammering, and the smell of the fresh sawdust created a very special atmosphere for me. Meanwhile, the teacher busily rehearsed with the students in the one-room schoolhouse that was soon transformed into a magical theater.

Letters from home arrived to update the families; some with good news and some with sad news. When a letter arrived, Bradlo families gathered to anxiously read about the developments from home. Letters usually contained family photographs, and these were delicately passed around for all to cherish. Yet, homesickness abounded. My mother often talked about saying goodbye to her most beloved family in 1933 saying, "I left behind my father, mother, brothers, and sisters to travel to a new country for a piece of bread."

One day in May of 1956, we were working on the spring seeding at the farm when a letter arrived from Europe. It contained tragic news. Dad's mother passed away and had already been buried. There was sadness in dad's voice as he shared the news with us and then we just carried on working. But I know that he was heartbroken. I am sure he hoped that he could one day return triumphantly home and make his mother's life better. Like the children of many immigrants, I have never met my grandparents nor heard their voices. That part of my life will never be complete.

The last resident left Bradlo in the late 1960s. However, the descendants of Bradlo's original homesteaders have not forgotten them. Over the past twenty-five years, they have placed markers around the town of Hearst, Ontario to remember their contribution to its history. To celebrate the 92nd anniversary of Bradlo's founding, a very special monument was installed to mark the site of the village. A large local northern Ontario granite rock weighing 11 tons is located at the corner of Ch. Bradlo Road and Ch. Caithness Road.

After 92 years, all of the original homesteaders have passed. Only a handful of the first children, now in their nineties, remain. Only three families live there now. Although Bradlo is almost totally abandoned, it remains a symbol of the Slovak immigrant experience in Canada between the world wars, and its spirit will live on forever in the hearts of the descendants.

The respect of Bradlo's original settlers for education was instilled in their children. Many like myself, went on to university, received college degrees, and went on to have professional careers. Integrity, work ethic, and strong family bond were the building blocks on which I have created my own life. I have been blessed with a wonderful wife Gloria, who is not only the love of my life but also my best friend. Together we have built a home where we raised our three children. As my mother often said- it takes two to succeed.

I hope that this book will be a window for Slovaks currently living in Slovakia, to look across that wide ocean, and connect with descendants of cousins who had left Slovakia for Canada almost one hundred years ago. We Slovaks in Canada gratefully extend our hand.

Rudy Bies *was born in Ontario in 1938 to Slovak parents as one of seven brothers and sisters. He spent his first 19 years on the Homestead in Bradlo, Ontario. Rudy has been practicing professional engineering for over 40 years and has had long career at Ontario Hydro and at Atomic Energy of Canada. As a proud Slovak Canadian, Rudy has spent countless hours researching and celebrating his heritage. He has recently written the 2nd edition of his book Bradlo and Other Slovak Pioneer Footprints in Northern Ontario and played an active role in the installation of the Bradlo Memorial Monument in Bradlo.*

Sweet Fried Cabbage for Halušky

- Oil or butter, for frying
- 1 onion, chopped
- 1 small head of cabbage, finely cut
- Salt
- Bacon, finely chopped (optional)

1. Heat the oil or butter in a large pan and add the onion. Cook over medium heat, until softened.

2. Add the cabbage, then salt to taste. Stir frequently, to prevent the cabbage from burning.

3. Add the bacon, if using. Cook until the bacon and cabbage are cooked.

4. The cabbage mixture can be stirred into halušky or cooked noodles of any kind.

A BOY FROM FIĽAKOVO

by Frank Lowy

"Great geopolitical forces were at work and there was nothing we could do."

I was just a boy when WW II disrupted my universe, pulled me out of my small Slovak hometown, and took me away from everything I knew. Since then, I have returned to Fiľakovo many times and walked its streets, trying to remember the smell of those sweet years before things turned ugly for the Jewish community of Slovakia.

I am 91 as I write this story. I am sitting in my study in Tel-Aviv, freeing my mind to float back to Fiľakovo in 1930, where I was born into a close-knit religious family, surrounded by a Jewish community of about 200 souls. They were my whole world. We and the others followed the Jewish calendar religiously, which centred around the local synagogue. Everyone contributed to its upkeep and towards the rabbi's salary. It was called a 'culture tax'. But let's return to me and my family.

Although I was born in the depths of the global depression, we were always clothed, fed, and educated. Our lives were simple and wholesome. We had fruit trees, grew vegetables, and drew water from a large handpump in the garden. I was bathed on the kitchen table, and us four children shared beds. From the front room facing the street, mother ran a grocery store selling sugar, bread, flour, and other staples. Bells were attached to the door and whenever we heard them tinkle, we knew a customer had arrived. I used to hear it a lot. As the youngest child, I spent most of my time during the first years of life with my mother. Her family, the Grunfelds, hailed from Revúca where they also ran a grocery store. The highlight of our year was taking a train to visit them in the summer. I still remember carefree play with my cousins, especially with the blue-eyed girls Renée and Rebecca. Our families didn't meet very often, but the distance between us was bridged with weekly letters full of domestic details and words of love.

My father, Hugo, was born into a large family of a former teacher. His father gave up teaching to become an innkeeper, so he could better support his family. The family moved to Fiľakovo where they lived behind the inn. When he passed away, my grandmother remained there with her daughter and family. Our lives were interwoven with theirs, and mother would often leave me to play with my cousin under the watchful eye of my grandmother.

Most of us lived humbly, but my father's brother, Leopold, was one of a handful of wealthy men in Fiľakovo. He earned

his fortune by running an exclusive agency for the products made by the town's stove and kitchenware factory. Leopold lived in a big house that we only visited once in a blue moon. I did not care much about that at the time. What fascinated me was his car in which I never got to ride. I had to manage with a bicycle that I was allowed to use to run errands for mother's shop. I was so small, I had to ride under the cross bar.

By 1936, it was time for me to attend school, play soccer with a ball made from socks during breaks, and head to a Hebrew class after school when the other children went home. I had to go on Sundays too, but occasionally a miracle happened. On those memorable days, father would turn up, talk to the Hebrew teacher and the next minute, I was released. Holding father's hand, we walked across the fields to the local soccer ground where the team of Fiľakovo, famous for its prowess in the district and beyond, was playing. Men of the Jewish community were big supporters and would sit together on the stand.

It is one of my most cherished memories to be there with father, freed from Hebrew class and watching our team surrounded by men we knew well. I treasure that moment, because I did not see much of my father in those days. He was impacted by the Great Depression and had to work as a travelling salesman for his brother, Leopold, during the week to make ends meet. He returned on Fridays, and I ran home after school to wait for him. Seeing him walk through the door gave me boundless joy. Sometimes, I would even wait at the railway station near our house and run into his arms.

It was a tranquil time in Fiľakovo. Although everyone knew we were Jews, for my first seven or so years, we were not harassed, and there was no official anti-Semitism. There were other minorities in our town too, but we rarely interacted. As far as possible, the Slovaks, the Hungarians, the Roma, and the Jews all kept to their own.

The country was led by Tomáš Garrigue Masaryk, a liberal whom we trusted and who appreciated the Jewish culture. In 1935, Edvard Beneš followed Masaryk's lead. He was a genuine liberal democrat, and we felt protected.

But then came 1938, and the earth beneath our feet started to tremble.

Great geopolitical forces were at work, and there was nothing we could do to stop them. Under the Munich agreement, Germany gained permission to occupy the Sudetenland, the

areas in the Czech lands that were a home to a large German minority. This happened just before my eighth birthday, and it left us exposed and nervous. Czechoslovakia was wounded, and soon Poland and Hungary would also start claiming a share of our weakened country.

Any remaining sense of security was shattered a few weeks after my birthday. The news of *Kristallnacht*, a pogrom against Jews throughout Nazi Germany, came as a shock. I could feel anxiety in our community. It was just the beginning. Soon after, Hungary took the Magyar-inhabited southern part of Slovakia and Carpatho-Ruthenia, and Slovakia claimed independence from Prague. All I could feel was raw fear.

In the turmoil, the borders closed and our annual and much looked forward to holidays to Revúca, now under Slovak rule, stopped. Our town fell under Hungarian rule and anti-Semitism rose steeply every day.

Suddenly, Jews were deprived of opportunities to work and own businesses or property. Mother was forced to take a non--Jewish partner into her grocery shop, so his name could appear on the license instead of hers. It was no longer possible for us to keep our heads down and get on with life. In such a small town, we became an immediate target. My friends and I were harassed on the way to and from school. It was humiliating and I was afraid, but I knew I could not afford to show weakness.

Uncle Leopold was forced to take a business partner too, but with Slovakia cut off and the future uncertain, trade was declining, and many were out of work. When Father lost his job, our house was at risk of being repossessed. I remember how distressed my parents were, but I also recall the enormous relief when mother's family came to the rescue. Her brothers filled a couple of suitcases with cash, traversed the border, and arrived in time to pay out the mortgage and save our house. The memory of that unquestioning family support—the warmth, generosity, and kinship. The feeling that when in need, the family would provide, has remained with me ever since. It is imprinted in my mind. Any problem for one was a problem for them all.

In 1942, we received chilling news. As part of a general round-up of Jews in Slovakia, mother's family was being deported. Several letters described the deportations and in April, mother opened a heartbreaking letter from her brother Géza. He was in despair about the plight of the children.

'I would very much like to ask you if you could take our dear children to be with you. Although I know you are not in an easy situation, one only pities the little ones. We can manage somehow. We could arrange to get them to [word deleted by censors] and you could come and meet them there, if we are still here at that time.'

Without a moment's delay, my parents despatched a trusted non-Jewish woman from the village to go towards Revúca to collect the children at a place near the border. The woman had cash to secure their passage, but they never arrived. The family had been deported the day before. In total, four families, each with three or four children, had disappeared and little information was available about where they had gone.

I was 11 and tried to imagine what might have happened to Renée and Rebecca. How could we help them? Mother was distraught. She spent much of her days crying and praying. There was a letter from one of the families and for a couple of months she held hope, but no letters followed, and eventually, mother was overcome by uncontainable grief. Sadness pervaded the house, with each child feeling the heavy weight of the immense loss. I was becoming aware of the precariousness of our existence and of ominous forces at work.

A few months later, Father decided we should move to Budapest where it would be easier to blend in among the one million inhabitants. The then-regent of the city was relatively protective of the Jews, allowing discrimination, but within limits. Our house and shop were sold, we packed up and joined our extended family that had been in Budapest for a year. After lodging with them for a few weeks, we found an apartment with a bathroom and heating, which was luxurious for us.

But my oldest brother, Alex, couldn't join us. He had been drafted into the Hungarian army as a labourer. Mother ran our home; I went to school; and Father, my older sister, and brother all found work. In some ways, this period was an interlude of happiness for us. Despite considerable anti-Jewish sentiment and restrictions, we could live openly. I could still go to school. Some Sundays, I even attended soccer matches.

The fragile equilibrium was blown apart on Sunday, March 19, 1944, when the Nazis entered Budapest with the sole intention of ridding Hungary of Jews. When I close my eyes, I can still see the fright in my parents' faces. They talked all night, plotting a way out of this impasse. In the morning, father went to the railway station to buy tickets to move us to the provinces, but his arrival at the station coincided disastrously with a raid by the secret police.

For days, I stood on the sofa next to the window, looking down into the street, hoping to see him returning.

We never saw him again.

We did not know where to turn. A relative suggested we buy false papers and split up. That is what we did, but there were no papers for me. As my sister and brother went off separately, mother and I went into hiding. Stories of our family's survival could fill an entire book...

Eventually, Budapest was liberated, and we found each other again. My oldest brother returned from the war, and the five of us clung together, waiting for father. Every day, we checked the Red Cross lists, questioned returning survivors, and followed all possible leads. As hope faded, we could see no future in Budapest and, with heavy hearts, we turned for 'home'. If father were alive, he would surely find us in Fiľakovo.

Jews had begun trickling back from the camps, and although only around 30 returned to Fiľakovo, none were welcomed, and none were spared the details of what had happened when the town was 'cleansed' of its Jews. When I heard what happened to Uncle Leopold, I could not sleep at night, and I knew this was not a place for us. Although he had lost his money by 1943, he was accused of hiding it and brutally beaten for not producing it. His body was broken and, barely conscious, he had to be carried to the trucks waiting to transport the Jews to a larger town, before sending them on to Auschwitz. This could no longer be our home. We packed our few belongings and went to Lučenec to turn over a new leaf and start again.

One of my brothers opened a shop there, and my sister met a lawyer called Paul Weiner. They married and began planning to move to Australia, but my other brother Janko was restless. He felt he had no identity. Although he was a Czechoslovak citizen, he felt neither Czech nor Slovak. He certainly did not feel Hungarian. He saw his future in Palestine, where he could recreate himself, be born again. As he left, he said, "In Palestine, I can be part of something I could claim as my own."

Soon after he left, Mother recognized the desolation of our life in Europe and said I should join him. To this end, I went to a Zionist-funded camp in Košice where I was taught about Palestine and Zionism. The Jewish Agency had for some years been organizing escape routes from central Europe to the Mediterranean where it bought or chartered ships to Palestine. There was nothing for me in Czechoslovakia—only bleak memories. What is more, I had missed many days of school and was not motivated to catch up.

I also felt a huge inner pressure to leave. Palestine offered a new beginning and a chance to be part of the Jewish drive to create a homeland.

I said goodbye to mother in early 1946. The sadness of separation was tempered with the hope of something new. Through the pain of parting, she assured me that we would all meet again in Palestine.

I travelled by train to Prague and then Paris with two dozen youngsters, chaperoned by the Jewish Agency. Just south of Marseille, at the port of La Ciotat, we boarded a ship that had been patched together and was barely seaworthy. Designed to carry 100, it had more than 750 souls on board with little food or water.

During one stormy night, it finally dawned on me what my decision meant. Mother had always been the still point in the turmoil of the world, and now I was alone, seasick, and frightened. I couldn't seek comfort from anyone. I was 15 and I was crying on the inside.

When I stepped ashore in Palestine, there were no questions, just an unspoken promise of belonging. I joined a small group of boys and girls who had survived the Holocaust. Together we worked in the fields in the mornings, attended lessons in the afternoons, and had our evenings free. It was a healing time for me.

Things changed dramatically in late-1947. The United Nations voted in favor of creating a Jewish State. The local Palestinians and surrounding Arab countries were in violent disagreement with this decision, and in 1948, when David

Ben Gurion declared independence, they all combined to attack the new State of Israel.

I had just turned 17 and signed up immediately to fight for the Biblical homeland I had learned so much about in Košice. Willing to endure any hardship, my group was selected to join the first commando unit in the Israeli army. As part of the Golani Brigade, it operated at night, behind enemy lines.

When the war was over, I found work on building sites, then worked in the post office while attending night school to learn accounting. That helped me secure a job in a bank. I was living with my brother Janko. Our free time was devoted to soccer, and life seemed to be "normal" again. Although I never said it out loud, every match took me back to father. We also missed Mother, more than words can describe.

Mother and other members of the family had moved to Sydney, Australia, and we yearned to be reunited. But Israel was brimming with youthful optimism, and we also wanted to stay. We agonised over the decision, but the pull of family was irresistible and in January 1952, I rushed into mother's arms at Sydney airport.

All I possessed was a small suitcase and a debt to cover my airfare to Australia. Soon I was delivering smallgoods all over Sydney. This job came with a small commission. The more I delivered and sold, the more I would make. So, I never stopped.

That year, at a party to celebrate the Jewish festival of Channukah, I met a beautiful 18-year-old woman called Shirley Rusanow who, for the next 66 years, would become my life partner. While I worked as hard as was humanly possible, she looked after our three sons, David, Peter, and Steven and ran our home. Shirley was our center of gravity, and while business often took me away, she was always there. She was my home.

Life went on, and I entered into a business partnership with an older European émigré, Janu Schwartz. It started as a small delicatessen. Over time, we grew it into a shopping center called Westfield, which then spread across Australia, into America, and the U.K. On some metrics, it became the largest retail real estate company in the world. My sons and I worked together like a business machine driving the company forward.

My love for soccer never faded. As my father had done for me, so I had ignited a passion for soccer in my sons. By 2003, Australian football (soccer) had fallen into disarray and its administration had collapsed. When I was asked to restore the sport to a professional level, I did not hesitate, first rebuilding the domestic league, then strengthening the national team and seeing it qualify for three successive FIFA World Cups. Soccer remains central in our lives and for me, it will always be an unbroken link to Fiľakovo.

For personal comfort, I always carried a photo of mother and father in my wallet to remind me of what was lost and why I should live life to the fullest. I also carried a photo of my blue-eyed cousins Renée and Rebecca. In the late-60s, these images were with me when I took Shirley to Fiľakovo for the first time. We stood on the pavement and looked at the old house.

I felt nothing. We walked to the railway station. Still nothing. Then I found the place where the Synagogue had stood, but there was no trace of it. The Communist Party had erased it from the map. Over the years we went back to Slovakia a few more times, finding nothing. Then, when the communist regime fell, there was a lighter mood in the town, and we braved to knock on the front door of our old house. To our amazement, we were invited in.

Suddenly, it all came alive for me!

I remembered it all, and with that, felt the stirrings of a connection.

I went back a few years later, this time with my sons and their wives. Just as we were leaving the town, we noticed the derelict Jewish cemetery and stopped. My sons and I climbed its high fences and found it overgrown with stones that had long since fallen.

After an hour of clearing weeds in the sun, we turned over the headstone of Jonah Lowy, the grandfather and inn keeper I had never known.

We set his stone upright and stood in silence, each aware that four generations of Lowy men were in one spot. Only father was missing. In faltering voices, we recited Kaddish, the traditional prayer for the dead.

The cemetery was the only sign that Jews had ever lived in Fiľakovo. It was an opportunity pleading to be taken. Janko agreed to fly there and stay a couple of months to arrange for it to be restored. This project awakened interest in the townsfolk and was, I think, the beginning of the recognition of what was lost.

By then, I had learned that Father had perished at Auschwitz for refusing to forsake his faith and in 2010, I managed to create a private memorial for him at the place where he died. With that, a part of me relaxed, but something was not right yet.

So, I went back to Fiľakovo. There is a small park where the synagogue once stood. I placed an obelisk there and dedicated it to the memory of our community that had been there since the early-1800s. The town enthusiastically organized a ceremony and with this, the lost community was acknowledged.

With my community recognized, I feel comfortable in Fiľakovo again.

I eat in its restaurants, and I am touched by the museum that displays a few artefacts someone had saved from the synagogue before it was destroyed. One of these artefacts is a seating plan that shows where my father used to sit.

I would like to thank Edita Berntsen a Slovak immigrant, lawyer, and Honorary Consul for Slovakia in Sydney, who has helped coordinate my reconnection on to Fiľakovo for the past 20 years.

When I was signing a contract for the town to maintain the memorial, a local citizen, Peter Sáfrány, offered to look after the cemetery as an act of grace. He asks no payment, but as we share a passion for soccer, I sponsor his club and the team I followed as a boy. That is another cycle closed.

Thereafter, I returned every year or so, bringing my grandchildren so they would know the story of their family.

In 2018, Shirley and I moved to Israel to live. She passed away peacefully in 2020, on the eve of the Jewish Festival of Channukah.

. . .

In 2021, Slovakia apologized to its Jews for the tragedy unleashed on them during those fateful and tragic years. As someone who lived through the sad times and survived the Holocaust, I appreciate this gesture and regard it as significant.

After losing much family in the Holocaust, **Frank Lowy** left his birthplace. He became a multi-billionaire and a philanthropist, but kept returning to Fiľakovo looking for traces of family. He restored the cemetery and, on the site of the demolished synagogue, erected a memorial to its lost Jewish community. As this community, including his father who perished in the Holocaust, had supported the town's football team, so did he. Sir Frank Lowy has been knighted by Her Majesty, Queen Elizabeth, and he holds the highest civilian honor of Australia and Israel, and the Gold Plaque of Minister of Foreign and European Affairs of Slovak Republic. When Slovakia apologized for the tragedy unleashed on its Jews, something in Frank relaxed.

Matzo Balls (Kneidelach)

- 2 large eggs
- ½ cup cold water
- ⅓ cup olive oil (traditionally, chicken fat was used)
- ½ TSP salt
- Pinch of pepper
- Finely minced parsley
- 1 cup matzo meal (ground-up matzo, a traditional Jewish unleavened bread)

1. In a large bowl, beat the eggs with a fork. Mix in the cold water and the olive oil.
2. Add salt, pepper, and parsley, and mix well.
3. Add the matzo meal and blend well.
4. Cover the bowl and refrigerate for 2-3 hours. The consistency will change.
5. Moisten both hands and form the mixture into balls about 1" in diameter.
6. Drop the balls gently into a big pot of boiling chicken broth.
7. Reduce the heat and let simmer for 30 minutes or more. The matzo balls will rise to the top. (If you make the balls bigger than 1", simmer them longer.)
8. Carefully remove the matzo balls from the broth with a slotted spoon, place them in a large bowl, then gently pour the soup over them.

WHAT MAKES MY ROOTS SO ALIVE?

by John Palka

> "When I was with my parents, I never spoke anything but Slovak. Slovak was the only language of home."

My roots in Slovakia are very deep. Except for our two daughters, their children, and two cousins in England, all the members of my family live in Slovakia. I know the history of my family back to the late 1600s. And I know all too well exactly how and why my parents and I had to leave Slovakia (then part of Czechoslovakia) twice, escaping first from the Nazis and then from the Communists. The United States has been a safe haven for me, and I love this country dearly, but those roots continue to bind me tightly to Slovakia even after over seventy years of living in the U.S. Being forced to leave home did not break those ties. Neither has living for so long in American society caused them to wither away.

What makes my roots so alive? Let me start with language, poetry, and song. When I was with my parents, I never spoke anything but Slovak. Where we were living made no difference; Slovak was the only language of home. It became so deeply ingrained in me that, even though I hardly spoke my mother tongue for the ten-year period between when my parents died (around 1980) and when we were able to start visiting Slovakia (around 1990), I remained totally fluent. I have no education in Slovak apart from half a year in first grade, second grade, and half a year in third grade, so my vocabulary is restricted when it comes to sophisticated fields, but at the same time Slovaks both there and here regularly remark on how pure my language is and some even try to identify which region it comes from. Is it Martin speech? Is it Mikuláš speech? For this I am very, very grateful to my parents!

They also wanted me to absorb as much of Slovak culture as possible, even while we were living in the United States. For example, my mother told me numerous children's stories in Slovak. *Varila mamička kašičku v maľovanom hrnčíčku...* (Mommy was cooking porridge in a little painted pot...) —a rhyme of nine or ten lines that she often recited to me at age four or five as I was going to bed in Chicago. The story is also often sung. Traditional hand motions go with the text and provide the storyteller or singer with an excuse to tweak each finger of the child's hand, to tickle its palm, and in the end to tickle it under the armpit! For me, this was meant to be a bed-time story! Well, it worked and, as you can see, I still know many of the words seventy-five years later.

Folk songs were an even bigger part of our family life. There was never an evening with guests when we did not sing one song after another for hours. My mother had a weak voice but an excellent memory, and she was the one who could produce all the verses. My father provided a rich voice and everyone, without exception, sang together. There were no songbooks or sheets. These were traditional songs that had become part of the Slovak national movement in the mid-nineteenth century. Slovakia is extremely rich in folk music, dance, and costumes. There is a great deal of regional variation in these, but there is also a core set of songs that most people know. Those are the ones we sang—and that I still love to sing whenever the occasion arises.

My parents wanted me to assimilate in America, to feel truly at home here, to have a successful career, not to feel like a foreigner. But they also wanted me to keep those deep roots alive and strong. The way they managed this was through making our home a Slovak home in which Slovak language and culture were completely natural.

They also wanted me to know the most important aspects of Slovak history, because they saw the history as part of the soil in which my roots were growing and because a number of my forebears had played prominent roles in this history. In addition, sweeping historical events were the cause of our family's emigration to the United States.

I was born in July of 1939, neither in Slovakia nor in America but in Paris. Why Paris? Because just two weeks earlier my mother had made her way to France from Slovakia, slipping out of the Slovak State that prevailed during World War II. In March of that year, under pressure from Hitler, Czechoslovakia had split into two portions: the Protectorate of Bohemia and Moravia, which was ruled directly from Berlin, and the Slovak Republic, generally known as the Slovak State, which was nominally independent. However, the government of the Slovak State was ultranationalist and pro-Nazi. The Slovak State couldn't do anything that Hitler actively opposed and was effectively a German vassal.

This affected my parents very directly. Not for religious reasons—we were Lutherans, not Jews, and thus were not subject to the extremes of anti-Semitism legislated by the Slovak government. And extremes they were. The Slovak government even voluntarily paid the German government a significant amount per capita to accept the tens of thousands of Jews whom it shipped out of Slovakia and into Germany.

My parents were affected for two other reasons. First, my mother's father, Milan Hodža, was one of twentieth-century Slovakia's most prominent political figures. He served as prime minister of Czechoslovakia during the years 1935 to 1938 and was the only Slovak to hold that position during the entire so-called First Republic, from the founding of Czechoslovakia in 1918 to its break-up in 1939; all the other prime ministers were Czechs. My grandfather was adamantly anti-Nazi. He was also a strong proponent of a united Czechoslovakia, whereas the pro-Nazi Slovak government was led by men who wanted to separate from the Czechs. For these reasons Milan Hodža was *persona non grata* to the new government. Long after going into exile, he was prosecuted by that government and was ultimately sentenced to eighteen years in prison for treason. They took the trouble to carry on a protracted legal process while the war was raging and Hodža was in exile! This attitude placed his immediate family in constant danger of arrest, and all of them got out of the country. My mother was the last to leave.

The other reason for my parents' departure was that my father, like so many of our family, was active in a burgeoning anti-Nazi resistance. I always knew that my father had not accompanied my mother to France and had not been present at my birth. However, it was only after my parents' deaths, when I was searching through family archives, that I finally understood why. It was because of my father's commitment to the underground anti-Nazi effort. He stayed behind in Slovakia because he was encumbering his share of a family-owned leather business in Mikuláš to obtain large amounts of cash. He smuggled this cash across the border into Hungary, and then across a second border into Yugoslavia, where he delivered it to the attorney Janko Bulík, a member of one of the centuries-old Slovak communities in Serbia. Bulík was the leader of an active anti-Nazi group in Belgrade whose main focus was to help escapees from Slovakia and from the Czech lands, many of them Jews, gain legal standing to enter Yugoslavia and stay there long enough to arrange for transportation to some other destination.

My father made three such trips, each time risking his life. Then one night he was awakened by the mayor of Mikuláš, who came to tell him urgently that he had just learned at a meeting with police officials that my father would be arrested the following morning and sent to the prison in Ilʼava. That prison was well-known as a staging point for extradition to Germany. My father took a few belongings, jumped on a midnight train, and made it safely to Belgrade. Later he finally came to join my mother and me in Paris.

Through Janko Bulík, my father obtained and brought with him a false passport and other documents that declared him to be Janko Pafković of Novi Sad in Serbia, not Ján Palka of Liptovský svätý Mikuláš in Slovakia. These documents allowed us to escape the watchful eyes of the Gestapo that was soon operating in Occupied France, where we were trapped for a year and a half.

At one point, however, we received an order to report within twenty-four hours to the Gestapo headquarters in Nice with no more than one suitcase per person. It was no secret what this meant—a concentration camp. Once again, my parents managed to get on a midnight train. It took us from Nice to Paris. In a few days, the French Resistance smuggled us across the border into Free France. From there, on the basis of that false Yugoslav passport, we made our way into pro-German Franco Spain. I celebrated my second birthday in Madrid. Finally, we reached neutral Portugal. My parents were able to get us on one of the last commercial flights from Lisbon, the last remaining open port in Europe, to New York. Thus began our first stay in the United States.

We spent most of the war years in Chicago. My mother, the prime minister's daughter, worked as a file clerk in an insurance agency. My father, the factory owner, worked to exhaustion on the assembly line in a factory whose owner had Slovak roots. We lived in a duplex whose Slovak owner had

immigrated from my mother's hometown of Sučany, near Martin. He was a modest house painter, but he had managed to accumulate enough money to buy this duplex. He and his family lived downstairs; we lived upstairs. Volta Elementary School was only a few blocks away. When I started kindergarten there, it was my first regular exposure to an English-speaking environment.

The language that was so important to my parents was not just a means of communicating. Starting toward the end of the eighteenth century, language came to be felt as central to the sense of identity of many European peoples, Slovaks among them. Here is one illustration of how this feeling manifested.

In Slovakia there is, in addition to the national anthem, a set of national songs that have a place in culture rather like that of "America the Beautiful" in the United States. By far the most frequently sung of all these songs is *Hej, Slováci* (O Slovaks!) The text was written in 1834, just as Slovak national awareness was gaining momentum. It was written by a Slovak passing through Czech Prague and set to a Polish melody, reflecting the close bonds among Slavic nations. The opening is all about language:

Hej, Slováci, ešte naša Slovenská reč žije,
pokiaľ naše verné srdce za náš národ bije,
. . .

O Slovaks, our Slovak language still lives,
as long as our faithful heart for our nation beats,
. . .

I absorbed this song, as does virtually every Slovak child, and I even have an audio recording of me singing it. I was seven and a half when we returned home to Slovakia right after the war. Before our departure from New York on the SS *America*, there was a farewell party at which one of our family's dear friends made a series of commemorative recordings on bright red plastic record disks that I still have. I am the star on two of them. This is how I know that I spoke English fluently but with a strong accent. At one point my mother's brother asked me to sing. I responded rather quietly with a dull church hymn, but he interrupted me. "Don't you know something livelier, something Slovak? How about *Hej, Slováci?*" And immediately my tone changed. I sang with a new voice: bold, rhythmic, and filled with energy. When I was finished, my uncle complimented me. "*Výborne,*" he said. "Excellent!"

We arrived in Czechoslovakia in December of 1946. After a few months of staying with my father's sister, Ľudinka, in Bratislava, we were able to move into the house that my parents had built in Liptovský svätý Mikuláš and where I have been many times in the years since the Iron Curtain fell. However, the Communist coup came in February of 1948, not much more than a year after our arrival. In April, just three months later, my father was arrested for alleged anti-state activities. It was a charge that potentially carried a death penalty but fortunately, after a few months of solitary confinement, he was released. Nevertheless, the factory of which he was part-owner was confiscated and he was followed by secret police all the time. In the face of this constant danger, in March of 1949 we escaped. This entailed literally crawling under a barbed wire fence that ran down the middle of a wide, ploughed-up strip of no-man's-land, mindful of the machine gun towers and searchlights that interrupted it at intervals. I was almost ten years old at the time, and I remember our escape vividly.

In December of 1949 we arrived as political refugees in the United States for a second time. It was just three years after we had left for our Slovak home, dreaming of a joyful future in the embrace of beloved family, culture, and society. This time we settled in New York, in the Jackson Heights section of Queens where many other refugees from Czechoslovakia had also found housing in modest apartments.

I graduated from P. S. (Public School) 69 in 1953, from high school in 1956, and from Swarthmore College in 1960. My mother worked for the Czechoslovak Desk of Radio Free Europe. My father tried hard to get an international export-import business rolling, based on his many old connections, but it never truly worked, and he retired at an early age. Through all these years, our family life was just like it had always been. There were no more children's stories, but the home language continued to be exclusively Slovak; when guests came, we sang the same songs we had always sung; and my mother continued to steep me in Slovak history.

At Swarthmore I met Yvonne, whose parents were immigrants from Switzerland. After we graduated, Yvonne and I spent a year in India and we married there. After we finished graduate school at UCLA in 1965, Yvonne in neuroendocrinology and I in neurophysiology, we returned to India for another year. Our first daughter, Rachel, was born there. Thereafter came academic careers, first for three years in Houston—where our second daughter, Tanya, was born—and then for more than thirty years in Seattle. Yvonne worked primarily at Antioch University Seattle, I at the University of Washington.

During this long period, we were separated from my parents, who stayed in New York until the very end of their lives when they joined us in Seattle. Whenever it was just my parents and I, I always spoke with them in Slovak, but we corresponded in English so Yvonne would be included and, of course, family conversations were all in English. I did not manage to pass the Slovak language on to our daughters, though they heard many recordings of Slovak folk songs and liked them a lot. But Slovakia was in no way forgotten.

In 1975–76 we spent a sabbatical year in Cambridge, England. In the spring of 1976, I applied for visas that would let us visit Czechoslovakia. I had applied for a visa several times before through the Czechoslovak Embassy in Washington but had always been denied. In London, however, everything went smoothly, and we had our visas by return mail!

It was an amazing visit. Twenty-seven years after I had crawled out under the barbed wire, I and my wife and children landed in Prague. We were met at the airport by my father's brother, Dušan Palka, a well-known writer of popular music, especially the so-called Slovak tango. After staying with him and his family for a few days, we went on to Bratislava, where we stayed with Aunt Ľudinka again, this time also with her son, and his wife. Ľudinka had managed to secure permits to travel abroad several times (through the clever bribery that was a routine part of life under Communism), so we had all met her in New York previously. We visited other family members in Bratislava and in Martin. We visited nearby Sučany and Rakša, where the Hodža family had centuries-old roots. We visited Mikuláš, where my parents' house had been confiscated by the government and turned into a childcare center. We met my best friend from childhood, with whom I had gone to school during that all-too-brief post-war interlude. We made a thrilling excursion to the Tatra Mountains. And we flew back to England with folk costumes (*kroje*) stitched specially for Rachel and Tanya that they treasured and wore for years on special occasions. They still have them.

All of a sudden, Slovak roots were a reality not only for me but also for Yvonne, Rachel, and Tanya—for all four of us. That sense has never faded. Rachel and Tanya visited again on their own (communicating in French) in 1985 when they were in college. Starting in 1990 we visited every year or two. Over the years, several members of our family came and stayed with us in Seattle, usually for educational purposes.

Everything changed again in 2002. During World War II, Grandfather Hodža, like my immediate family, had ended up in the United States. He died in 1944 and was buried in the Bohemian National Cemetery in Chicago. In 2002, responding to the promptings of historians, the Slovak government decided to bring his remains home and re-bury them in the cemetery in Martin, which serves as the Slovak national cemetery. This was done with great ceremony and intense press and television coverage. Our whole family, including several grandchildren, participated in Chicago. Then Yvonne and I flew to Bratislava on the official government airplane, traveling with the government delegation and the press corps. Amidst ceremonies at the Bratislava airport we were greeted by the prime minister, Mikuláš Dzurinda, and I had my first taste of being pulled aside for radio and television interviews, all in Slovak, of course. At the end of the day, we were taken by limousine to Martin for the final extended ceremonies. The conclusion came two days later with the actual lowering of the casket into the grave that also held my grandmother's remains and was graced with a new headstone.

Of course, life could never be the same after events such as these! Visits to Slovakia became even more frequent. We took our daughters and their families a number of times. After a great deal of research, I wrote a book about my family in the context of Slovak history. It came out in Bratislava in 2010 as *Moje Slovensko, moja rodina* and in the United States in 2012 as *My Slovakia, My Family*. The last time I visited Slovakia was in 2019, on a detour to our oldest granddaughter's wedding in England. Whether I will be able to go again remains to be seen.

In 2017, Yvonne and I moved. We had lived in the Pacific Northwest for nearly fifty years, around thirty in Seattle and, after we retired from academia, another twenty on one of the nearby islands, Whidbey Island. Now we were living on the outskirts of Minneapolis, minutes away from Tanya and her family and a few hours' drive away from Rachel and her family. Here, we found a very active Czech and Slovak community, including several wonderful organizations. Soon we were involved in a song circle, and a book club, and a variety of performances and social events. The great majority of immigrants here are Czech, but they are extremely inclusive of Slovaks and are interested in the added perspective that

I am able to bring. Czechoslovakia went through a totally peaceful Velvet Divorce effective January 1, 1993, and for the first time ever Slovakia became a truly independent country. Fortunately, in the years since then Slovakia and the Czech Republic have become the best of neighbors, with a huge amount of interchange at home and heartening cooperation between their official legations abroad. This extends to the immigrant communities. It's a model relationship.

I have been blessed with an extraordinarily rich life. Its early years were traumatic in many ways, especially for my parents. Losing one's homeland under duress, especially losing it twice, is bound to leave scars. Once we really settled in the United States, however, my parents' dreams came true. They raised a son who has felt at home here, has raised a loving family, had a successful career, and in the process never, ever separated from his Slovak roots. Those life-filled roots have had a strong impact on the next generation, and on the generation after that. If my parents could see us, I'm sure they would be holding hands and smiling!

John Palka, *a retired professor of biology, is a first-generation immigrant to the United States. His parents and he were driven out from home twice for political reasons. The family was culturally and politically prominent for many generations. His grandfather, Milan Hodza, was the only Slovak Prime Minister of democratic Czechoslovakia. As a result, John grew up in a home where Slovak culture and traditions, including the language, were vibrantly alive. This intimate connection with Slovakia has enabled John to maintain active ties with his extensive family, friends and colleagues there.*

Christmas Sauerkraut Soup (Kapustnica)

- 2 lbs. sauerkraut, preferably with juice
- Beef or chicken stock made from 3 bouillon cubes, and prepared according to package instructions
- 6 prunes
- 1 *klobása* (or any Eastern European sausage), kept whole
- Handful of peppercorns, tied up in cheesecloth, for easy removal
- Handful of dried mushrooms (preferably *porcini*), soaked in warm milk and then strained, reserving the milk
- 1 TBSP all-purpose flour
- 1 cup sour cream
- 1 potato, peeled

1. Place the sauerkraut, stock, and prunes in a large pot, and boil for 1 hour over low heat.
2. During the last 20 minutes, add the sausage, peppercorns, and mushrooms (without the milk).
3. After 20 minutes, remove the sausage to a plate.
4. In a medium bowl, thoroughly mix the flour into 2 TBSP of the mushroom milk. Then add the sour cream and mix until smooth. Slowly and evenly stir into the soup.
5. If the soup is too thin or too sour, grate in one raw potato and continue cooking until the potato has softened.
6. Cut the cooked sausage crosswise into moderately thin slices, add back to the soup.
7. The flavor improves if the soup is served on the day after it is prepared. Keep chilled overnight and warm before serving. Avoid boiling so the sour cream does not curdle.

EPILOGUE

From Bird of Passage to Returnee: In Honor of My Great-Grandfather Juraj Pták

By Dr. Zuzana Palovic

Some 750,000 brave Slovak men, women and children left behind the world they knew for a world they did not, ready to work hard, earn money and return home. One of them was my great-grandfather, Juraj Pták.

Born in 1878 in a small village on the outskirts of Martin, he jumped on the trend and joined the hundreds of thousands of hungry and desperate, but also ambitious, young men, ready to turn their dreams into reality.

Determined to provide a better life for himself, Juraj journeyed up to Bremen, Germany, where he boarded a steamship in steerage set for America. He was only 21 years-old, and arrived in the port of New York in 1899, with a whopping 18 USD in his pocket. He was part of the legions of cheap Eastern European workers who arrived on US shores, ready to meet the demands of the coal mines.

However, Juraj was not just a cog in somebody else's machine. He was a man of vision. Like many of his fellow journey men—humble, strong-willed farmers from the Old World, he aspired to earn the golden $1,000. And then, return to Slovakia a rich man, capable of building a life greater than that of his father.

The experience changed him.

A village boy thrust onto a trans-Atlantic journey, he watched blue whales come up to the ship as they sailed across an open and endless ocean. He saw the wonders of a New York City skyline and was welcomed by the Statue of Liberty. He also faced the cruel side of American capitalism, working long hours deep underground in the coal mines. He risked his life for pay daily and witnessed tragedy when a close friend and neighbor died in the mines next to him. Evidently human life was cheap in the 1900s.

Still, my great-grandfather persevered. Making the most of what he had, and eventually returning to Slovakia with hard-earned cash in his hand, he secured his footing in his homeland by purchasing land and livestock and was blessed to find a wife. Life in the Slovak countryside looked idyllic, but if they were to survive as a new family, more land and cows were needed.

Juraj undertook the perilous voyage to America once more in 1905—this time as a seasoned migrant and married man. He moved on from the coal mines to the steel mills and continued to keep his head down and work hard. The goal was to make more cash, to secure more land and, of course, to return to his beloved Slovakia.

The New World transformed *amerikáni*. They grew fond of beer that replaced homemade spirits, as well as city fashion and innovations that made their lives and homes more comfortable. But more than that, America taught Slovaks to develop an active interest in reading newspapers and books, and in educating themselves. Self-development translated into an altered perception of the world and their place in it. They no longer felt like passive victims of unfortunate circumstances; these returning Slovaks started to see themselves as makers of their own lives.

My great-grandfather, Juraj, was one such change-maker. A humble petty farmer, he used capital that he earned abroad to improve his lot in life. He introduced tools and techniques to his fields that made his work more efficient. He fitted his home with fine furniture and welcomed innovation. He stayed true to who he was but never forgot about his sojourn to America—sharing stories of the New World with his eight children and teaching them of a different life across the ocean. He served as an example to the family and the community that change was not only possible, but necessary. He showed them that things no longer had to be done the way they had always been done. What a shift of mindset!

My great-grandfather was an *amerikán*.

Although Juraj Pták's "American Dream" was cut short, he made his Slovak dream happen. He lived a happy, honest, and wholesome life in the Slovak countryside, surrounded by his children and grandchildren. They may have never been born had he chosen to stay on in America.

It was thanks to his decision to return, that I too can call Slovakia my home.

His spirit lives in me and inspires me to travel and explore. Every time I visit the harbor of New York, I take a moment to reflect on my forefather, his courage, his resilience, and his sacrifice as a migrant.

I am his descendant, and I am proud of it.

Zuzana Palovic
Founder of Global Slovakia

Afterword

"Immigration is a voyage that lasts for many generations. Someday soon, a generation will come along that what will link hands again with the culture left behind, and in a kind of circle complete the fragmentary journey so far, and so painfully, traversed."

Michael Novak, Cleveland State University, 1978[1]

The stories in this book reveal a fascinating, complex, and rich image of an important history. It is a history of countless families in Slovakia, in the Americas and beyond.

Was Slovak migration a success? It was, and it wasn't. Countries that gained and nurtured Slovak talent reaped the benefits. Slovakia, on the other hand, lost much of its population that went on to build, advance, and strengthen other nations.

Those who left Slovakia, came to the New World in high hopes. They made money but many died young in the mines and the mills. A migrant's life was cheap. With time, however, the Slovaks learned the power of unity. They organized protests and joined unions. They fought for better working conditions, and their lives improved.

Entire Slovak colonies rose next to the factories and mills and as children were born, so was the immigrants' hope for

---

[1] Megles et al, 1978

a better future. Some chose to work alongside their fathers and grandfathers, doing hard work in exchange for a stable life and secure paycheck. Others opted to expand and explore new professions. In the end, they were all valuable citizens.

Slovaks in the New World greatly contributed to the Czechoslovak effort. Czechoslovakia might have never existed without them. The founding of the country in post-WW I Europe was truly a miracle and it laid the groundwork for an independent Slovakia to be born less than a century later.

Despite growing up across the ocean, most never forgot where they came from. They proudly kept their culture and values alive and passed them down in Slovak customs, songs and recipes. Many opted to marry a Slovak, while never giving up on the dream of one day returning to the old country. Others were so dismayed by the poverty in their homeland that they seldom talked about it and never wanted to return. Regardless of intent, most Slovaks-Americas maintained their ethnic bond, continuing to make Slovak food and celebrate Slovak rites and rituals, including Christmas and Easter customs.

The advance of the Cold War and the division of the world into good and evil, made it easier or even necessary to forget the homeland. The communities were shut down and most Slovak-Americans opted to blend in instead. Nevertheless, a love for Slovakia was passed on.

Today some 2 million Americans alone identify as Slovak descendants and over three decades after the collapse of the Iron Curtain, many are looking—to reconnect with their heritage and roots but also with Slovakia, the land of their predecessors.

Is this true for you?

You may live an ocean apart from your ancestral homeland, but you carry the Slovak legacy in your blood. Your roots are a gift, forged in the fire of hardships and triumphs that your ancestors endured to transplant and birth your lineage in the New World.

You now thrive multiple generations strong as Americans, Canadians, Argentinians or even Australians. Yet, a tree can grow only as high as its roots.

May you cherish your Slovak origins and pass on your roots.

Zuzana & Gabriela
Global Slovakia
www.globalslovakia.com

Photographs & Illustrations
(in order of appearance)

Page 8 Sherman, Augustus F. (1905-1914) 'Slovak woman and children, Manuscripts and Archives Division, The New York Public Library.

Page 15 Levick, Edwin, 'Immigrants on at Atlantic Liner', 1906, Washington D.C., Library of Congress, Prints and Photographs Division.

Page 39 Antwerpen, New York Ocean Liner Ticket, Museum Kasigarda.

Page 43 Str. Oceanic, 1900-1905, Washington D.C., Library of Congress, Prints and Photographs Division.

Page 47 (top to bottom) Anonymous, 'Steerage Passengers Taking Life Easy on an Ocean Liner', 1900-1905, Washington D.C., Library of Congress, Prints and Photographs Division.

Ellis Island, 1950-1920, Washington D.C., Library of Congress, Prints and Photographs Division.

'Emigrants Coming up the Boardwalk from the Barge', Ellis Island, 1902, Washington D.C., Library of Congress, Prints and Photographs Division.

Page 48 (top to bottom) *Physicians Examining a Group of Immigrants*', *1900-1910*, Washington D.C., Library of Congress, Prints and Photographs Division.

Page 49 Anonymous, 'Emigrants coming to the Land of Promise', 1902, Washington D.C., Library of Congress, Prints and Photographs Division.

Ship Manifest, 1909, Barbara Ulkus family archives.

Page 52 Anonymous, 'Welcome to the land of freedom', 1887, Washington D.C., Library of Congress, Prints and Photographs Division.

Page 53 Lunch on top of 30 Rockefeller Plaza in Manhattan, 1932, the man on the very right is Slovak Gusti Popovič, who sent his wife a postcard with this photograph on which he wrote: "Don't worry, my dear Mariska, as you can see, I'm still with a bottle."

Page 54 Remittance receipt, Barbara Ulkus family archives.

Page 57 'Miner Working in Coal Mine', 1909-1932, Washington D.C., Library of Congress, Prints and Photographs Division.

Page 58 (top to bottom) Virginia coal mines, David Barna family archives.

A sign from Fayette County, Pennsylvania, represents many of the languages common in the Pennsylvanian coal mines, including English, Hungarian, Italian, Slovak, and Polish; Collection of the Senator John Heinz History Center.

Page 60 (top to bottom) Mahony City Colliery, Mahony City, Pennsylvania, David Barna family archives.

Article about a coal mine explosion in Mahanoy City, Pennsylvania.

Page 61 Hine, Lewis Wickes, 'Noon hour in the Ewen Breaker, Pennsylvania Coal Co.', Breaker Boys series, 1911, Pennsylvania, Washington D.C., Library of Congress, Prints and Photographs Division.

Page 64 Pennsylvania—the mining troubles in the Schuylkill region—attack on the coal and iron police by a mob of Polish strikers, at Shenandoah, February 3d / from a sketch by Joseph Becker, 1888, Washington D.C., Library of Congress, Prints and Photographs Division.

Page 65 Davis, Jackson, 'Miners Cabins', Digital Public Library of America.

Page 66 (top to bottom) *Dayton Daily News*, Dayton, Ohio, May 24, 1902, Library of Congress

Lincoln Journal Star, Lincoln, Nebraska, September 22, 1920, Library of Congress.

The Day Book., Chicago, Illinois, March 7, 1917, *Chronicling America: Historic American Newspapers*, Washington D.C., Library of Congress.

The Daily Telegram, August 15, 1914, Library of Congress.

New York Daily Tribute, March 28, 1909, Library of Congress.

Page 68 Coal miners buying groceries in company store, West Virginia, 1938, Washington D.C., Library of Congress, Prints and Photographs Division

Page 71 Steve Dobrovich, Arkansas, USA, Frank Dobrovich family archives.

Page 82 Ruthenian Church in Northfork, Elkhorn, West Virginia, David Barna family archives.

Page 84 The Milokaj family from Spiš, Perryopolis, Pennsylvania, Museum Kasigarda.

Page 89 At a Slovak grocery store, 1930s, Eva Vargo family archives.

Page 91 A page from *Praktičný Slovensko-Anglický Tlumač* (*The Practical Slovak American Interpreter*), compiled by Paul Kadak, 1905.

Page 93 Slovak and Carpatho-Rusyn Organizations in the U.S. from 1883 to 1960, Kasigarda Museum of Emigration from Slovakia.

Page 95 Delegates of the 1934 Convention in Cleveland, Ohio, enjoy a baseball game played between *Jednota* members, *Jednota*.

Page 103 Slovak And Carpatho-Rusyn Churches in North America from 1870 to 1955, Kasigarda Museum of Emigration from Slovakia.

Page 110 Milan Rastislav Štefánik at the meeting of the Bohemian National Alliance and the Slovak League in Washington D.C., 1917, Czech Centennial Chicago.

Page 111 (top to bottom) Tomáš Garrigue Masaryk in Chicago, 1917, Czech Centennial Chicago.

The Chicago Daily Tribune, May 6, 1918.

Page 113 The Pittsburgh Agreement signed in Pittsburgh on May 31, 1918.

Page 119 (top to bottom) Lumber Camp I., Ruel Ontario, 1923, Lukča and Marejka family archives.

Lumber Camp II., Ruel Ontario, 1923, Lukča and Marejka family archives.

School in Bradlo, 1934, Rudy Bies family archives

Page 121 (top to bottom) A monument in Bradlo (plaque) honoring its Slovak settlers, Rudy Bies family archives.

A monument in Bradlo (stone) honoring its Slovak settlers, Rudy Bies family archives.

Page 130 John Mager (seated top center) and his Pennsylvania coal mining crew, early 1920s, Ken Duda family archives.

Page 133 Nicholas (Potproč) Duda (left) with partner at his Montana coal mine, early 1920s, Ken Duda family archives.

Page 139 White-shirted Nicholas Duda with sons John and little Cliff at fence to right of bucking horse, Montana, 1920, Ken Duda family archives.

Page 141 Elizabeth and Nicholas Duda with daughter, Margaret, 1910s. Ken Duda family archives.

Page 144 U.S. Army soldier Clifford Duda before WW II battles in Africa and Europe, early 1943, Ken Duda family archives.

Page 146 John and Anna Mager family at Pennsylvania home, Elizabeth on her mother's lap, 1925, Ken Duda family archives.

Page 150 Sophie and Andrew Partak, Sr. with their first child Sylvia in front of the Partak's Tavern, Andrew Partak, Jr. family archives.

Page 155 Ján Partok's parents Mária and Serafin and brother Anton, Jablonka, Slovakia, Andrew Partak, Jr. family archives.

Page 156 Mária and Ján Partok on their wedding day, Andrew Partak, Jr. family archives.

Page 157 Partak's Tavern at 651 Garnsey Ave, Joliet, Illinois, USA, Andrew Partak, Jr. family archives.

Page 158 Interior of Partak's Tavern during Andrew and Sophie Partak's wedding celebration, Andrew Partak, Jr. family archives.

Page 161 Anna (Nana) Obšitník in one of her many custom-made dresses, Andrew Partak, Jr. family archives.

Page 168 The first four of Valentine's great-grandchildren born in America, circa 1920.

Left to right: Louis, Rudolph (back), John, Jr., Anna, Paul Kostyak family archives.

Page 177 John and Mary Kostyak, circa 1909, Emma Lou Kostyak Walter family archives.

Page 178 Ann Kostyak, John Kostyak, Rudy Kostyak (back), Frank Kostyak, Mary Miskovics

Kostyak, Louis Kostyak and Margaret Kostyak, circa 1926, Paul Kostyak family archives.

Page 179 Page from the *National Slovak Society* policy on John Kostyak for $1,000, circa 1921, Paul Kostyak family archives.

Page 180 Michael Miskovics, Mary Miskovics, and John Kostyak in the backyard of Haberman

Avenue in Mt. Washington, Pennsylvania, USA, circa 1943, Emma Lou Kostyak Walter family archives.

Page 181 First family meeting in Lendak, 2013, Paul Kostyak family archives.

Page 182 Eva Stucko, Audrey Stucko family archives.

Page 191 Eva with her sister Mary and niece Anna, Audrey Stucko family archives.

Page 192 The Stucko clan enjoying a meal at Eva's home, circa 1950s, Audrey Stucko family archives.

Page 193 Eva joking around with daughter Mary and son-in-law Joe, Greenpoint, New York, USA, Audrey Stucko family archives.

Page 194 Eva with her son Metro, Audrey Stucko family archives.

Page 198 Margaret Zulick Seles, wearing traditional *kroj*, Jeanne Zulick family archives.

Page 205 Andrew Zulick and Irene Fello on their wedding day, 1918, Jeanne Zulick family archives.

Page 206 (top to bottom) Irene Zulick feeding chickens with sons Andrew and John, Jeanne Zulick family archives.

Irene Zulick with her mother, Borbála Fello, on the Zulick farm in Ashford, Connecticut, USA, Jeanne Zulick family archives.

Andrew and Irene Zulick with daughter, Margaret, on their farm in Ashford, Connecticut, USA, Jeanne Zulick family archives.

Page 212 Edward and Ellen Monovich in their kitchen in Brownsville, Pennsylvania, USA, Easter, circa 1991, Edward Monovich family archives.

Page 219 Ede Jozsef Mohnovics, circa 1913, illustrated reconstruction of an old photograph by Edward Alexander Monovich.

Page 220 Edward Peter Monovich carrying his *koláče* and other Easter specialties to church for

blessing before Easter dinner, circa 1991, artistic rendering by Edward Alexander Monovich.

Page 228 Nicolas and Felix Kovanič in Vienna, Austria, circa 1905, Albert Kovanis family archives.

Page 232 Three generations of Kovárik family in Gbely, Slovakia, 1947, Albert Kovanis family archives.

Page 237 Kovanič-Kovárik wedding in Belaire, Ohio, USA, 1915, Albert Kovanis family archives.

Page 241 (top to bottom) Felix and Johanna Kovanic with their son Albert Jr., 1941, Albert Kovanis family archives.

Felix and Johanna Kovanis, Albert Kovanis family archives.

Page 243 Kovárik reunion in Gbely, Slovakia, 1997, Albert Kovanis family archives.

Page 250 John Lazovi and Mária Martinková on their wedding day, 1920, Pennsylvania, United States, Beverly Clifford family archives.

Page 253 Self-subsistence of the family, artistic rendering by Tucker Jaroll.

Page 258 Items rescued from the ancestral family home, Beverly Clifford family archives.

Page 264 Janoš Figlar, Lisa Alzo family archives.

Page 270 Janoš working at US Steel Duquesne Works, artistic rendition by Tucker Jaroll.

Page 280 Marcela Fajmonova (on the right) with sister, Ana, and brother, Enrique, María Elena Jurado family archives.

Page 282 12-year-old Marcela at her First Communion, María Elena Doello Jurado family archives.

Page 288 Anne (Bies) Siska standing in doorway of the Bradlo School House, 1949, Bies family archives.

Back row (left to right): Jean Martin, Gertrude Martin, Mary Sevc, Cecile Martin, Armand Martin, Rudy Bies, Joe Bunsko, John Bies, unknown, Bill Bies, Front Row Anna Sevc.

Page 291 Ján Bies in the Army, Myjava, Slovakia, Bies family archives.

Page 292 Judita (Kostkova) Bies, Cleveland, Ohio, USA, circa 1908, Olga Stevenson family archives.

Page 296 Anna Bies and her daughter Olga, Myjava, Slovakia, 1932, Bies family archives.

Page 297 Bradlo Wood Cutter (Feranec), circa 1934, Bies family archives.

Page 300 Anna Bies holding baby Bill, Rudy Bies and John Bies Jr., 1942, Bradlo, Ontario, Canada, Bies family archives.

Page 302 Bradlo Monument Blessing, July 30, 2022, Bies family archives.

Left to right: Ambassador of the Slovak Republic to Canada, Vit Koziak, Robert Bies, Rudy Bies, Gloria Bies, Aidan Boyd, Michael Boyd, Barbara (Bies) Boyd. Connor Boyd. Dog Cona.

Page 306 Frank Lowy, Frank Lowy family archives.

Page 309 Frank (in the middle) with parents and siblings, Frank Lowy family archives.

Page 311 Frank with his mother, Frank Lowy family archives.

Page 321 Knighted by Her Majesty, Queen Elizabeth II., 2017, Frank Lowy family archives.

Page 324 John Palka with parents, John Palka family archives.

Page 330 The Yugoslav passport, issued to the imaginary Janko Pafković of Novi Sad, Serbia, John Palka family archives.

Page 331 Three generations of the family shortly after Milan Hodža arrived in the United States, 1942, John Palka family archives.

Left to right: Irena Hodžová, holding John Palka dressed in a Slovak outfit; Milan Hodža, Irena Palková, Ján Palka.

Page 337 Family reunion in Liptovský Mikuláš, 2012, John Palka family archives.

The family gathered under the statue of Michal Miloslav Hodža, grandfather Hodža's uncle. It stands in front of the Lutheran church where he served as the minister. M. M. Hodža is regarded as one of the most influential figures in the so-called Slovak National Awakening of the 19th century.

Bibliography

Alexander, J. G. (2007). *Daily life in immigrant America, 1870–1920*. Greenwood.

Alexander, J. G. (1981). Staying Together: Chain Migration and Patterns of Slovak Settlement in Pittsburgh prior to World War I. *Journal of American Ethnic History*, vol. 1, no.1, pp 56-83.

Bahna, M, (2011) *Migrácia zo Slovenska po vstupe do Európskej únie*, Bratislava: Veda.Bakay-Záhorská, M. and Králová, Z. (2015) 'The Compatriot Magazine Jednota': A Mirror of Hundred-Year History of Slovak Immigrants in the USA, *XLinguae Journal*, vol. 8, no. 3, pp. 66-75.

Bell, T. (1941) *Out of this Furnace*, Pittsburgh: University of Pittsburgh Press.

Bicha, K. D. (1982) 'Hunkies: Stereotyping the Slavic Immigrants, 1890–1920,' *Journal of American Ethnic History*, 2(1), 16-38.

Brnich, M. J. and Kowalski-Trakofker, K. (2010) 'Underground Coal Mine Disasters 1900–2010: Events, Responses, and a Look to the Future', in Brune, Jurgen (ed.) *Extracting the Science: A Century of Mining Research*, Littleton, Englewood, Colorado: Society of Mining, Metallurgy, and Exploration, pp. 363-372.

Carnegie, A. (2006) *Autobiography of Andrew Carnegie: With the Gospel of Wealth*, Seven Treasures Publications.

Cude, M. (2014) 'The Imagined Exiles: SlovakAmericans and the Slovak Question during the First Czechoslovak Republic', in *Studia Historica Gedanensia*, vol. 5, pp. 287-305.

Čulen, K. (2007) *The History of Slovaks in America*, St. Paul, Minnesota: Czechoslovak Genealogical Society International.

Čupka, M. (2022) *What is huncút?* Bratislava: Barecz & Conrad Books.

Derfiňák, P. (2016) 'Cholerová epidémia na severovýchone Uhorsku v rokoch 1872-1873', in *ANNALES HISTORICI PRESOVIENSES*, vol. 16, issue 2, Inštitút histórie: Filozofická fakulta Prešovskej university.

Dziak, R. (2012) *The Czechoslovak legions in World War I.*, Marine Corps University, Quantico, Virginia.

Gerber, D. (2011) *American Immigration: A Very Short Introduction*, Oxford: Oxford University Press.

Godál, M. (2020) *Slovak immigration and return migration from the United States during the late 19th and early 20th centuries*, Masaryk University.

Jakešová, E. (1997) *The Impact of Emigrants and Re-emigrants on Slovak Society (1880's–1920's)*, Bratislava: Slovak Historical Institute.

Javor, M. (2022) *Interview with Martin Javor*, 10 January, Prešov.

King, R. (2000) 'Generalizations from the history of return migration', in Bimal, G. (ed.) *Return migration: Journey of hope or despair*, Geneva: International Organization for Migration, pp. 7-55.

Kosa, J. (1957) 'A century of Hungarian emigration 1850–1950', *The American Slavic and East European Review*, vol. 16, no.4, pp. 501-514.

Koser, K. (2007) *International migration: A very short introduction*, Oxford: Oxford University Press.

Kopanic, M.J. (1990) 'The Slovak Community of Cleveland: Historiography and Sources', *Ethnic Forum*, v.10, nos. 12, pp. 8397.

Kopanic, M.J. (2003) 'The Slovaks', in David C. Hammack, John J. Grabowski, Diane L. Grabowski (eds) *Identity, Conflict, and Cooperation: Central Europeans in Cleveland, 1850–1930*, Cleveland: Western Reserve Historical Society, pp. 249-306.

Kopanic, M.J. (2009) 'The Beginnings of Slovak Fraternal Societies in the USA', *Naša rodina*, vol. 21, no. 4, pp. 147-156.

Kopanic, M.J. (2011) 'With Feet Planted in Two Lands: An Overview of Emigration to North America from Czechoslovakia', *Slovo*, vol. 12, no. 1, pp. 10-13.

Kováčová, A. (2014) *Po stopách slovenskej minulosti Budapešti*, Budapest: Výskumný ústav Celoštátnej slovenskej samosprávy v Maďarsku.

Magocsi, P. R. (2015) *With their back to the mountains*, Budapest: CEU Press.

Magocsi, P. R. (2018) *The people from nowhere (2nd edition)*, New York: Carpatho-Rusyn Research Center.

Megles, S., Tybor, M. and Stolarik, M. (1978) *Slovak Americans and Their Communities of Cleveland*, Cleveland: Cleveland State University.

Miháľ, O. (2005) *Slovaks in Canada from Vojvodina*, Vaughan, Ontario: Slovak Canadian Cultural and Heritage Centre.

Miháľ, O. (2003) *Slovaks in Canada*, Vaughan, Ontario: Slovak Canadian Cultural and Heritage Centre.

Novak, M. (1996) *The guns of Lattimer*, London: Routledge.

Palovic, Z. (2018) *The Great Return*, Bratislava: Global Slovakia. Pollack, M. (2016) *Americký cisár*, Krásno nad Kysuvou: Absynt.

Pop, Ivan (2020) *Malé dejiny Rusínov*, Bratislava: Združenie inteligencie Rusínov Slovenska.

Roos, D. (2019) 'America's First Immigration Law Tried (and Failed) to Deal With Nightmarish Sea Journeys', *History*, March 1.

Slovenský, J. (1887) *Americký tlumač ku naučeňu še najpotrebňejších, začatečných známosco chz anglickej rečipre uherských slovákoch v Amerike žijucích* (American interpreter), Pittsburgh, Pennsylvania: Náklad Amerikanško slovenských novin.

Stolarik, M. M. (1976) 'From field to factory: The historiography of Slovak immigration to the United states', *International migration review*, vol. 10, no. 1, pp. 81-102.

Stolárik, M. M. 2015. *Kde je môj domov? Slovenské prisťahovalectvo do Severnej Ameriky (1870–2010)*. Žilina: Žilinská univerzita

Stolarik, M. M. (1997) 'Slovak-Americans in the Great Steel Strike', *Pennsylvania History: A Journal of Mid-Atlantic Studies*, vol. 64, no. 3, pp. 407-418.

Stolarik, M. M. (1992) 'Slovaks in Canada and the United States, 1880–1990, Similarities and Differences', *Historické štúdie*, vol.34, Bratislava: Historical Institute of the Slovak Academy of Sciences.

Stolarik, M. M. (2012) *Where Is My Home?: Slovak Immigration to North America, 1870-2010*, Bristol: Peter Lang.

Stolarik, M. M. (1988) *The Slovak Americans*, New York: Chelsea House Publishers.

Stolarik, M. M. (1967). *The role of American Slovaks in the creation of Czecho-Slovakia, 1914–1918* (Doctoral dissertation, University of Ottawa (Canada)).

Stolarik, M. M. (1976) 'From field to factory: The historiography of Slovak immigration to the United states', *The International Migration Review*, vol. 10, no. 1, pp. 81-102.

Stolarik, M. M. (1994) 'Slovak fraternal-benefit societies in Pennsylvania', *Pennsylvania Folklife*, vol. 44, no.2, pp. 18-83.

Šustek, D. (2009) *Do Ameriky*, Bratislava: Zlatý fond denníka SME.

Šustek, D. (2009) *Obrázky z amerického života*, Bratislava: Zlatý fond denníka SME.

Zahra, T. (2016) *The great departure: Mass migration from Eastern Europe and the making of the free world*, New York: WW Norton & Company.

We would like to thank the following institutions and their expansive archives:

Kasigarda Museum of Emigration from Slovakia

Ellis Island National Museum of Immigration

The Library of Congress

Appendix

Slovak Success in North America

Most Slovaks arrived in their new homelands with nothing material in hand. These men and women would work hard for years, even decades, before they could afford decent homes and elegant clothes. But Slovaks are defined by their resilient and resourceful nature. With time, these Slovak settlers took to the opportunities that the New World offered and went on to build empires of their own. Here are a few of success stories from Slovak emigrants and their descendants.

Štefan Banič

Inventor of the early parachute. He constructed and tested a prototype of his parachute in Washington, D.C., by jumping from a 41-floor building and subsequently from an airplane. His patented parachute became standard equipment for U.S. pilots during World War I. Banič emigrated to the United States from western Slovakia in 1907 and returned to the homeland in 1920.

Jon Bon Jovi

Singer, songwriter, guitarist, whose grandmother was born in Pennsylvania to Slovak immigrants.

Michal Bosák

Banker, philanthropist, and sponsor of the Czechoslovak independence movement from eastern Slovakia. This immigrant of Rusyn origins was not even 40 when he became the president of the National Bank in Olyphant, Pennsylvania, with permission to issue bank notes. Bosak's name appeared on 5-, 10-, and 20-dollar bank notes issued on June 25, 1907. He was a fervent campaigner for the Slovak cause, and in 1917, organized a million-dollar collection to "agitate for the independence of Slovakia."

Eugene Cernan
Astronaut, fighter pilot, and a grandson of immigrants from northern Slovakia. He walked on the Moon in December 1972.

Stephen Ditko
Comic-book artist, best known for co-creating the superhero Spider-Man. Ditko is the son of Rusyn immigrants from eastern Slovakia.

David Grohl
American rock musician: drummer for Nirvana and vocalist/ guitarist for the Foo Fighters. Grohl is the descendant of emigrants from Slovakia.

John D. Hertz
Businessman and philanthropist, owner of the Hertz Corporation, born in Slovakia. He emigrated with his parents, settling in Chicago, Illinois. He founded the Yellow Cab Company in Chicago in 1915 and later ventured into the car rental business, naming it after himself.

Angelina Jolie
American actress, filmmaker, humanitarian, and daughter of actor John Voight. Voight's grandfather was born in Košice and emigrated to the United States in 1895.

Travis Kalanick
Cofounder and CEO of Uber, whose grandfather came to the United States from eastern Slovakia.

Diana Krall
Celebrated Canadian jazz singer whose great-grandparents emigrated from Slovakia at beginning of the 20th century. She has sold more than 15-million albums worldwide.

Jozef Murgaš
Inventor, Catholic priest, and pioneer of wireless telegraphy. He holds 1,212 U.S. patents and achieved the first full

wireless telegraphic transmission in history. He was born near Banská Bystrica and emigrated to the United States in 1896. Murgaš was nicknamed the Radio Priest.

Paul Newman

World famous actor, film director, philanthropist, and son of an immigrant from eastern Slovakia.

John Roberts

A lawyer and jurist who began serving as the chief justice of the U.S. Supreme Court in 2005. His great-grandparents came from eastern Slovakia.

Štefan Roman

Prominent mining engineer, industrialist, and captain of the Canadian mining industry of Rusyn origin who emigrated to Canada from eastern Slovakia in 1937. He is known as the Uranium King, who became one of the richest Slovaks of all time.

Michael Strank

An emigrant who came to the U.S. from eastern Slovakia with his Rusyn parents. He distinguished himself as a U.S. Marine Corps sergeant, losing his life in World War II at Iwo Jima, Japan. Sergeant Michael Strank was pictured in an iconic photo in which he leads his men—in raising the American flag atop Mount Suribachi.

Jessie Ventura

Actor, professional wrestler, former governor of Minnesota, and a grandson of immigrants from Slovakia.

Jan Vilček

Prominent biomedical scientist, inventor, educator, and philanthropist who was born in Bratislava and emigrated to the United States in 1964. He published over 350 papers in scientific journals, was awarded over 40 U.S. patents, and established the Vilcek Foundation to increase public awareness of the artistic, scientific, and professional contributions of immigrants in the U.S.

Andy Warhol

Visual artist, film director, producer, and son of Rusyn immigrants from eastern Slovakia. He became a leader of the pop art movement and an icon of American pop art.

Wall of Gratitude

This book was supported by the following persons, in honor of their ancestors and their emigration journeys.

- Mike Kudlac, in memory of Pavel Kudláč and František Koberčik
- Elizabeth Massura, in memory of John Massura and Sophie Olla
- Andy Strenio, in memory of George Strenio and Maria Dorich
- Kevin Stamber, in memory of Joseph Gresko and John Matta
- Karen Chorba, in memory of George Yousko and Anna Yavos Yousko
- Sharon Ferguson, in memory of John Palko and Mary Hanincik
- John A. Kolodgy, in memory of Franciscus Joseph Kolodzey and Charles Stephen Kolodgy
- Mark Tarby, in memory of Matthias Tarbaj and Michal Zubko
- Stephen Stumpp, in memory of Michal Sivcso and Barbola Harvan
- Elizabeth Kirsch, in memory of John Csacsko and Elizabeth Micak

- Priscilla Klein, in memory of Stephanus Tomasik Charles Tomasik
- Barbara Ulkus, in memory of Michael Malinak and Anna Vira
- Julae Kubus, in memory of Andreas Kubus
- Judy Richards, in memory of Jozef Lukač and Frantisek Palovčik
- Mary Frances Zelenak, in memory of Joseph Zelenak and Andrew Grohol
- Paul Kostyak, in honor of Karen Melis and Vlado Flak
- David Rafaidus, in memory of Emilia and George Rafaidus
- Carol Fedorchak, in memory of Anna Franko Zoldak and Susan Sabol Hajdučko Fedorchak

This book was made possible thanks to the support of generous men and women, who understand that remembering the Slovak emigration journey is an important part of history, in the New World and Slovakia alike.

We extend our appreciation to Paul Kostyak, Misbah Shah, Bob Lesko, John Adnan, Peter Stastny, Christopher Straurovsky, Jerome Kraisinger, John Selecky, Beverly Kajaria, Czechoslovak Genealogical Society International, Czech & Slovak Cultural Center of Minnesota, James Gajewski, William Owen, Daniel Kopchick, Sarah Kish, Mark Tranovich, Natalie Zett, Richard Morris, Jonathan Lukca, Mary Frances Zelenak, David Baron, Steve Zlatos, Allison Snyder, Matthew-Peter Buthrie, Diane Brent, James Dubelko, Agnes Zabik, Susan Salley, Andrew Zvara, Audrey Hughes, Trina DiMario and Mary Lou Cavallini for their support.

We would like to express our deep gratitude to Professor John Palka who has believed in the mission of Global Slovakia since its inception, and who has been helping us share Slovakia with the world with his counsel and support over the years.

We would also like to thank our amazing team of volunteers, who have significantly contributed to the *Slovak Settlers* project with their skills, passion and time. In the process, they also helped to raise awareness of Slovak settlers worldwide.

Thank you, Deah Partak, Chris Stifel, Tucker Jaroll, Sean Kovarovic, James Ashley Mayer and David Grega for bringing this emigration history to life through podcasts, art and our book trailer.

Thank you, Helen Fedor, Dana Dorčáková, Nicholas Rando, Erin Lillywhite, and Aaron Borrelli for your guidance, ideas, organizing and editing skills.

Lastly, a big and very special thank you to Deah Partak for her tireless passion in helping to see the *Slovak Settlers* book come to fruition, and for leading our outstanding crowdfunding campaign! We surpassed our funding goal by 292% thanks to her dedicated efforts.

Dear supporters, it was an honor to share the journey of completing this book with you.

GLOBAL SLOVAKIA

Global Slovakia is a not-for-profit, non-governmental organization whose purpose is to share Slovakia with the world.

It was founded in 2017 by two Slovak scholars who are experts on their home country. Zuzana Palovic has focused on migration in Central and Eastern Europe; Gabriela Bereghazyova has focused on political and socials patterns within Slovakia.

Under the leadership of Palovic and Bereghazyova, Global Slovakia has produced and published several books, and has been widely represented in national and international media. The organization has also played a key role in recent changes in the Slovak Citizenship Act, giving Slovak descendants easier access to becoming Slovak citizens.

At Global Slovakia, we support and encourage Slovak descendants to reconnect with their roots. As a descendant, you are eligible for the Slovak Living Abroad Certificate (SLA) and perhaps also for Citizenship by Descent. We have already helped applicants to comply with SLA and CBD requirements, in addition to nurturing their connection to Slovakia.

www.globalslovakia.com

GLOBAL SLOVAKIA WEBINARS

Discover Slovakia with us!

GLOBAL SLOVAKIA WEBINARS

Global Slovakia launched its webinar series in 2020. Our monthly webinars by donation explore a range of themes from Slovak history and culture to contemporary affairs. These online events often feature guest speakers, and continue to grow in popularity. Our largest webinar drew an international audience of more than four hundred.

www.globalslovakia.com

GLOBAL SLOVAKIA ACADEMY

Global Slovakia Academy was founded by Global Slovakia in 2020 to meet growing international interest, particularly among Slovak descendants in Canada and the US. The academy offers 12 online programs, each of which is designed to explore Slovakia from a unique angle. These entertaining programs bring together valuable information that is difficult to source in English, and present it in an easy-to-digest, fun way.

www.globalslovakia.com

Our Books

SLOVAKIA: THE LEGEND OF THE LINDEN

Slovakia: The Legend of the Linden introduces an artistic rendition of the national story of Slovakia. It anchors the country's history in the significance of its national tree and symbol—the Linden.

THE GREAT RETURN

The Great Return documents the dramatic changes that took place at the beginning of the 21st century when western Europe opened its borders to the countries from behind the former Iron Curtain. Since then, more than 100 million citizens, including Slovaks, gained the freedom to move across Europe without a visa or passport. *The Great Return* documents the stories of those who chose to go abroad to learn and then, return to Slovakia.

CZECHOSLOVAKIA: BEHIND THE IRON CURTAIN

Czechoslovakia: Behind the Iron Curtain was published in 2019 to mark the 30th anniversary of the Velvet Revolution, that ended more than 40 years of communism in the country. Featuring the work of renowned documentary photographers, this book brings to life the experience of Slovaks behind the Iron Curtain.

SUPER SLOVAKS

Super Slovaks / Super Slováci is a bilingual English-Slovak book for young readers. It presents the stories of 50 Slovaks whose actions in some way benefitted their country and the world.

Our Book Partners

OFFICE FOR SLOVAKS LIVING ABROAD

www.uszz.sk

THE FIRST CATHOLIC SLOVAK UNION OF THE UNITED STATES OF AMERICA AND CANADA

FIRST CATHOLIC SLOVAK UNION
FCSU FINANCIAL

The First Catholic Slovak Union of The United States of America and Canada (FCSU) is a non-profit fraternal organization headquartered in Independence, Ohio, USA. FCSU was founded in Cleveland in 1890 by eleven Slovak immigrants with the guidance of Rev. Štefan Furdek. The FCSU's original purpose was to help Slovak immigrants to deepen their religious faith, protect their language and heritage, and provide an insurance fund for those working in and near Cleveland's dangerous factories. Today the FCSU offers competitive annuities, wealth transfer, and life insurance services to 50,000+ members throughout North America. It continues to support fraternal activities that preserve shared values of faith, family, and heritage.

www.fcsu.com

SLOVAK AMERICAN SOCIETY OF WASHINGTON, D.C.

SLOVAK AMERICAN SOCIETY
OF WASHINGTON D.C.

The Slovak American Society of Washington, D.C. is a nonprofit 501(c)(3) organization that promotes Slovak culture and history, and fosters fellowship among those who are of Slovak heritage or who have an interest in Slovakia. We host numerous educational, cultural, and social events to bring together those interested in maintaining a connection to Slovakia and actively support initiatives to promote freedom, democracy, and prosperity in Slovakia.
www.dcslovaks.org

NATIONAL CZECH & SLOVAK MUSEUM & LIBRARY

The NCSML preserves, presents and transcends unique stories of Czech and Slovak history and culture through innovative experiences and active engagement to reach cross-cultural audiences locally, nationally and internationally. The NCSML is an innovative leader in lifelong learning, community building and cultural connections. We encourage self-discovery for all ages so that the stories of freedom, identity, family and community will live on for future generations.
https://ncsml.org/

SLOVAK-AMERICAN CULTURAL CENTER

The Slovak-American Cultural Center (S-ACC) was founded in 1967 in New York City as a not-for-profit organization to preserve Slovak heritage in the United States for the Slovak-American community; promote Slovak cultural, scientific, and athletic activities at home and abroad; and to promote the achievements of Slovak-Americans in the United States and abroad. Over the years, the organization has had many notable accomplishments including organization of large-scale classical concerts, art exhibitions, providing scholarships and continuing the tradition of hosting the annual The Slovak Ball. For more information on our events visit: **www.SlovakAmericanCC.org**

+421 FOUNDATION

The +421 Foundation enhances relations between the Slovak people and the world by showcasing the cultural richness of Slovakia to International audiences and by creating opportunities for mutually beneficial interaction in the cultural sphere and beyond.
https://www.plus421.org

JOHN & HELEN TIMO FOUNDATION

John & Helen Timo Foundation brings together Carpatho-Rusyns who are dedicated to ancestors and traditions, and are committed to educating others and promoting their treasured culture and faith.

THE NATIONAL SLOVAK SOCIETY OF THE UNITED STATES OF AMERICA

The National Slovak Society of the United States of America (NSS) is a non-profit 501(c)(8) fraternal benefit society located in McMurray, a southern suburb of Pittsburgh, Pennsylvania, USA. The Society was founded in Pittsburgh on February 1890 under the leadership of Peter V. Rovnianek who assembled leaders of five different Slovak organizations making it the oldest Slovak fraternal benefit society in the United States of America. The NSS was founded as a nondenominational organization to provide a means for financial security for its members and their families and to promote the Slovak culture. Today, the NSS offers life insurance and annuity products for its 40,000 members and continues to support and promote the Slovak culture through our Slovak Heritage Museum and fraternal activities by its members across the country.
www.nsslife.org

INOBAT

InoBat is a revolutionary electric battery company that leads in research, development, manufacturing, supply and recycling of cutting-edge electric batteries. Its 'cradle to cradle' approach results in tailor-made products, that meet and exceed the needs of the global automotive industry. From design to delivery and to the recycling of electric batteries, Inbobat is a wholistic company- that embodies the principles of circular economy.
https://www.inobat.eu/

About the authors

ZUZANA PALOVIC, Ph.D.

Zuzana is a daughter of Slovak immigrants. She was born in communist Czechoslovakia, before her family fled the Iron Curtain to Canada, where she was raised and educated. Although she lived far away from her homeland, Zuzana never forgot her roots.

Dr. Palovic studied in the United States and was a NCAA Division I athlete. She continued her education in Europe and completed her doctoral studies in the United Kingdom, where she studied migration.

Zuzana returned to her native homeland in 2018 and established Global Slovakia. She has authored and co-authored five books. Moreover, Dr. Palovic was the co-founder of the One Slovak Family initiative that championed a law change in the Slovak Citizenship Act to make it accessible to Slovak descendants.

GABRIELA BEREGHAZYOVA, Ph.D.

Gabriela was born in socialist Czechoslovakia and raised in independent Slovakia where she completed a master's degree in Cultural Studies. This is where she first came across the history of Slovak emigration and the stories of *amerikáni* that planted the first seeds of interest in this legacy.

Gabriela continued her education at prestigious universities in the United Kingdom where she developed her unique approach to exploring, understanding and sharing Slovakia's long historic legacy with the world.

An expert on social patterns in Slovakia, and a Director of Global Slovakia, she is dedicated to promoting Slovakia's history and culture, and helping Slovaks around the world to reconnect with their ancestral homeland.

GLOBAL SLOVAKIA
AGÁTOVÁ 1323
905 01 SENICA
SLOVAKIA
www.globalslovakia.com

Volume I. first published in 2023
Zuzana Palovic and Gabriela Bereghazyova assert their moral right to be identified as the authors of this work.

English version © Zuzana Palovic and Gabriela Bereghazyova 2023
Front Cover Artwork © Zuzana Hudakova
Artwork © Tucker Jaroll and Sean Kovarovic
Graphic Design © Zuzana Chmelová
Editors: Margaret Bendet, Erin Lillywhite, Aaron Borrelli, Helen Fedor

ISBN 978-1-7374054-7-4

All rights reserved. No part of this book may be reproduced or transmitted in any form or by any means, electronic or mechanical, including photocopying, recording, or by any information storage and retrieval system, without permission in writing from the publisher.

www.ingramcontent.com/pod-product-compliance
Lightning Source LLC
Chambersburg PA
CBHW010824070526
44583CB00022B/2921